International Human Rights
in the 21st Century

International Human Rights in the 21st Century

Protecting the Rights of Groups

Edited by
Gene M. Lyons and
James Mayall

ROWMAN & LITTLEFIELD PUBLISHERS, INC.
Lanham • Boulder • New York • Oxford

ROWMAN & LITTLEFIELD PUBLISHERS, INC.

Published in the United States of America
by Rowman & Littlefield Publishers, Inc.
A Member of the Rowman & Littlefield Publishing Group
4720 Boston Way, Lanham, Maryland 20706
www.rowmanlittlefield.com

P.O. Box 317, Oxford OX2 9RU, United Kingdom

British Library Cataloguing in Publication Information Available

Library of Congress Cataloging-in-Publication Data

International human rights in the 21st century : protecting the rights
of groups / edited by Gene M. Lyons and James Mayall.
    p. cm.
    Includes bibliographical references (p.) and index.
    ISBN 0-7425-2352-7 (cloth) — ISBN 0-7425-2353-5 (paper)
    1. Human rights. I. Lyons, Gene Martin, 1924– II. Mayall, James.
JC571 .I5918 2003
323.1—dc21   2002011579

Printed in the United States of America

♾ ™ The paper used in this publication meets the minimum requirements
of American National Standard for Information Sciences—Permanence of
Paper for Printed Library Materials, ANSI/NISO Z39.48-1992.

Contents

Preface

This book had its origins in a meeting at Dartmouth College in the fall of 1998 to assess the fiftieth anniversary of the Universal Declaration of Human Rights. At the time, we recognized the widespread significance of the declaration and the subsequent covenants that, together, make up an international bill of rights and, most important, have become widely accepted as an integral part of normative behavior in international relations. But we also recognized that the declaration and the covenants largely focus on the protection of individual rights and give only indirect attention to the rights of groups, their culture, language, and identity, which have become increasingly violated, especially since the end of the Cold War.

In the months that followed, we became convinced that the problems of group rights deserve special attention, particularly (but not exclusively) in cases of weak and divided states where human rights have been brutally violated because of ethnic or religious differences and where the position of women has been consistently degraded. The last decade of the twentieth century also provided a series of cases of failed and divided states where the international community had intervened, in the first instance, to provide humanitarian assistance, but in a number of cases, to attend to the wider processes of nation building, including the protection of human rights for individuals and for groups. The record of intervention is mixed but nevertheless serves as a significant background to anticipate the problems of international human rights in the twenty-first century, most particularly the rights of groups.

We therefore took the initiative to assemble the scholars who have contributed to this book and to convene two working sessions, the first at the Centre of International Studies at the University of Cambridge and the second at the John Sloan Dickey Center for International Understanding at Dartmouth College. We are grateful to the two centers for financial support that

enabled us to bring the project together. We are also grateful to the participants for their willingness to join us. Each of us is, of course, responsible for
his or her own contribution, but we all profited greatly from the sharp and
challenging interactions at the meetings in Cambridge and Hanover. In
essence, our purpose has not been to be definitive but rather to introduce
perplexing issues that should occupy the attention of scholars and statesmen
for much of the century that has now started. We hope that we have succeeded.

List of Acronyms

ASEAN	Association of Southeast Asian Nations
AU	African Union
CEDAW	Convention on the Elimination of All Forms of Discrimination against Women
CIM	Commission Interamericana de Mujeres (Inter-American Commission of Women)
CIS	Commonwealth of Independent States
CmEDAW	Committee for the Elimination of Discrimination against Women
COE	Council of Europe
CSW	Commission on the Status of Women
DAW	Division for the Advancement of Women
ECHR	European Convention on Human Rights
ECtHR	European Court of Human Rights
ECOSOC	Economic and Social Council
ECOWAS	Economic Community of West African States
EU	European Union
FGM	Female genital mutilation
GATT	General Agreement on Tariffs and Trade
HCNM	High Commissioner for National Minorities
ICC	International Criminal Court
ICCPR	International Covenant on Civil and Political Rights
ICESCR	International Covenant on Economic, Social, and Cultural Rights
ICJ	International Court of Justice
ICTY	International Criminal Tribunal for the Former Yugoslavia
ILO	International Labor Organization
IMF	International Monetary Fund

INSTRAW	International Research and Training Institute for the Advancement of Women
IRO	International Refugee Organization
KLA	Kosovo Liberation Army
NATO	North Atlantic Treaty Organization
NGO	Nongovernmental organization
OAS	Organization of American States
OAU	Organization of African Unity
ONUC	United Nations Operation in the Congo
ONUMOZ	United Nations Operation in Mozambique
OSCE	Organization for Security and Cooperation in Europe
PDD	Presidential Decision Directive
RENAMO	Mozambiquan National Resistance
RPF	Rwandese Patriotic Front
SWAPO	South West Africa People's Organization
UDHR	Universal Declaration of Human Rights
UNAMIR	United Nations Assistance Mission for Rwanda
UNASOG	United Nations Aouzou Strip Observer Group
UNAVEM	United Nations Angola Verification Mission
UNCHR	United Nations Commission on Human Rights
UNESCO	United Nations Educational, Scientific, and Cultural Organization
UNGOMAP	United Nations Good Offices in Afghanistan and Pakistan
UNHCR	UN Office of the High Commissioner for Refugees
UNIFEM	United Nations Development Fund for Women
UNIIMOG	United Nations Iran–Iraq Military Observer Group
UNITA	National Union for the Full Independence of Angola
UNITAF	Unified Task Force
UNMEE	United Nations Mission in Ethiopia/Eritrea
UNMOP	United Nations Mission of Observers in Prevlaka
UNMOT	United Nations Mission of Observers in Tajikistan
UNOMIG	United Nations Observer Mission in Georgia
UNOMUR	United Nations Observer Mission Uganda-Rwanda
UNOSOM	United Nations Operation in Somalia
UNSF	United National Security Force in Western New Guinea
UNTAC	United Nations Transitional Authority in Cambodia
WTO	World Trade Organization

I

FROM INDIVIDUAL TO GROUP RIGHTS

1

Stating the Problem of Group Rights

Gene M. Lyons and James Mayall

The United Nations approved the Universal Declaration of Human Rights in 1948. The declaration spawned two international covenants, one on civil and political rights and the other on economic, social, and cultural rights. Together, the declaration and the two covenants comprise an international bill of rights, a set of norms and procedures, which the great majority of states have ratified. More specific treaties have also been developed—for example, to protect the rights of women and children and rid the world of racial discrimination. Together, these commitments make human rights a matter of international concern and governments liable to the international community for their implementation. All of this is a formidable accomplishment over the past fifty-plus years. What, then, is the problem?

The problem is twofold. First, governments continue to violate their treaty obligations, the international community is divided on how to compel states to meet their commitments, there are tensions between different sets of rights, and the treaties run up against the claim of sovereignty by governments to deal with domestic problems without outside interference. Second, increasing controversies over the rights of groups have complicated the original focus on the rights of individuals and the relationship between the state and the individual. This is especially true in the case of the rights of minorities, indigenous peoples, and women that were originally neglected in creating a baseline for the international human rights regime when the Universal Declaration was written. The liberal approach that drove the first series of human rights agreements has been overtaken as individual rights become increasingly entangled in group rights whenever the rights of individuals are violated because they are members of ethnic or religious minorities or of indigenous people or because they are women.

This double-edged problem was vividly exposed with the end of the Cold War, which was followed by two developments that heightened the international visibility and political salience of human rights. First, the fall of the Soviet Union raised the political stock of multiparty democracy, leading to the widespread hope that the majority of states would now opt for a democratic constitutional order with full protection of human rights. The second was the resurgence of a series of fierce ethnic and/or religious conflicts in which there was systematic and widespread abuse of fundamental rights. The scale of these humanitarian catastrophes inevitably faced the international community with the question of how it should respond and—since most of these conflicts were within the borders of sovereign states—what basis there was for intervention into what were essentially matters of "domestic jurisdiction."

It was the desire to trace the implications of these developments for the future of the international human rights regime that provided the focus for our book. Democracy and human rights are not identical concepts (as several of our contributors reminded us), but they overlap. Most important, if democratic politics are to replace authoritarian systems, it is crucial that fundamental human rights are entrenched in the workings of society in reality and not merely in theory. If they are not, there will be no incentive for those who lose an election, for example, to accept the results. It is possible, as Jack Donnelly argues in his chapter in this book, that the original liberal regime can be adapted to cover new concerns about the rights of groups without invoking new sets of obligations. But it is not obvious, particularly in deeply divided societies where democratization, while often perceived as a solution to civil conflict, can as easily become a major part of the problem if the interests of minorities are ignored and they continue to fear being treated like second-class citizens with the obliteration of their cultural practices and language.

This is the underlying rationale for concentrating on the rights of groups in the chapters that follow; the protection of group rights is a necessary part of any attempt to democratize troubled societies, especially those that are deeply divided. The reason is that, in such societies, constitutional guarantees of individual citizen rights and the rule of law may not be sufficient to overcome communal and/or sectarian identities and rivalries. This is the essential argument in the chapter on minority rights by Jennifer Jackson-Preece, no less than in the chapters that follow on indigenous peoples by Hurst Hannum and the rights of women by Eva Brems. If it can be shown, for example, that the existing liberal framework cannot lend itself to accommodating issues of great importance to women as women, this will provide powerful support for taking group rights more seriously than they have been in the past. Also, as "native" to the country in which they live, indigenous peoples insist that they are not minorities, a distinction that makes more psychological and historical than logical sense. From the point of view of human rights, however, the campaign of indigenous peoples for autonomy rather than secession is not a direct threat to the sovereignty of states and, paradoxically, may give them more room for maneuver in domestic politics than other minorities enjoy.

Ideally, the international community should attempt to widen the basis of human rights both to serve as a prerequisite of credible democratic government and to reassure marginalized groups of the legitimacy of democratic freedoms and politics by guaranteeing the rights of their identity. What happens, however, when all efforts to persuade governments to protect human rights through diplomatic channels fail? Or when a government is too weakened or corrupted to fulfill its obligations under international treaties? These are the questions that led us to consider the human rights dimension of international intervention, the second focus of the book. The strict proscriptions placed on the use of force under the United Nations Charter would seem to rule out intervention to respond to violations of human rights (as much as for any other reason) except under very limited circumstances: a threat to international peace and security as agreed to by the Security Council. Should this proscription be lifted, and if so, when? Under what conditions should the violations of human rights be interpreted as a threat to international peace? Have the interventions authorized by the Security Council, especially after the Cold War, created a new set of common interests in the international community?

These questions are the center of the chapter by Nicholas J. Wheeler. Whether justified or not, the international community has intervened in a number of conflicts since the end of the Cold War in which the violation of human rights has not been the only reason but has certainly been a major justification. Similarly, reconstruction efforts in countries where the Security Council has authorized UN operations have provided that the civil and political order be rebuilt on the basis of protection of fundamental rights and democratic institutions. How successful have these efforts been, and to what extent do they provide support for the view that international society is evolving toward greater solidarity with regard to the meaning and significance of human rights? The evidence reviewed in the chapter by Marc Weller allows us to reach tentative conclusions on this issue.

The contributors in this book all agreed that the world has moved beyond the narrow confines of the paradigm that accepts a natural law basis for human rights and almost exclusively emphasizes the rights of individuals, especially in relation to states. This is not to deny the importance of liberalism as an argument for human rights. As Jack Donnelly explains in his chapter, the original liberal approach has taken us a long way, providing us with an ambitious regime that contains a far-reaching code of human rights and a series of procedures, both formal and informal, to monitor their implementation. The question is whether the existing regime can be expanded to include group rights or whether a new set of obligations need be added. Liberalism has never been a static philosophy with a canonical set of texts and prescribed dogmas, however. Just as John Stuart Mill was persuaded by reflection and experience repeatedly to extend the list of public goods that could not be provided by the unfettered market,[1] we are convinced that the next fifty years needs an expanded framework of analysis, within or beyond the present regime, if the aim of extending human rights to those who are denied them is to succeed.

HUMAN RIGHTS THROUGH HISTORY

In many respects, human rights have only been a major issue in international politics since World War II. From the emergence of modern states in the seventeenth century, human rights have essentially been a matter between the state and its people, with the behavior of states protected from outside interference by the doctrine of sovereignty. Sovereignty, moreover, has been a bedrock of the international system. Peace and stability among states were based on the premise that states recognized each other's sovereignty and agreed not to intervene into each other's domestic affairs. Nevertheless, sovereignty, beyond its legal dimensions, has never been uniform or absolute. Some states—to mimic George Orwell's *Animal Farm*—are more sovereign than others, and states have frequently been committed by treaty to treat their people more benignly than they might have otherwise wished.[2]

From the beginning, for example, the international community has attempted through treaties to protect minorities from being repressed by states. The treaties that made up the peace of Westphalia, coming as they did at the end of the religious wars, prevailed on states to ensure the right of all groups to follow the religion to which they belong. The imposition on state policy to protect minority rights extended into the nineteenth century when the major European powers put pressure on the Ottoman Empire to protect Christian minorities (through military threats as well as treaties). During the nineteenth century, the international community—via the Concert of Europe—also made inroads on the principle of sovereignty in abolishing the slave trade and providing for the protection of the wounded and sick in war in the first Geneva conventions of 1864.

Protection of minorities was also written down in a series of treaties signed at the end of World War I to protect minorities in the several countries being formed out of the broken-up Austro-Hungarian Empire. Nevertheless, the ambitious attempt by Japan to insert a provision outlawing racial discrimination in the 1919 conference was summarily rejected by the other powers as a breach of the principles of sovereignty and noninterference. All of the efforts to protect minorities, moreover, were subject to the will of state authorities, and the widespread violation of minority rights in the years between the two world wars was ugly testimony to the weakness of the system. This history provides much of the background to the chapter by Jennifer Jackson-Preece on the revival of interest in, and debate about, minority rights.

By 1945, the behavior of Nazi Germany so horrified the world that there was little resistance to adding a provision in the UN Charter that, among its major aims, the United Nations would promote "universal respect for, and observance of, human rights and fundamental freedoms for all without distinction as to race, sex, language, or religion." Certainly the Holocaust, the systematic attempt to eradicate the Jews of Europe, was the most appalling of Nazi crimes. The Nazis' arrogant claim of being a superior race and the deep fears that they engendered throughout the countries that they occupied created widespread support for raising human rights to a new level of international concern. The ideals of human rights had already been given positive direction by the "Four Freedoms" speech of Franklin Delano Roosevelt in 1941, in which the American president called for a world with freedom of speech and worship and equally freedom from want and fear.

The human rights provisions in the UN Charter are still limited by the recognition of sovereignty and especially the admonition in paragraph 2.7 that "nothing contained in the present Charter shall authorize the United Nations to intervene in matters which are essentially within the domestic jurisdiction of any state." As we noted earlier, the one exception to this limitation is when the Security Council under Chapter VII authorizes enforcement measures. When, in effect, the Security Council finds that a threat to international peace and security exists, states are not protected by the doctrine of sovereignty and can be held directly accountable for violations of human rights. In the years since 1945, the expansion of the human rights regime has not only threatened to erode the concept of sovereignty but, especially since the end of the Cold War, has on several occasions led the Security Council to adopt a widened interpretation of "international peace and security" as the basis for action under Chapter VII of the Charter. In the process, the narrow meaning of security as protection of attack from another state is slowly shifting. Increasingly, threats to world peace emerge from internal conflicts that directly affect neighboring states and, as they become more violent and especially as they involve gross violations of human rights, also draw in the interests and resources of major states, individually or in support of internationally sanctioned coalitions.

THE EXPANSION OF HUMAN RIGHTS

One of the first actions taken by the United Nations when it was organized in 1945 was to establish a working commission to prepare what came to be the Universal Declaration of Human Rights. From the time the Universal Declaration was adopted in 1948, it has been widely accepted by states and has become part of customary international law.[3] The declaration, by itself, is a statement of highly endorsed intentions but is not operational in the sense of providing processes and institutions for the execution of its aims. The task of writing a covenant to implement the provisions of the declaration became mired in the conflict between civil and political rights, on the one hand, and economic, social, and cultural rights on the other. The Western states strongly supported civil and political rights on two grounds. First, they emphasized constraints on governments, which are seen, in the tradition of Western political philosophy, as a constant threat to personal liberty. Second, because governments were so constrained, political and civil rights could be expressed negatively and in a form that, in principle, could be upheld in the courts.

The West was more divided on economic, social, and cultural rights, which implied an active role for government. Such rights were strongly supported by the Western European states with important socialist constituencies, as well as the Soviet bloc and, as they gained independence, by the developing countries of Asia and Africa. The United States, however, led the opposition to raising these rights to a level of obligation that governments owed to their citizens. As a result, it was agreed in the early 1950s to proceed by drafting two covenants, in effect separating the two sets of rights. It was not until 1966 that the documents were ready for signature, and while they have been widely ratified, the United States did not ratify the civil and political rights covenant until 1992 and has never ratified the covenant on economic, social, and cultural rights.

Meanwhile, a series of anti-Semitic attacks in various parts of the world in the early 1960s again raised the spectrum of the Holocaust and renewed interest in writing, first, a declaration and then a "convention on the elimination of all forms of racial discrimination."[4] The momentum was initially carried forward by the civil rights movement in the United States and by newly independent African states that used the negotiations as a mechanism through which to mobilize political support against the apartheid government in South Africa. Here again, American enthusiasm receded as conservative groups in the United States feared that international human rights treaties, in general, would not only give the federal government increased power over the individual states but would also give government the authority to limit the right of freedom of expression, guaranteed in the First Amendment of the U.S. Constitution.

Despite American reservations, the convention on eliminating racial discrimination was also opened for signature in 1966 and was widely ratified. The campaign against apartheid, moreover, took on a life of its own and continued condemnation was intensified in resolutions of the UN General

Assembly, the Commonwealth, and, after the Sharpeville massacre in 1960, periodically even the Security Council. Cumulatively, these pressures forced South Africa into diplomatic isolation. The Western powers, however, continued to veto attempts by the Security Council to impose economic sanctions under Chapter VII of the Charter in an attempt to disrupt South African trade relations and deprive the country of essential imports.

In 1977, after the murder of the black consciousness leader Steve Biko by the South African Security service, Western opposition faded, and the Council imposed a mandatory arms embargo. From the mid-1980s, partly in response to pressure from the Commonwealth and the prosanctions lobby in the U.S. Congress, but primarily from private financial interests acting for prudential reasons, the net was tightened. To what extent international condemnation and economic sanctions ultimately contributed to the fall of apartheid is very much an open question. Nonetheless, the case was one in which the shield of sovereignty was purposefully breached by the international community and served as a precedent for the more substantial challenge to the principle of sovereignty that has resulted from Security Council activities in the 1990s.

The United Nations has also become an instrument for human rights initiatives beyond racial discrimination. A convention against genocide had already been signed in 1948 and was joined by "a convention against torture and other cruel, inhuman or degrading treatment or punishment" in 1984. Nevertheless, the difficulty of implementing these efforts to criminalize gross violations of rights became most evident in the 1990s: For one, the international community failed to intervene to prevent the genocidal massacre of Tutsi in Rwanda in 1994; for another, the UN Security Council established a weak "security zone" that proved ineffective in deterring the killings in Srebenica in 1995; and, yet again, it intervened too late in Kosovo in 1998 to prevent what amounted to a wide campaign of "ethnic cleansing" of the Kosovar Albanians by the Serbs (which was followed by the Serbs fleeing from their homes when the Albanians returned in the wake of the NATO-led intervention into the Kosovo conflict). At the same time, the relevance of the torture treaty was sharpened in 1998 when it became the basis for a Spanish judge exercising the right of universal jurisdiction to bring the former Chilean dictator, General Augusto Pinochet, to trial for crimes against humanity while he was head of state.

Held in house arrest in Britain, the general was judged to be medically unfit to stand trial and subsequently sent back to Chile rather than extradited to Spain. Nevertheless, building on the earlier Nuremberg trials and the more recent Security Council decisions to create ad hoc criminal courts for Bosnia and Rwanda, as well as the agreement in 1998 to set up a permanent international criminal court, it will no doubt be claimed in the future that the Pinochet case confirmed that the principle of "sovereign immunity" can no longer be invoked to protect political leaders from taking personal responsibility for violating the human rights of their people. Indeed, the apparent precedent was immediately noted: the Pinochet case was rapidly followed by the trial of Hissène Habré in Senegalese courts, for human rights violations committed while he was president of Chad. Moreover, the indictment and ultimately the transfer of the Yugoslav leader, Slobodan Milošević, to the international tribunal in The Hague in 2001, reinforced the concept of personal responsibility, notwithstanding questions raised by the ambiguities surrounding the application of "universal jurisdiction."

EXTENDING HUMAN RIGHTS

For all the expansion, there is still considerable controversy over the universality of human rights. At the UN human rights review conference in Vienna in 1993, representatives from Asian states, especially, insisted that the international bill of human rights was essentially a "Western" creation, and its provision had to be adapted by others in accordance with their own belief systems and cultural backgrounds. Admittedly, many Asian human rights groups lobbied against their own governments at Vienna in favor of a universal standard. Nonetheless, it is clear that some cultures hold a narrower range of views on the relations between the individual and the community than in the West and that others see different traditional roles for women in their society. The strong pressure to abandon the idea of the universality of human rights in favor of some kind of "cultural relativism" may have been largely opportunistic, but not wholly so. At the same time, developing countries, led, in many respects, by China, insist that modernization and democratization are long-term processes that may require curtailment of political rights in ensuring the social stability essential for economic growth.

The truth is that the "internationalization" of human rights has more rapidly expanded in prosperous Europe where a European Court of Human Rights has been established that serves as an appeals court when litigants have exhausted national systems of justice.[5] Not only has its jurisdiction been dramatically broadened, but decisions of the European Court are binding on participating member states. In Europe, the cause of human rights was also advanced by the Helsinki Accords, a series of agreements signed in 1975 between the Soviet Union and its allies and the Western members of the North Atlantic Treaty Organization (NATO) and the European Union. The Helsinki discussions began as an attempt by the Soviet Union to get some kind of recognition of its hegemony in Eastern Europe. During the course of long negotiations, the West insisted on a set of human rights provisions essentially involving the uniting of divided families, which the USSR finally accepted. The human rights "basket," as it came to be called, was exploited by private human rights groups in the West to make contact with dissidents in the Eastern countries. The dissidents, in turn, mobilized by leaders like Vaclav Havel in Czechoslovakia and Andrei Sakharov in the Soviet Union, took the accords as a basis for pressing for freedom of association and expression and, with material support from western contacts, contributed to the fall of the communist regimes.

More broadly, however, human rights have been further extended in three ways. First, there has been a vast expansion of international activity in protecting refugees and providing humanitarian assistance in countries devastated by civil conflict.[6] These are areas, while distinct unto themselves, that clearly overlap with human rights. Even while World War II continued, programs had been developed to deal with the hundreds of thousands of refugees, largely from Eastern Europe, who had been driven from their homes and, in many cases, taken into Germany as forced laborers. In the years after the war, the International Refugee Organization (IRO) at first began to repatriate these displaced persons, but as the governments of Eastern Europe fell into communist hands, the agency adopted programs of resettlement for those who were opposed to returning to their homeland for political reasons.

Intended as a temporary agency to handle World War II refugees, the IRO was slowly dissolved. But the continuing increase in refugee populations, initially driven by the first Arab-Israeli war and by the Korean conflict, led to the creation of the UN Office of the High Commissioner for Refugees (UNHCR) under a 1951 convention that also established criteria for determining refugee status. Over the years, UNHCR has dealt with millions of refugees in Asia, especially as a result of the disruptions brought on with the Vietnam struggle and in Africa as countries were shaken by internal conflicts, largely ethnic in character. Indeed, by the 1990s, the problem was expanded, principally in Africa, by the addition of millions of internally displaced persons who were not qualified as refugees since they were not forced out of their home states, but whose rights had been seriously violated and were no less destitute, having lost all of their possessions in the horror of civil war. According to UN figures, by 1996, there were more than twenty-five million internally displaced persons—up from around three million in the early 1980s—in fifty-three countries.[7]

Second, the problems of refugee protection and humanitarian assistance have also become entwined with the evolution of UN peacekeeping. During the Cold War, the UN had developed peacekeeping procedures to deploy lightly armed troops between the forces of conflicting states, but only with the prior agreement of the antagonists and their commitment to seek a peaceful settlement of their dispute. When the Cold War ended, consensus became more possible in the Security Council, and in a series of cases involving weak and divided states, the Council authorized UN intervention without prior approval of the warring sides, to go far beyond traditional peacekeeping. A major objective in the operations in a ruptured state such as Bosnia, for example, was, first, to provide humanitarian assistance and, once drawn in, to go on to protect ethnic minorities from further brutalization. Peacekeeping came to include a range of functions from intervening between conflicting factions to caring for the weak and homeless, protecting the distribution of relief supplies, policing war-stricken cities, and supervising elections once hostilities have been pacified. Marc Weller and Nicholas Wheeler develop a deeper analysis of these cases in their chapters.

Third, the international human rights regime—the treaties, international organizations, and networks of nongovernmental agencies—is an essential part of a normative framework for state behavior that has been developing since the Universal Declaration was written and expanding since the Soviet system collapsed. States that have defied human rights standards, whether they signed the human rights treaties or not, are under pressure to comply. Democratic practices and the state of human rights, for example, are criteria for the admission of former communist states of Eastern and Central Europe, into the European Union, as they were earlier for the Council of Europe. Democracies have also replaced military regimes throughout most of Latin America and are holding their former rulers to account for violations of human rights. On his return to Chile, for example, Pinochet was stripped of his immunity and only escaped judicial inquiry on violations to human rights by reason of medical unfitness. In Africa, the ending of apartheid in South Africa remains a significant triumph in the struggle for equality despite the way human rights are trampled elsewhere in the violence of internal wars. In Asia, freedom of expression and association are spurred on by the spread of free markets despite serious setbacks, such as the economic retrenchment and military resistance that unsteadied the democratic election in Indonesia that followed the forced resignation of the longtime dictator, Suharto.

By the end of the twentieth century, human rights had become a major issue in international politics. It had also become an extremely complicating issue since human rights has to be understood within a broad context; that is, they get linked up with a full spectrum of other economic and social issues. For one thing, the several sets of human rights have to be seen in relation to one another. This is most obvious in the relations between civil and political rights, on the one hand, and economic, social, and cultural rights, on the other. Perhaps the point is oversimplified, but the right to express one's views and the rights of association may have little meaning to many people who suffer severe poverty such as one finds in many parts of Africa and Asia. This need not compromise the universality of human rights. But it does reinforce the imperative to provide economic rights and ensure that there is "freedom from want" as well as freedom of speech and assembly.

There is more: Human rights are also involved in the choices that states make in deciding on economic policies. Today, globalization is driving states to adopt open markets and remove restrictions on the free movement of capital. Such deregulation increases the difficulties in pursuing income redistribution policies. There are pressures on developing countries to privatize their industries, reduce government expenditures, and construct a society that facilitates social mobility. The United States, of course, is the prime example of a country in which social mobility is a central feature of economic development. Nonetheless, whatever the other merits of free markets, the United States can only provide a long-term model for the rest of the world. Besides suffering from large disparities in income in its own population, it is a continental state with abundant natural resources that, over time, provided unusual opportunities for a large immigrant and generally mobile population. In contrast, in many parts of the world, there is deep and desperate poverty and layers of custom and culture that cannot be so readily shed—snakelike—in the interests of wealth creation. Under what is effectively a new international economic orthodoxy that eschews welfare and prizes mobility, those who have the most difficulty in climbing the ladder of social and economic success without government support are very often those who suffer the harshest discrimination: minorities, indigenous people, and women. Moreover, if they choose to pack up and migrate, they risk being classified as economic refugees, not eligible for international protection, and turned back at the borders of more prosperous countries.

HUMAN RIGHTS IN THE NEXT FIFTY YEARS

A major purpose in this book is thus to inquire into two sets of human rights problems that are certain to be at the center of international attention during the next fifty years: the increasing evidence of group identity as a principal source of human rights violations, and the intervention of the international community in emergency cases in which there are gross violations of rights. Jennifer Jackson-Preece, Hurst Hannum, and Eva Brems develop the problem of group rights in depth in their chapters. The chapters by Marc Waller and Nicholas Wheeler examine the problems that international society encounters in responding to violations of rights in a world that is still highly "pluralist" where states continue to pursue narrowly conceived interests. Jack Donnelly treats both sets of problems in the more theoretical introductory chapter.

Donnelly, in the first place, identifies the focus on individual rights in what he calls the "Universal model," in effect, the international human rights regime that emerged with the Universal Declaration and subsequent Covenants. This is particularly evident in article 27 of the covenant on civil and political rights, which guarantees the right to pursue one's own culture, religion, and language but only in terms of the rights of individuals and not of social groups. All of this despite the reality that people do not live as "isolated, atomistic individuals" but as social beings who cannot effectively exercise rights of culture, religion, or language alone but only as members of a larger group. Arguing that the Universal model assumes the collective nature of individual rights, Donnelly insists that there is no need, as others advocate, for an additional system of group rights.

Second, Donnelly maintains that, as a matter of practice, the Universal model leaves implementation to the member states. In this sense, human rights are ultimately subject to the policies of governments, even though they increasingly have come "to express many of the highest political aspirations" in international society. Certainly it is fair to say that, in formulating policies, most governments have to take the international human rights regime into account since their actions are bound to be measured against the standards of the regime by other governments, by nongovernmental organizations (NGOs), and by the international media, as well as sectors of their own public. Nonetheless, this still does not ensure that considerations of human rights will outweigh other factors and be decisive in the policies that governments adopt or that there is as yet a sufficiently strong consensus of what human rights mean to make international society effective in influencing national priorities. A major task for the future, Donnelly concludes, is to develop more effective methods for implementing the existing human rights regime rather than adding to it.

In her chapter, Jackson-Preece also argues that the human rights regime is dominated by a concern for individual rights. This emphasis has come about not only because of the strong influence of Western political philosophy but also because of the weight given to the interests of states in international society. Attachment to the state, particularly in the form of citizenship, is given preference over affiliation with other communities, whether clans or ethnic groups. For that matter, the one group right that is specified in the UN Charter and the human rights treaties is the right of self-determination. It is as if the choice for any ethnic group is either to become completely assimilated into the dominant culture of the state in which they live or to achieve separate statehood. Certainly the UN Charter gave less attention to the right of self-determination than had the Covenant of the League of Nations, but for understandable political reasons. In the case of the covenant, a major objective was to eliminate the presence of minorities as a source of European conflict by granting them statehood, particularly with the breakup of the Austro-Hungarian Empire. As for the Charter, self-determination was by now extended beyond Europe to the rest of the world, where it was deliberately downplayed since the major European states wished to postpone the breakup of their empires and delay the rush toward decolonization. However, decolonization did occur, more rapidly than anyone expected, largely within boundaries that had been set down by the colonial powers. Self-determination was effectively defined as European decolonization, a formula that was obviously in the interest of those who had won control of the state and who had no interest in ceding territory to their opponents. Most of the new states created in this way included different ethnic groups who, after the unifying excitement of independence, began to compete for power and domination.

It is nonetheless important to take note, as Hurst Hannum does in his chapter, that unlike other minorities, there has been little inclination by indigenous people to exercise a right of secession. Living on the margins of society, they have usually asked for the protection of their rights within the state and have especially been concerned with their rights to the land on which they live. Indigenous people can be clearly identified in North and South America, in the Arctic regions, and in Australia and New Zealand where native people were forced off their land and segregated by invading Europeans who proceeded to establish permanent settlements and dominate the political life of the developing state. The problem is more complex in Asia and Africa where there are native people forced on to the margins of society, but not so strongly differentiated from the dominant groups. Indeed, as Hannum reports, a declaration of the rights of indigenous people is being drafted at the United Nations without clearly defining to whom it applies.

Both Jackson-Preece and Hannum conclude that a major challenge to human rights is to create "pluralist" societies that enfold different groups of people, living together with tolerance—and even respect—for the very differences that set them apart. In this regard, their conclusions intersect with Donnelly's discussion of the difficulties of moving states toward policies of tolerance and even further to nondiscrimination and eventually to multiculturalism as the ultimate response to pluralist societies. The problem is no less complicated when we add the issue of gender. While there were no distinctions in the way that the Universal Declaration and the two covenants were written, it could not be taken for granted that in implementing their provisions, states would deal with men and women on an equal basis. For that matter, a convention on the political rights of women was opened for ratification as early as 1953 and a separate convention on the elimination of all forms of discrimination against women in 1979. As Eva Brems emphasizes in her chapter, the drive for women's rights has advanced in two directions: to ensure that the two covenants apply to women as they do to men and to protect the special rights of women that derive from their own experience—for example, protection from sexual harassment and special provisions in cases of maternity.

More recently, as Brems discusses, the quest for women's rights is leading to a transformation of the human rights regime that involves an overall rethinking of the kind of society in which people live, a transformation, for example, from a largely male-dominated, highly assimilationist society to a society in which women—and minorities, whether ethnic, religious, or indigenous—play a fuller and more productive part in the normal practices of daily life. This kind of transformation—spurred on by feminist critiques and moving in the direction of the kind of multiculturalism that Donnelly identifies as a long-range goal—is only beginning but, Brems contends, will become increasingly influential in the years to come. More immediately, the story of women's rights has already dramatically illustrated how the growing influence of nonstate actors has influenced the overall development of human rights and, by practice, the character of international society. Beyond the conventions that have been promulgated, improvement in women's status has been the focus of a series of global conferences, beginning in Mexico City in 1975. These conferences have been especially useful in creating a vibrant network of women's groups throughout the world, a prime example of how private economic and social movements have contributed to the expansion of human rights and been a prime means of encouraging, even goading, governments toward cooperation.

In her chapter, Brems's discussion of the role of NGOs echoes the analysis in the chapters by Jackson-Preece and Hannum. As all three chapters point out, NGOs perform a series of functions in international society: they serve as "lobbies" at the international level and at the national level, they conduct independent investigations of human rights violations, they publicize the human rights policies and practices of governments, and they mobilize public opinion to support human rights activities at home and abroad. Transnational movements operate where governments cannot either because of the fear of destabilizing political or economic relations with other governments or because they themselves are violating the rights of their own citizens. Governments are, more often than not, the targets of NGO investigations. At the same time, it is just as important to remember that NGOs are private organizations, and, as valuable as they are, there may be questions about whom they represent, how they are accountable for their activities, and how they are funded.[8]

In the end, as much as NGOs have enriched international society, they have not changed its fundamental structure or the central role within it played by states. It is well to remember that, whatever the increasing role of private social and economic movements in giving it central purpose, international society is a society of states that have different and often opposing interests. There is thus real question whether, as Wheeler points out, the society of states is capable of developing a collective capacity for human rights enforcement. Both Wheeler and Marc Weller give special attention to the course of international relations since the end of the Cold War, especially international operations to intervene in internal conflicts in divided states in which there have been widespread violations of human rights. Their verdict is mixed: on the one hand, these operations provide considerable evidence of the willingness of international society to override the limits of sovereignty and hold political leaders directly responsible when human rights are violated; on the other hand, the decision to intervene has often been weakened (or abandoned, as in the case of Rwanda) by an unwillingness to support operations with the human and material resources necessary to accomplish their objectives.[9]

Wheeler tackles the problem in the broader sense, setting up his chapter as a dialogue among three views of international society: realism, pluralism, and solidarism. Realists, in the first instance, assume that states pursue narrowly conceived interests in an otherwise anarchic world in which power, principally measured by material resources, determines relations with other states. Pluralists see states no less as separate self-serving actors, but, in this case, they are constrained in their relations with others by common interests in maintaining stability largely through diplomatic exchange and a willingness to comply with international agreements. Finally, solidarists argue that the bonds of international society have been strengthened beyond the claims of pluralists by the threat that weapons of mass destruction pose for people everywhere, by the worldwide connections created by modern science and technology and the expanding global economy, and by the common interests that emerge from the need to protect the world environment from further degradation and from the commitment to human rights in the international treaties that have been ratified since the Universal Declaration.[10]

In many respects, Wheeler argues the case for solidarism. Nevertheless, he is constrained in identifying an evolution from pluralism by the indecisive response of international society to violations of human rights in recent internal conflicts. There has been as much failure as success, and here he is joined by Marc Weller, who looks at these conflicts—in Africa, the Balkans, Asia, and Central America—from the perspective of the internal politics of the countries involved as much as the politics among the states in international society. Weller demonstrates in considerable detail how traditional "first-generation" peacekeeping has developed into more complex operations with the end of the Cold War. He illustrates the variety of functions that so-called international peacekeeping forces have come to perform. In East Timor and Kosovo, for example, they have been charged with the direct administration of government affairs; in other cases, they have reconstituted public agencies, provided police protection for local government to operate, monitored the transition from violence to stability, encouraged reconciliation among opposing factions, and served to prevent further outbreaks of violence. Weller agrees with Wheeler that a major weakness in international "peacekeeping" comes from the unwillingness of the major states in international society to provide the necessary resources and to realize that internal conflicts in often poor and underdeveloped countries can only be resolved over a long period of time; major donors want cheap and quick results. In Weller's case, he also contends that it can take considerable time to bring about a sufficiently strong consensus among the conflicting parties to reconstitute their society along more democratic lines and to agree on the concrete shape of a new political structure.[11]

All together, the chapters in this book do what most scholarly contributions do: they raise more questions than answers. For that matter, there may not be answers in the narrow, direct sense. What the chapters give us is a sense of direction that it would be sensible to take if we are to extend the effectiveness of the international human rights regime over the next fifty years: for one thing, to move toward "pluralist" societies in which different ethnic or religious groups can live together in peace and tranquility with genuine respect for the differences among them; and, on the other hand, to strengthen the move toward "solidarism" in international society by reinforcing incentives for states to absorb the international human rights regime into their internal rules and practices. In this regard, the book takes a position whether or not all of us see it in quite the same way. We think that human rights enhance the dignity of people and that violations reduce us to the crudest and cruelest of human relations. We will want to return to these issues in the concluding chapter, not to bring them to a close but rather to provide a basis for a continuing discussion on questions that are bound to occupy scholars and statesmen for some time to come.

NOTES

1. J. S. Mill, *Principles of Political Economy* (Oxford: Oxford University Press, 1999), chap. 13.

2. For a recent study of sovereignty, see Stephen D. Krasner, *Sovereignty: Organized Hypocrisy* (Princeton, N.J.: Princeton University Press, 1999). Krasner's review is valuable, however doubtful his argument that, because the notion of sovereignty has never been absolute, nothing has substantially changed since the settlement of Westphalia.

3. See Johannes Morsink, *The Universal Declaration of Human Rights: Origins, Drafting and Intent* (Philadelphia: University of Pennsylvania Press, 1999). For a general review of human rights in international relations, see R. J. Vincent, *Human Rights and International Relations* (Cambridge: Cambridge University Press, 1986); Jack Donnelly, *International Human Rights* (Boulder, Colo.: Westview, 1998); and David Forsythe, *Human Rights in International Relations* (Cambridge: Cambridge University Press, 2000).

4. See Gene M. Lyons, "In Search of Racial Equality: The Elimination of Racial Discrimination," in *Global Issues in the United Nations Framework*, ed. Paul Taylor and A. J. R. Groom (London: Macmillan, 1989).

5. For a review of the European experience, see Philip Alston, ed., *The European Union and Human Rights* (Oxford: Oxford University Press, 1999).

6. The refugee question is covered in Gil Loescher, *Beyond Charity: International Cooperation and the Global Refugee Problem* (Oxford: Oxford University Press, 1993).

7. For an analysis of the internally dispossessed, see Francis M. Deng, *Protecting the Dispossessed* (Washington, D.C.: Brookings Institution, 1993).

8. For a broad review of the role of NGOs in several issues areas, see Margaret E. Keck and Kathryn Sikkink, *Activists beyond Borders* (Ithaca, N.Y.: Cornell University Press, 1998).

9. Several early cases are discussed in James Mayall, ed., *The New Interventionism, 1991–1994* (Cambridge: Cambridge University Press, 1996). The more general relationship between sovereignty and international intervention is analyzed in Gene M. Lyons and Michael Mastanduno, eds., *Beyond Westphalia? State Sovereignty and International Intervention* (Baltimore: Johns Hopkins University Press, 1995).

10. Since the events of September 11, 2001, when terrorists destroyed the World Trade Center in New York and rammed an aircraft into the Pentagon in Washington, D.C., the campaign against terrorism has been called a "common cause" of the international community, at least by the U.S. government. There is, nonetheless, some uncertainty whether all states, even those cooperating with the United States would agree on a definition of who are terrorists.

11. Both sets of problems may be critically affected by the experience of the international community in rebuilding the state of Afghanistan, but at this stage of writing (late 2002), it is still too early to come to any judgment.

2

In Defense of the Universal Declaration Model

Jack Donnelly

The global human rights regime is rooted in the 1948 Universal Declaration of Human Rights and its later elaborations, especially the 1966 International Human Rights Covenants. These documents reflect what I will call "the Universal Declaration model" of international human rights. In this chapter, the first four sections outline the model and argue that today it stands on an overlapping consensus on a political conception of justice based on the notion of equal concern and respect. The following five sections develop a liberal defense of this vision, focusing on issues of group rights (which appear centrally in the chapters by Eva Brems, Hurst Hannum, and especially Jennifer Jackson-Preece) and on the central role of the state in implementing these rights (a shortcoming emphasized in the chapters by Marc Weller and Nicholas Wheeler).

THE UNIVERSAL DECLARATION MODEL

Four elements of the Universal Declaration model deserve emphasis: its focus on rights; the restriction to individual rights; the balance between civil and political rights and economic, social, and cultural rights; and national responsibility for implementing internationally recognized human rights.

Human Rights

Internationally recognized human rights are rights, a particular sort of social practice.[1] To have a right to *x* is to be *entitled* to *x* and authorized to

20

make special claims to enjoy x should it be threatened or denied. Although all rights have correlative duties, they are not reducible to those duties. Social and political duties, and the values they seek to realize, are vitally important. But they need not be—and throughout most of history have not been—rooted in the entitlements of right holders. Not all important objectives are best realized through the practice of (human) rights.

Human rights are those rights held simply because one is a human being, goods, services, and opportunities to which everyone is entitled. Because one either is or is not a human being, human rights are held equally by all. Because one cannot stop being human, no matter how inhuman one's behavior or the treatment one is forced to endure, they are inalienable rights. Human rights are also commonly spoken of as universal rights. This universality is more prescriptive than descriptive.[2] The claim of "universal" human rights is that all human beings *ought* to be treated in these ways, not that they are or have been, or that these norms are (let alone have been) accepted everywhere.

Individual Rights

All the rights that appear in the Universal Declaration and the covenants are, with the exception of self-determination of peoples, rights of individuals, not corporate entities. Enumeration of rights thus typically begin "Every human being . . . ," "Everyone has the right . . . ," "No one shall be . . . ," or "Everyone is entitled. . . ."

Even where one might expect groups to appear as right holders, they do not. For example, article 27 of the International Covenant on Civil and Political Rights (ICCPR) reads, "In those States in which ethnic, religious or linguistic minorities exist, persons belonging to such minorities shall not be denied the right, in community with the other members of their group, to enjoy their own culture, to profess and practise their own religion, or to use their own language." Individuals belonging to minorities, not minorities (collective entities), have these rights. The chapter by Jackson-Preece challenges the adequacy of this approach, which I defend later.

Individual rights, however, are a *social* practice. Individual and group rights differ in who holds the right—individuals or corporate actors—not in their sociality. *All* (individual human) rights are inescapably social. A's right to x with respect to B establishes and operates through social relationships. Rights-bearing individuals alone cannot effectively implement their rights, let alone make for themselves a life worthy of human beings.

The Universal Declaration model envisions individuals deeply enmeshed in "natural" and voluntary groups ranging from families through the state. Internationally recognized human rights impose obligations on the state, regulate relations between citizens and states, and require the state and society for their realization. Many (most?) human rights, although held by individuals, can only be enjoyed collectively. Consider, for example, workers' rights, family rights, and minority rights, which are defined by social groups or roles, as well as rights as diverse as political participation, freedom of association, social insurance, and free and compulsory primary education.

Civil and Political and Economic, Social, and Cultural Rights

Another striking feature of the Universal Declaration model is the balance between civil and political and economic, social, and cultural rights. Nothing in either covenant suggests priority for one set of rights. The Universal Declaration does not even make a categorical distinction.

Although the relationship between civil and political and economic, social, and cultural rights was a matter of intense ideological controversy during the Cold War, today there is little disagreement that, as article 5 of the 1993 Vienna Declaration puts it, "All human rights are universal, indivisible and interdependent and interrelated." For example, as of November 16, 2000 only 8 states were party to just one of the covenants, while 137 were parties to both.[3] Debate focuses instead on short- and medium-run priorities and the most effective means to realize economic and social (and civil and political) rights. Such debates, however, are not a central concern of this volume. Therefore, I will simply assume the interdependence and indivisibility of all internationally recognized human rights.

National Implementation of International Human Rights

A further distinctive feature of the Universal Declaration model is the national implementation of internationally recognized human rights. "Everyone has a right to x" in practice means "Each state has the authority and responsibility to implement and protect the right to x within its territory."

The Universal Declaration was formulated as "a standard of achievement," a set of aspirational norms that left states with full sovereign authority to implement human rights within their territory. The "enforcement" procedures of the covenants—periodic reports to committees of experts[4]— did not significantly alter this allocation of responsibility. Norm creation has been internationalized, but implementation remains largely with sovereign territorial states.

The normative adequacy of this statist approach to implementation is a central matter of controversy within this volume, especially in the chapters by Marc Weller and Nicholas Wheeler. I return to it myself later in this chapter.

HEGEMONY AND SETTLED NORMS

The next several sections provide a series of increasingly deep and substantive, and thus increasingly controversial, justifications of the Universal Declaration model. I begin with a descriptive, empirical claim: Human rights have become a hegemonic political discourse, or what Mervyn Frost calls "settled norms" of contemporary international society,[5] principles that are widely accepted as authoritative within the society of states. Both nationally and internationally, political legitimacy is increasingly judged by and expressed in terms of internationally recognized human rights.

The six leading international human rights treaties (on civil and political rights; economic, social, and cultural rights; racial discrimination; discrimination against women; torture; and the rights of the child) had an average of 154 parties at the end of 2000.[6] Even more notable is the penetration of human rights into bilateral, multilateral, and transnational diplomacy. In the 1970s, considerable controversy still raged over whether human rights were even an appropriate concern of foreign policy. As late as 1980, only a handful of states had explicit international human rights policies, and most of those usually were supported only with verbal and symbolic policy instruments. Today, however, human rights are a standard subject of bilateral and multilateral diplomacy.

Human rights norms and values are also penetrating more deeply into a growing number of national societies. Both governments and their opponents appeal to human rights not only much more frequently but more centrally than just a few decades ago. Compare, for example, the terms of debate and the range of political options considered nationally and regionally today in Latin America, Africa, and Asia with those in the 1960s and 1970s.

This does not mean that human rights have been enthusiastically embraced everywhere. For many, they are a "default option,"[7] accepted only because the leading competitors have been delegitimized. Even cynical uses pay tribute to the moral imperative of a commitment to human rights. And as the Helsinki Final Act illustrates, such norms can take on an independent life of their own, with consequences very different from those intended by cynical endorsers.

The prominence of human rights in contemporary international society is not unrelated to their endorsement by the world's leading power, the United States, and its principal allies. The Universal Declaration model, however, also responds to some of the most important social and political aspirations of individuals, families, and groups in most countries of the world. Human rights dominate political debate not only because of the support of materially dominant powers but also because a wide range of states, groups, and individuals at least quasi-voluntarily accepts them. They have authority, as well as the backing of force, and thus have become internationally hegemonic in a Gramscian sense of the term.

AN OVERLAPPING CONSENSUS ON
INTERNATIONAL HUMAN RIGHTS

John Rawls distinguishes "comprehensive religious, philosophical, or moral doctrines" from "political conceptions of justice."[8] Because the latter address only the political structure of society, defined (as far as possible) independent of any particular comprehensive doctrine, adherents of different comprehensive doctrines may reach an "overlapping consensus" on a political conception of justice.[9] I will argue that there is an international overlapping consensus on the Universal Declaration model.[10]

The idea of overlapping (rather than complete) political (rather than moral or religious) consensus offers a plausible answer to the question "How is it possible that there can be a stable and just society whose free and equal citizens are deeply divided by conflicting and even incommensurable religious, philosophical, and moral doctrines?"[11] This answer seems especially attractive in a "postmodern" world skeptical of foundations. It also has special attractions for a culturally and politically diverse pluralist international society.

Moral theories and other comprehensive doctrines have rarely (until recently) been founded on human rights. For example, human rights, despite their political prominence, have played a tiny part in the history of (Western) moral theory.[12] Nonetheless, human rights can be relatively easily derived from many moral theories; for example, they can be seen as encoded in or derived from the natural law, as political means to further human good (utility), or as political institutions designed to produce virtuous citizens. The increasing political prominence of human rights over the past few decades has led more and more adherents of a growing range of comprehensive doctrines to endorse human rights—but (only) as a political conception of justice. For example, Muslims of various political persuasions in many parts of the Islamic world have in recent decades developed Islamic doctrines of human rights that are strikingly similar in substance to the Universal Declaration.[13]

Although internationally recognized human rights "do not depend on any particular comprehensive religious doctrine of human nature,"[14] they are not compatible with all comprehensive doctrines. Claims such as those in the covenants that "these rights derive from the inherent dignity of the human person" or in the Vienna Declaration that "all human rights derive from the dignity and worth inherent in the human person" set the range of possible comprehensive doctrines within an overlapping consensus. The link between human rights and comprehensive doctrines, although loose, is a matter of substance, not just procedural agreement. Certain comprehensive doctrines are in principle excluded from the consensus. Most important, human rights, because they are held equally by all human beings, are incompatible with all fundamentally inegalitarian comprehensive doctrines.

EQUAL CONCERN AND RESPECT

Elsewhere,[15] drawing heavily on Ronald Dworkin,[16] I have shown that the full list of rights in the Universal Declaration and the covenants is easily derived from the requirement that states treat each citizen with equal concern and respect. Here I will argue that the practice of equal and inalienable rights held by all human beings can be seen as a political conception of justice based on equal concern and respect that has been accepted in significant measure for intrinsic or moral reasons, not just as a modus vivendi.[17]

Human rights are both constitutive and regulative norms. We are most immediately familiar with their regulative aspects: "No one shall be subjected to torture or to cruel, inhuman or degrading treatment or punishment"; "Everyone has the right to work, to free choice of employment, to just and favorable conditions of work and to protection against unemployment." Even more important, though, human rights constitute individuals as a particular kind of political subject, as citizens entitled to a government that will recognize, implement, and protect their human rights. By defining the requirements and limits of legitimate government, they constitute states fit to govern rights-holding citizens.

The equality of all human beings leads "naturally" to a political emphasis on autonomy. To justify denying or severely restricting individual autonomy almost necessarily involves an appeal to inequality. Equal and autonomous rights-bearing individuals are entitled to make fundamental choices about what constitutes the good life (for them), with whom they associate, and how. The state must treat such individuals with equal concern and respect.

A list of (human and legal) rights reflects a particular understanding of the meaning of equal concern and respect, based on a substantive conception of human dignity, of the conditions required for human flourishing. Human rights promise to (re)shape political and social relations so that this moral vision will be realized. Equal, inalienable rights held by all against state and society provide a mechanism to realize a world of equal and autonomous human beings. The effective implementation of the specified rights will *produce* the envisioned person/life (assuming a certain coherence and practicality in that vision).

The underlying vision of human possibilities in the Universal Declaration model cannot be separated from the political principles and institutions by which those possibilities are to be realized. Human rights thus are simultaneously a "utopian" vision and a set of institutions—equal and inalienable rights—for realizing at least an approximation of that vision. The substantive attractions of this particular "realistic utopia"[18] go a long way toward explaining the hegemonic power of the Universal Declaration model.

DEFINING LIBERALISM

Equal concern and respect, understood as a political conception of justice, can be endorsed by a variety of comprehensive doctrines. I turn now to one, liberalism. In so doing, the chapter moves from description to an increasingly prescriptive argument. Starting from the common association of human rights with "Western liberalism," both in their historical development and in contemporary political practice, I argue that (a particular type of) liberalism provides a strong normative foundation for the substance of the Universal Declaration model and for its continuing refinement and elaboration in the coming decades.

Although "liberalism" is a complex and contested set of orientations and values, it is *relatively* uncontroversial to say that it is rooted in a commitment to liberty, freedom, or, in the formulation I prefer, autonomy. More particularly, liberals give central political place to *individual* autonomy, rather than the liberty of society, the state, or other corporate actors. Liberals see individuals as entitled to "govern" their lives, to make important life choices for themselves, within limits connected primarily with the mutual recognition of equal opportunities for others.

Liberalism also is specially committed to equality—although most liberal (and nonliberal) theories and all liberal (and nonliberal) societies ultimately permit substantial economic, social, or political inequality. Liberty is seen not as a special privilege of an elite but as (in principle) available to all. Equal liberty for all is at the heart of any liberal political vision.[19]

Figure 2.1 categorizes liberal theories along two dimensions: the extent to which they emphasize rights or the good (or virtue or some other value) and the substantive "thickness" of their conceptions of those core values.

John Locke is the seminal figure in the strand of liberalism that grounds the commitment to equal liberty on natural, or what we today call human, rights. Its roots go back at least to Leveler and Digger arguments during the English Civil War. Immanuel Kant, Thomas Paine, and Jean-Jacques Rousseau were leading eighteenth-century proponents. John Rawls and Dworkin are prominent recent American representatives.

Liberalism, however, also has a strong historical association with utilitarianism, a good-based theory. The roots of this tradition run back at least to

Rights Based   Good Based

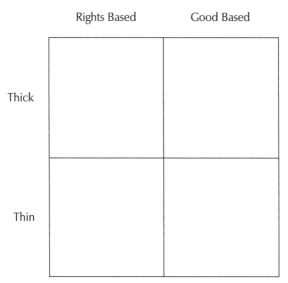

Figure 2.1   A Typology of Liberal Theories

Thomas Hobbes, but the seminal figure is Jeremy Bentham. It was the dominant vision of liberalism in Britain in the nineteenth century. A microeconomic version underlies contemporary "neoliberal" market-oriented economic reforms. My purpose here is to advance a rights-based liberal defense of the Universal Declaration model. Good-based conceptions, however, make human rights at best a second-order or derivative political principle. Therefore, although many good-based liberals participate in the overlapping consensus on international human rights, their views will not be considered here.

In fact, microeconomic, utilitarian neoliberalism is fundamentally opposed to the liberal human rights perspective I defend. Its logic of efficiency is aggregate, and thus collectivist, in sharp contrast to the logic of individual human rights.[20] Neoliberal equality involves political indifference to competing preferences—unbiased treatment in the marketplace—rather than guaranteed access to essential goods, services, and opportunities. Neoliberal structural adjustment is *very* different from the welfare states of Europe and North America with which the Universal Declaration model has (rightly) been specially associated.

Turning to the second dimension of our typology, the range of recognized rights, three important contemporary variants of rights-based liberalism can be identified. At the end points of the continuum are what I label "European" (or social democratic) or "minimalist" (or libertarian) liberalism, with the "American" variant lying somewhere in the middle.

A liberalism compatible with the Universal Declaration model must be strongly egalitarian, must actively embrace an extensive system of economic and social rights, and must reflect a robust (procedural and substantive) conception of democracy.[21] The European welfare state is the leading practical exemplar of such a position, especially in its social democratic conception. It is distinguished by a dual emphasis on the equal enjoyment of all human rights by all members of the political community and an extensive list of economic and social rights. *All* internationally recognized human rights are seen as entitlements of individuals—social and political claims that impose duties on the state and society—rather than mere liberties. Even with recent welfare state retrenchments, all the states of Western Europe lie toward the top left of figure 2.1. At the bottom left of the figure lies a minimalist liberalism that emphasizes individual personal liberties and includes only a short list of economic and social rights. Some circles refer to this as "classical" liberalism. In the United States, it is perhaps most neutrally described as "libertarian."

Minimalist liberalism's truncated list of human rights is substantively incompatible with the Universal Declaration model. Whatever its historical or philosophical merits, it is best seen as a critique of the substance of the Universal Declaration model, despite the considerable overlap on civil and political rights. For the past half century, *no* liberal democratic regime in Western Europe and North America, not even the United States, has pursued libertarian minimalist policies.

An important "intermediate" rights-based perspective emphasizes personal and civil liberties, a modest list of economic and social rights to be provided by a welfare state, and primarily procedural democracy. This "American" vision is much more willing than the libertarian to restrict personal liberties in order to remedy invidious inequalities. It also is somewhat more sympathetic to the idea of state action to assure minimum access to social and economic goods, services, and opportunities. The American welfare state is much less robust than those of Europe. In the United States this perspective is usually referred to as "liberal," pejoratively by the right. I will treat it as the thinnest plausible liberal conception of the Universal Declaration model.

"American" and "European" liberalisms are both committed to a democracy that operates only within the substantive requirements of equal human rights for all and to a welfare state that supplements a market system of production with substantial "welfare state" redistribution, again in order to assure equal human rights for all.[22] I will use *liberal* without qualification to refer to this shared political ideal of the liberal democratic welfare state and the underlying vision of equal concern and respect.

LIBERAL APPROACHES TO
GROUP DIFFERENCE

A standard, and theoretically important, complaint against liberalism is its excessive individualism. Most liberals, and the Universal Declaration model, do generally deny *human* rights to groups. They assume that individuals will exercise their rights collectively, as members of both "natural" and voluntary groups, not as atomistic or deracinated individuals.

All liberal regimes in practice recognize *legal* rights of groups ranging from businesses and trade unions, to churches and civic associations, to bowling leagues and hunt clubs. A great range of internationally recognized human rights are of special interest and value to marginalized or despised groups. For example, freedoms of thought, conscience, religion, opinion, and expression protect group, as well as individual, difference. Family rights, including the right of parents to choose the kind of education given to their children, protect the transmission of group beliefs and practices.

Nonetheless, issues that some see as matters of "group rights" are addressed by liberals and by the Universal Declaration model primarily through individual rights. In this and the following two sections, I argue that a liberal individual rights strategy to remedying the sufferings of members of despised, oppressed, or disadvantaged groups remains viable in the contemporary world.

Nondiscrimination

Liberal approaches to difference span a continuum lying between two very different kinds of communitarianism. At one end are communitarians that allow or require the state to impose civil and legal disabilities against members of certain groups. At the other end are visions of a society of "separate but equal" groups. Where communitarians see individuals and the social options available to them, as appropriately defined in significant measure by their group membership, liberals argue that group affiliations ought to be largely irrelevant to the rights and opportunities available to individuals.[23] Each individual, irrespective of race, gender, religion, or any other group affiliation, should be treated equally.

Nondiscrimination is thus the liberal starting point for addressing issues of group difference. The Universal Declaration model's general prohibition of discrimination is powerfully supplemented by a set of civil liberties (e.g., rights to freedom of expression, belief, and assembly) that specify particularly important activities where the state must respect individual liberty, whether that liberty is expressed in private or in public, alone or in association with others.

We can distinguish three ideal type interpretations of the requirement of nondiscrimination, which I will call toleration, equal protection, and multiculturalism. Toleration requires not imposing disabilities on individuals based on (voluntary, ascriptive, or imposed) group membership or disapproved behavior associated with a group.[24] It involves a principled political decision not to impose special burdens on (members of) despised groups. But they may still be marginalized and socially excluded.

Equal protection requires active efforts to ensure that members of disadvantaged or despised groups enjoy the (equal) rights that they formally hold. At minimum it involves an active effort to assure that people are not excluded from goods, services, and opportunities that would be available to them were they not members of despised or disadvantaged groups. In its stronger forms—affirmative action and even certain kinds of reverse discrimination—equal protection seeks to assure that members of targeted groups achieve full legal and political incorporation into society.

Equal protection, however, allows a neutral, even negative, evaluation of diversity. Multiculturalism positively values diversity, implying policies that recognize, celebrate, preserve, or foster group differences. Rather than attempt to abstract from group differences, as in toleration and equal treatment, those differences are highlighted and positively valued, within a general context of equal concern and respect.

Liberal Neutrality and the Protection of Difference

Its respect for and endeavors to assure the realization of the human rights of its citizens define the legitimacy of the liberal state. The purposes of the state thus ordinarily are subordinated to the rights of its citizens. This subordination is often expressed in the claim that the liberal state must be neutral with respect to the values, purposes, and life plans of its citizens, insofar as they are rooted in protected autonomous exercises of human rights. This formulation of the requirement of nondiscrimination places the emphasis on respect for individual autonomy.

Liberal neutrality, however, is not a sign of indifference to the decisions of citizens. It reflects an active commitment, embedded in the principle of equal concern and respect, to fostering citizens' enjoyment of their rights. Neutrality operates only within the boundaries of human rights.

To require identical treatment of all individual or group differences would be morally perverse. Consider, for example, the consequences of tolerating pedophiles, violent racists, those who derive pleasure from kidnapping and torturing strangers, and religious missionaries committed to killing all those they cannot convert. Such differences fall outside the range of the overlapping consensus and thus should not be treated neutrally by a liberal state.

As Charles Taylor notes, "liberalism can't and shouldn't claim complete . . . neutrality."[25]

Political liberalism's overlapping consensus does not (and should not) include all possible views. "Liberalism is not a possible meeting ground for all cultures, but is the political expression of one range of cultures, and quite incompatible with other ranges."[26] Neutrality, in other words, should be seen as an expression of the core value of equal concern and respect.

The liberal state is required to be neutral with respect to (i.e., not discriminate against) exercises of human rights. It need not be neutral to those activities not protected by human rights. It is required *not* to be neutral towards activities that infringe or violate human rights.

For example, a (liberal) state must not discriminate against any religion but need not be neutral toward (show equal concern and respect for) all conceptions of the purpose of sport (which are not ordinarily understood to be protected by internationally recognized human rights). Equal concern and respect for all political beliefs is required, but not for all beliefs about the origin of life. Creationism based on a literal reading of Genesis, for example, must be protected insofar as it reflects an exercise of human rights to freedoms of religion and speech. It need not—probably should not—be treated equally in science classes or natural history museums.

Each state/society has considerable latitude in how it treats, for example, particular minority religions. It would be completely consistent with international human rights standards to (merely) tolerate minority religion *a,* while actively supporting the majority religion and minority religion *b.* Such decisions fall within the margin of appreciation left to states by the broadly stated norms of the Universal Declaration. States may choose to treat all religions identically—for example, no state support for any, as in the United States—but that is required neither by the Universal Declaration model nor by liberalism, as I am using that term here.

As Michael Walzer nicely puts it, liberalism thus understood is "permissive, not determinative." It allows for a state committed to the survival and flourishing of a particular nation, culture, or religion, or of a (limited) set of nations, cultures, and religions—so long as the basic rights of citizens who have different commitments or no such commitments at all are protected.[27]

There is not merely a place for difference within liberalism. The protection of (many forms of) difference is one of its most important political objectives.

Freedom of Association and Guaranteed Participation

Nondiscrimination, however, is only one part of the liberal approach to difference. Remedying systematic discrimination usually requires collective action, which in the Universal Declaration model is enabled by rights to freedom of association and democratic political participation. Furthermore, active participation in society—including a right to work, understood as a right to economic participation—is an intrinsically important value, an essential aspect of (personal or group) autonomy.

Nondiscrimination protects a sphere of personal/group liberty and offers protection against suffering imposed for group membership. Freedom of association and rights of participation make individual members of the public entitled to act individually and collectively, with others of their own choosing, to realize their visions of the good life.

Taken together, nondiscrimination and freedom of association, broadly understood, provide a wide-ranging and coherent set of protections for groups and individuals rooted in the core (liberal and human rights) values of equality and autonomy. This liberal approach is not without difficulties.

Freedom of association, because it is a right of individuals, models group membership as a "voluntary" exercise of the protected autonomy of its members. Descriptively, this is obviously inaccurate for groups whose identity is in significant measure externally imposed. It may also be problematic groups marked by biological signs such as skin color or sex—although, it must be emphasized, race and gender are social constructs, not natural categories.

Nonetheless, the liberal approach has considerable leverage even in such cases. When individuals are subjected to suffering without any voluntary association with the group in question, nondiscrimination often will provide the appropriate remedy. When, for example, women or racial minorities begin to act collectively to realize their interests or protect their rights, freedom of association usually moves to the forefront of the struggle for equality and social justice.

GROUP HUMAN RIGHTS: A SKEPTICAL VIEW

Without denying the achievements and attractions of this liberal approach, the chapters by Eva Brems and Jennifer Jackson-Preece argue for supplementing it with group human rights. In this section, I pose seven questions that I think should lead us to be extremely wary of such a move.[28]

1. How do we identify the groups that (ought to) hold human rights? Not *all* groups have human rights. Consider, for example, states, multinational corporations, gangs, and barbershop quartets.

New substantive (individual or group) rights typically emerge as responses to the appearance or recognition of new "standard threats" to human dignity.[29] Consider, for example, the rise of the practice of disappearances in the 1970s and the ensuing international response. This standard threat provides a self-limiting character to such expansions of the list of internationally recognized human rights. But group human rights are distinguished by right holder, not the substance of the threat/right. There is thus a serious danger of excessive proliferation of human rights.

Suppose that we were to agree that group human rights for, say, minorities would be desirable. By what criteria can we restrict group human rights *only* to minorities? This is not necessarily an intractable problem, but it is an important one to which advocates of group rights seem to have largely ignored.

The most obvious criterion—namely, a long history of ongoing, systematic suffering—would yield group human rights for women; racial, ethnic, religious, and linguistic minorities; indigenous peoples; homosexuals; people with disabilities; the aged; children; and the poor, to mention just some of the more prominent groups. Pretty much everyone except prosperous white males—and many of them as well—would have group human rights. Such a radical expansion of right holders and associated claims of rights seems to me extremely problematic.

2. Having identified group x as a potential holder of human rights, what particular substantive rights does/should x have? Certainly it is not enough that x wants r in order to establish a (human) right of x to r.[30] On what ground can we say that others owe r to x *as a matter of (human) rights*?

The most limited move would be to recognize those rights needed to enjoy already-recognized human rights. These, however, would be only temporary, remedial measures and thus probably best seen as practical measures to achieve nondiscrimination. A more interesting (because more genuine) class of group rights would appeal instead to the particular character of the group or to values or attributes not already recognized. Claims of threatened values that merit group human rights protection need to be evaluated on a case-by-case basis. My point for now simply is that in order to avoid debasing the currency of human rights with a flood of new, unregulated coinage, advocates of such rights ought to face a considerable burden of proof.

3. Who exercises group rights? Rights work not simply by being voluntarily respected by duty bearers but, most important, by being claimed or otherwise exercised by right holders. Governments exercise the rights of states; the rights of business corporations, by shareholders, directors, and managers. Who ought—and is able—to exercise, for example, minority rights, understood as rights of a group?

The problems of group agency may be modest for small, concentrated, and homogenous groups with a strong tradition of collective action. (Indigenous peoples come readily to mind.) When the group is largely voluntary (e.g., some religious minorities), the officers of the association (e.g., a clerical hierarchy) may be a plausible agent. But where the group is "natural," ascribed, or coercively defined and maintained, agency is likely to be highly problematic, especially when the group is large or heterogeneous.[31] The "solution" of having group rights exercised by individuals or associations of group members, beyond its irony, raises serious questions as to whether such rights really are *group* rights, rather than exercises of individual rights.

4. How do we handle conflicts of rights? Although all rights conflict with at least some other rights or important social interests, introducing group rights will not only increase the number of conflicts but will create competition between qualitatively different kinds of rights that is likely to be unusually intense. How should we respond to native North American tribes that discriminate against women who claim equal treatment? Related issues may be raised by defining who is (and is not) in the group. Especially problematic from a human rights perspective are efforts to block or punish exit from the group.

5. Are the purported group rights necessary? Is the problem a lack of group rights or rather inadequate efforts to implement individual human rights? Most often it seems to me the latter. Once more, the burden of proof ought to lie with advocates of the rights.

6. Why should we expect group rights to succeed where individual rights have failed? If a government refuses to respect the individual rights of a despised minority, often—although not always (discussed later)—it will be hard to imagine it being convinced to treat those people better as members of a group. In fact, if group rights emphasize the difference between "us" and "them," might this not lead to worse treatment?

7. Are group *rights* the best way to protect or realize the interests, values, or desires of a group? "Proponents of collective rights . . . often seem to move in a rather cursory way from the claim that communities are good things to the claim that communities have rights."[32] We must demand an argument for protecting the value in question through the mechanism of rights. In particular, we must ask whether the global recognition of a new group *human* right is either necessary or desirable. At this point, we begin to circle back to the questions of *which* groups ought to be added to a list of internationally recognized holders of *which* human rights.

None of these problems is fatal. Many are largely matters of "negative externalities," undesirable unintended consequences, where the required calculus of costs and benefits may vary dramatically with circumstances. Some group human rights may overcome all of these problems. (Later I suggest that this is true for at least some indigenous peoples.) Nonetheless, I think that the preceding discussion does caution prima facie skepticism toward (although not automatic rejection of) most (but not necessarily all) group human rights claims.[33] At the very least, we should insist on clarity in specifying the "gap" in the Universal Declaration model that is being addressed and careful attention to unintended consequences of the proposed remedy.

WOMEN, MINORITIES, AND
INDIGENOUS PEOPLES

In this section I briefly examine human rights claims for three groups that receive extended discussion in later chapters: women, minorities, and indigenous peoples.

Women

Although women have a sad history of near-universal, systematic suffering in virtually every area of the globe, the idea of group human rights for women is fatally undermined by problems of collective agency for a diverse group that includes half of humanity.[34] It is also unclear what rights women as a group might be held to possess. Unless we accept gender roles that postulate qualitative differences between men and women, all the obvious candidates for special women's rights seem best formulated in gender-neutral terms.[35]

For example, family rights, reproductive rights, or protection against domestic violence are not special rights of women. Although the majority of adult victims of violence in the home are women, this no more makes protection against domestic violence a (group) right of women than the fact that the majority of those exercising (or suffering violations of) trade union rights are men makes the right to bargain collectively a (group) right of men. The principle in each case is independent of sex or gender: no one should be subject to violent assault by anyone, including a domestic partner; everyone is entitled to bargain collectively.

In practice, women in all countries continue to suffer (more or less severe) deprivations and indignities *as women*. But this simply does not entail the appropriateness, let alone the necessity, of group human rights. Compare workers who suffer as workers and political dissidents who suffer as dissidents. In each case the suffering arises from coercively imposed norms that create a subordinate status group.

Let us grant women special collective human rights. Why should we expect these rights to be better implemented than already-established rights? Especially in light of the insurmountable problems of collective agency, such rights would most likely turn out to be, at best, irrelevant abstractions—when they were not used by patriarchal forces to divert attention and resources from efforts to establish true nondiscrimination and equal participation for women in all aspects of society.

Minorities

To evade controversy over the term *minorities*,[36] I will follow article 27 of the ICCPR and restrict discussion to ethnic, religious, and linguistic minorities.[37] The established international approach to minority protection rests on the dual pillars of nondiscrimination and "measures to protect and promote the separate identity of the minority groups."[38] Protecting and promoting minority identity, and its political expressions in the form of minority autonomy, is the principal locus of potential group rights claims.

Religious minorities, however, present a *relatively* easy case for a liberal, individual rights approach. Freedoms of religion, expression, and association ordinarily will provide a context for perpetuating religious identity, particularly in conjunction with established international human rights norms that provide family control over the type of education children receive.[39] Furthermore, "church" structures, which are readily conceptualized in terms of freedom of association, are an obvious mechanism for collective action, without the need for additional group rights.

Ethnic and linguistic minorities may pose more serious problems. Language rights for linguistic minorities may be especially problematic because almost all aspects of public life are touched by language.[40] If serious social or economic disabilities are associated with use of a minority language, mere toleration is unlikely to be enough to preserve group identity.

Even in these cases, though, nondiscrimination, freedom of association, and family education rights provide considerable leverage. For example, one could readily argue that it is discriminatory to provide access to public services—including schooling—only in a dominant language. Single-language public media might also be seen as involving invidious linguistic discrimination. Whether such measures are adequate is an empirical, not a theoretical, issue.

My sense, however, is that advocates of group rights for minorities are likely to see the preceding paragraphs as "missing the point." They are interested in protections for group identity that go well beyond those provided by strong and effective measures of nondiscrimination and freedom of association.

Consider Jacob Levy's typology of cultural rights: exemptions, assistance, self-government, external rules restricting nonmembers, internal rules controlling members, recognition or enforcement of traditional rules, minority representation in government bodies, and symbolic acknowledgment of worth or status.[41] Nondiscrimination and freedom of association principally encompass measures involving exemptions, assistance, symbolic acknowledgment, and some forms of external rules on outsiders. Group rights claims, by contrast, are most likely to lie in the other categories.

Are *all* minorities, as a matter of human rights, entitled to, for example, self-government or guaranteed group representation in governmental bodies? A just society certainly may legitimately choose to grant some form of self-government to particular minorities. But is it a human rights violation if the society does not? I can see no reason why minorities, or any other group, should be universally entitled to self-government, or even guaranteed group representation. And I am aware of no morally attractive principle that would grant such rights to minorities that does not also grant them to an impractical large number of other groups as well.

Should minority communities have guaranteed legal rights to discipline members? Again, the precise form of the question is important. We are interested here in legal rights. (Members of the community are already free to shun those who violate group norms.) Because we are dealing with a putative human right, the issue is not whether it is permissible or desirable in particular cases to recognize such legal rights, but whether all minorities everywhere are entitled to such powers over their members.

Given space constraints, let me simply suggest that such rights are likely to be least problematic when the minority can be understood as a free association of individuals. The group readily conceives voluntary membership as implying acceptance of discipline. By allowing effective exit options, conflicts between the human rights of individuals and the group rights of minorities can be moderated to perhaps acceptable levels.

Under any other interpretation, individual rights would be subordinated to the group rights of the minority. I can see no reason why minorities should have such superior rights, which are, I think rightly, denied to other groups. In any case, if this is where the argument takes us, we are no longer talking about modest supplements to the Universal Declaration model. These are major changes that require the sort of argument that few advocates of group human rights for minorities even attempt to make.

I am not, let me repeat, challenging the idea of minority rights as they are already established in the major international human rights instruments (i.e., as individual rights that provide special protections to members of minority groups). I am not even challenging group rights of minorities. For example, the Singaporean practice of reserving legislative seats for representatives of Hindu and Malay communities clearly is (and ought to remain) defensible on human rights grounds. Rather, I am questioning the idea of group *human* rights for minorities.

Singapore's system of reserved legislative seats, or India's much more extensive system of reservations for (members of) scheduled castes and tribes, falls within the realm of discretion allowed states in discharging their human rights obligations and coordinating them with the pursuit of other important social purposes. Although such practices have been controversial, both nationally and internationally, they are not clearly prohibited by the Universal Declaration model. But neither are they required. And it would be a serious error to view the absence of such reservations—or any other group rights of minorities—as a violation of human rights.

Protecting Group Identity

This liberal approach to difference may, it must be acknowledged, lead to the weakening, or even demise, of some minority (and other group) identities. Group identities, however, are not now, and I think ought not become, subjects of international human rights protection. Only individual autonomy gives rise, and value, to the sorts of identities that must be respected by others. Any particular identity is entitled to protection only because it is an expression of the rights and values of those who carry it.

Others may choose to value difference for its own sake or for the social benefits that diversity provides. They are required, as a matter of human rights, only to respect the decisions that people choose to act on for themselves, within the limits of their rights. Neither individually nor collectively do others have a right to impose any particular identity on a resistant individual or group because, for example, their ancestors bore that identity or because particular social roles are widely endorsed.

In almost all societies almost all adults have multiple identities. It is for such real, and realistically complex, human beings[42] to balance the varied roles and histories that shape their life. Such choices are, of course, conditioned and thus in some (relatively uninteresting) sense not "free." But if equal treatment and freedom of association are fully realized, those choices can appropriately be seen as autonomous exercises of internationally recognized human rights.

In a social and political environment marked by equal treatment and freedom of association, groups of all sorts have a "fair" opportunity to compete in shaping the identities of "its" members. If a particular identity is valued sufficiently, it will survive, perhaps even thrive. If not, then it will not. That is the way it should be.[43] The only alternative is to say that identities are things that can rightly be imposed on those who reject, deny, or seek to modify them. This is not an extension of the Universal Declaration model but a rejection of its foundations.

People should be—and through the rights of nondiscrimination, freedom of association, and a variety of other internationally recognized human rights are—entitled to develop, express, and modify their identities, acting both individually and collectively.[44] No particular identity ought to be entitled to special protection *as a matter of human rights* beyond that which derives from the (individual and collective) choices of its members.

Nonetheless, where equal treatment and effective freedom of association are systematically violated, there may be no viable alternative to minority self-government. Where it can be plausibly argued that equal treatment is decidedly less likely without minority self-government, then that may indeed be the best human rights strategy. But this does not make minority self-government a human right. Rather, it is a local political decision about means of implementing internationally recognized human rights, within the margin of discretion allowed by international human rights norms. Such instances of minority self-government are best understood as extensions of the right to nondiscrimination, rather a new class of human rights. When such rights come to be implemented territorially, turning an oppressed minority into a potentially oppressing majority (e.g., Kosovo), vigilance is required to minimize unintended negative human rights consequences.

Indigenous Peoples

Indigenous peoples may be seen as posing an extreme example of just such a situation where effective equal treatment, perhaps even survival, requires a group right to self-government. To simplify the discussion, let us imagine an indigenous community with the following characteristics.[45] The community is small if not a face-to-face society, at least one in which the lineage of most members is known to most other members. It is geographically and cultur-ally largely separate from the mainstream society. Mainstream institutions thus appear to most members of the community as alien. Because there are also regular contacts with the "outside" world, we can think of those who reside in the community as having chosen to stay. Finally, the indigenous community is fragile, in the sense that well-established mainstream institu-tions (e.g., private property in land) would *as an unintended consequence* radically alter the community's way of life in a fashion that most members would reject if given a choice.

In such circumstances, it seems plausible to argue that the indigenous com-munity has chosen a way of life. That choice demands, on its face, a certain degree of respect from mainstream society and institutions, extending in at least some cases to accommodation and protection of the chosen way of life. In fact, in the conditions I have outlined there would appear to be no effective alternative to group rights involving both considerable self-government— which would be facilitated by the group's small size, geographical concentra-tion, and cultural history—and restrictions on the activities of nonmembers, in light of the fragility of the indigenous community and its way of life. Fur-thermore, the negative externalities of these particular group rights are mod-est, imposing severe burdens on relatively few outsiders in return for immense benefits to the group and its members.

The broader significance of this "exception" bears noting. Even if most claims for group human rights are profoundly defective, no particular claim can be rejected without examining its merits in detail. Even where skepticism is the appropriate general attitude, every claim for recognizing a new human right deserves careful scrutiny.

Systematic threats to human dignity change over time. In addition, our understandings of the nature of the life worthy of a human being, and of the practical meaning of equal concern and respect, may change. Although I am critical of most proposed additions to the list of internationally recognized human rights, I am profoundly sympathetic to the collective project of this volume of exploring gaps in and needed additions to the Universal Declaration model. The Universal Declaration and the covenants may be (for us, now) authoritative, even definitive. It would be tragic, however, were we to see them as the last word on international human rights.

INTERNATIONAL HUMAN RIGHTS AND THE STATE

However skeptical of group human rights one might be, we cannot overlook the deep, although usually obscured, communitarianism in the Universal Declaration model. As we saw earlier, states are the near exclusive instrument for implementing internationally recognized human rights. The assumed political community for the practice of human rights, in the current hegemonic understanding, is the sovereign territorial state. In effect, one group, the state, is privileged over all others. And even in the post–Cold War world, state sovereignty generally insulates governments that fail to discharge their human rights obligations from coercive international action.

The Universal Declaration model in effect transforms human rights into rights of citizens, a transformation that is explicit in classical contractarian theorists such as Hobbes and Locke. The rights that one enjoys thus depend heavily on accidents of birth or residence, especially in a world with huge legal and practical barriers to migration. Because life opportunities vary both dramatically and systematically from country to country, the resulting inequalities are largely indefensible, on moral grounds, from a human rights perspective.[46]

The priority given to states in the Universal Declaration model thus should be seen as practical rather than moral or theoretical, a concession to the international political reality of the primacy of sovereign territorial states. Rather than a political conception of justice in the strong sense of a view endorsed for largely intrinsic reasons, it is instead a political modus vivendi endorsed largely for instrumental reasons.

If the Universal Declaration model's essential character is cosmopolitan rather than nationalist, the challenge we face is to push the hegemonic understanding away from this near exclusive reliance on states for implementation, to move beyond this morally defective modus vivendi. The developing post–Cold War practice of humanitarian intervention, discussed in the chapter by Wheeler, represents one small but significant step in that direction.

The limitations of contemporary practice should not be underestimated. Even today, the best we can say is that humanitarian intervention in the face of genocide or extreme humanitarian emergency is legally permissible (but not required). As Kosovo clearly indicates, the permissible modalities of such intervention remain contentious. Furthermore, there seems to be little evidence that this exception is spilling over into other, more common kinds of gross and systematic human rights violations.

Nonetheless, the international immunity of the state has been punctured. And a strong argument of an emerging (substantive, not merely instrumental) overlapping consensus can be made. For these kinds of violations, the relevant community for protecting human rights seems to be becoming the society of states, supplemented, perhaps, by regional communities.

We should remember, however, that not all forms of cosmopolitanism have the same, or even necessarily positive, human rights consequences. For example, the cosmopolitan vision of certain evangelists of global capitalism is profoundly problematic from a human rights perspective. Therefore, without minimizing the threats to human rights that states pose, it is no less important to remember that the state is our principal contemporary mechanism for implementing and enforcing human rights. Most people still enjoy most of their internationally recognized human rights through the agency or mediation of the states of which they are a national. We thus should be wary of antistatist arguments, such as those by neoliberal international financial institutions, until we have been convinced that an alternative to state provision of human rights—civil and political rights no less than economic and social rights—has been identified and has plausible prospects of being put in place.

In summary, I have tried to suggest that the principal human rights tasks facing us today lie not in developing new rights but rather in better implementing the rights enumerated in the Universal Declaration and the covenants. Even in the area of implementation, without denigrating the possibilities represented by new supranational institutions, much more is to be gained by directing our limited resources to protecting and perfecting existing state-based mechanisms. Rather than substantially alter the Universal Declaration model, the key to human rights progress in the coming decades lies in more creative, and more effective efforts by states, citizens, and other national and international actors to implement and enforce it.

NOTES

1. For further conceptual analysis, see Jack Donnelly, *Universal Human Rights in Theory and Practice* (Ithaca, N.Y.: Cornell University Press, 1989), chap. 1, and James W. Nickel, *Making Sense of Human Rights: Philosophical Reflections on the Universal Declaration of Human Rights* (Berkeley: University of California Press, 1987).

2. Donnelly, *Universal Human Rights*, 1–2, 121–22.

3. See www.unhchr.ch/pdf/report.pdf. Although the United States is a party only to the civil and political covenant, ideological attacks on economic and social rights have largely disappeared from American diplomacy. Furthermore, the recent American emphasis on markets is regularly defended by their greater capacity to deliver economic welfare and by arguments of long-run interdependence between economic and political freedom. In practice, the United States has an extensive welfare state that protects a wide (although by no means adequate) range of economic and social rights. For an argument that economic rights have been central to the Western liberal approach to human rights since Locke, see Donnelly, *Universal Human Rights*, chap. 5.

4. For overviews of the international implementation machinery, see Jack Donnelly, *International Human Rights*, 2d ed. (Boulder, Colo.: Westview, 1998), chap. 4, and David P. Forsythe, *Human Rights in International Relations* (Cambridge: Cambridge University Press, 2000), chap. 3. For an authoritative examination of international human rights reporting, see Philip Alston and James Crawford, eds., *The Future of UN Human Rights Treaty Monitoring* (Cambridge: Cambridge University Press, 2000).

5. Mervyn Frost, *Ethics in International Affairs: A Constitutive Theory* (Cambridge: Cambridge University Press, 1996), 104–11.

6. See www.unhchr.ch/pdf/report.pdf.

7. I take this term from Claus Offe, who used it at a conference on globalization and human rights at Yale University in the spring of 1999.

8. John Rawls, *Political Liberalism* (New York: Columbia University Press, 1996), xliii–xlv, 11–15, 174–76; and *The Law of Peoples* (Cambridge, Mass.: Harvard University Press, 1999), 31–32, 172–73.

9. Rawls, *Political Liberalism*, 133–72, 385–96.

10. My arguments, however, should be read as drawing on, rather than simply elaborating, Rawls; as Rawlsian, but in some details different from Rawls.

11. Rawls, *Political Liberalism*, 133.

12. No major moral philosopher prior to World War II took human rights as a moral primitive. More recently, Alan Gewirth stands as a moderately prominent exception that proves the rule. See *Human Rights: Essays on Justification and Applications* (Chicago: University of Chicago Press, 1982).

13. See, for example, the Arab Charter of Human Rights, adopted by the Arab League in 1994 (www1.umn.edu/humanrts/instree/arabhrcharter.html) and the Cairo Declaration on Human Rights in Islam (www1.umn.edu/humanrts/instree/cairodeclaration.html). For recent scholarly discussions, see, for example, Shaheen Sardar Ali, *Gender and Human Rights in Islam and International Law: Equal before Allah, Unequal before Man?* (Boston: Kluwer Law International, 2000); Mahmood Monshipouri, *Islamism, Secularism, and Human Rights in the Middle-East* (Boulder, Colo.: Rienner, 1998); Ahmad Moussalli, *The Islamic Quest for Democracy, Pluralism, and Human Rights* (Gainesville: University Press of Florida, 2001); and Norani Othman, "Grounding Human Rights Arguments in Non-Western Culture: Shari'a and the Citizenship Rights of Women in a Modern Islamic State," in The East Asian Challenge for Human Rights, ed. Joanne R. Bauer and Daniel A. Bell (Cambridge: Cambridge University Press, 1999).

14. Rawls, *Law of Peoples*, 68. Although Rawls refers here explicitly to a short list of rights composed principally of life, liberty, property, and formal equality (65), the argument holds for the Universal Declaration model more generally. See also 78–81.

15. Donnelly, *Universal Human Rights*, 71–73.

16. See Ronald Dworkin, *A Matter of Principle* (Cambridge, Mass.: Harvard University Press, 1985), chap. 8.

17. For the importance of this distinction, see Rawls, *Political Liberalism*, 145–50.

18. Rawls, *Law of Peoples*, 11.

19. It is often argued that liberals (and nonliberals as well) face an inescapable trade-off between liberty and equality. Even if true, this underscores the commitment of liberalism to both values. What distinguishes liberal theories is their commitment to equal liberty for all, rather than, for example, equality for all or liberty for some. Different liberal theories have very different accounts of the meaning of "equal liberty for all." Even where liberals accept substantial inequality, it requires special defense—Rawls's "difference principle" (*A Theory of Justice* [Cambridge, Mass.: Harvard University Press, 1971], 65–73) is a much-discussed example—and is subject to liberal (as well as nonliberal) critique. Dworkin, *Matter of Principle*, chap. 9, offers an especially forceful argument for the centrality of equality to liberalism.

20. See Jack Donnelly, "Human Rights, Democracy, and Development," *Human Rights Quarterly* 21 (August 1999): 608–32, at 626–30.

21. On the complex relations between democracy and human rights, with an emphasis on their differing logic, see Donnelly, "Human Rights," 619–21.

22. For a further development of these claims, see Donnelly, "Human Rights," 619–21, 627–31.

23. I certainly do not want to deny that many people approach others significantly, even primarily, in group terms. But this sociological fact—to the extent that it is indeed a fact—has little moral force. In fact, I would suggest that "othering" group identities is the human rights problem, not a potential solution.

24. I do not mean to suggest that this thin conception is the only, let alone the best, conception of toleration. It simply marks an endpoint on the continuum of approaches to nondiscrimination I consider here. For a characteristically subtle study of toleration, see Michael Walzer, *On Toleration* (New Haven, Conn.: Yale University Press, 1997).

25. Charles Taylor, "The Politics of Recognition," in *Multiculturalism: Examining the Politics of Recognition*, ed. Amy Gutmann (Princeton, N.J.: Princeton University Press, 1994), 62.

26. Taylor, "Politics of Recognition," 62.

27. Michael Walzer, "Comment," in *Multiculturalism: Examining the Politics of Recognition*, ed. Amy Gutmann (Princeton, N.J.: Princeton University Press, 1994), 99–100.

28. To be as clear as possible at the outset, I want to emphasize that I do not argue that we should treat any of the issues raised in this or the following section "on a purely individual basis" (Kristin Henrard, *Devising an Adequate System of Minority Protection: Individual Human Rights, Minority Rights and the Right to Self-Determination* [The Hague: Martinus Nijhoff, 2000], 241). I have already emphasized the essentially social character of human rights. I argue only against groups as holders of

human rights. I am not arguing categorically against recognizing legal (rather than human) rights for groups.

In addition, I am concerned here only with group rights that are not reducible to individual rights. (Compare Marlies Galenkamp, *Individualism versus Collective Rights: The Concept of Collective Rights* [Rotterdam: Rotterdams Filosopische Studies, 1993].) Such irreducibly group rights pose a real and significant challenge to the Universal Declaration model that ought to be taken seriously however we evaluate it.

29. Henry Shue, *Basic Rights: Subsistence, Affluence, and U.S. Foreign Policy* (Princeton, N.J.: Princeton University Press, 1980), 29–34.

30. Compare Marlies Galenkamp, "The Rationale of Minority Rights: Wishes Rather Than Needs?" in *Do We Need Minority Rights? Conceptual Issues*, ed. Juha Raikka (The Hague: Martinus Nijhoff, 1996).

31. For a thoughtful and balanced philosophical discussion of the problem of group agency in the context of rights, see James W. Nickel, "Group Agency and Group Rights," in *Ethnicity and Group Rights*, ed. Ian Shapiro and Will Kymlicka (New York: New York University Press, 1997).

32. Michael Hartney, "Some Confusions Concerning Collective Rights," in *The Rights of Minority Cultures*, ed. Will Kymlicka (Oxford: Oxford University Press, 1995), 203.

33. For a sympathetic approach to at least some group rights issues, from a liberal perspective that draws heavily on Will Kymlicka, *Multicultural Citizenship: A Liberal Theory of Minority Rights* (Oxford: Oxford University Press, 1995), see Maleiha Malik, "Communal Goods as Human Rights," in *Understanding Human Rights*, ed. Conor Gearty and Adam Tomkins (London: Mansell, 1996). Malik also gives thoughtful consideration to the limitations of individual rights strategies for realizing communal goods.

34. Groups of women in particular localities or concerned with particular issues may have the necessary collective personality. Nondiscrimination and freedom of association usually will allow such groups to act effectively.

35. The obvious exception is childbearing. Not all women choose to or are capable of bearing children. The relevant group then would be (potentially) pregnant women. Any group (or individual) rights that they might have would involve only minor additions to the Universal Declaration.

36. See chapter 3 by Jackson-Preece in this volume and, more extensively, Henrard, *Minority Protection*, 16–55.

37. Racial minorities have been treated in international human rights law separately (and with a greater sense of importance and urgency). Other minority groups have been largely excluded. On homosexuals, see Jack Donnelly, "Nondiscrimination and Sexual Orientation: Making a Place for Sexual Minorities in the Global Human Rights Regime," in *Innovation and Inspiration: Fifty Years of the Universal Declaration of Human Rights*, ed. Peter R. Baehr, Cees Flinterman, and Mignon Senders (Amsterdam: Royal Academy of Arts and Sciences, 1999). In international human rights law, it is decidedly *not* the case that all "minorities," in the broad sense of that term, are treated equally.

38. Henrard, *Minority Protection*, 8.

39. This right is explicitly recognized in all three of the major international instruments: Universal Declaration, article 26; ICESCR, article 13.3; ICCPR, article 18.4.

40. For an overview of linguistic human rights issues, see Tove Skutnabb-Kangas and Robert Phillipson, "Linguistic Human Rights, Past and Present," in *Linguistic Human Rights: Overcoming Linguistic Discrimination* (Berlin: Mouton de Gruyter, 1995).

41. Jacob T. Levy, "Classifying Cultural Rights," in *Ethnicity and Group Rights*, ed. Ian Shapiro and Will Kymlicka (New York: New York University Press, 1997), 25.

42. As Jeremy Waldron notes, many advocates of group rights and minority cultures instead assume that individuals are (if not exclusively, at least primarily) members of a single, coherent, even homogenous "culture." "Minority Cultures and the Cosmopolitan Alternative," in *The Rights of Minority Cultures*, ed. Will Kymlicka (Oxford: Oxford University Press, 1995), 105–8.

43. This does not preclude active state support for the group in question. But such support should be seen as an expression of the values and choices of the society as a whole, operating through established political practices, rather than a matter of group human rights.

44. I find particularly attractive Waldron's suggestion ("Minority Cultures," 112) that we think of personal identity "not in terms of hierarchical management, but in terms of democratic self-government of a pluralistic population."

45. I claim only that some indigenous peoples approximate such a model.

46. For a brief argument to this conclusion, focusing on the issue of open immigration, see Joseph H. Carens, "Aliens and Citizens: The Case for Open Borders," in *The Rights of Minority Cultures*, ed. Will Kymlicka (Oxford: Oxford University Press, 1995).

II

THE CASE FOR GROUP RIGHTS

3

Human Rights and Cultural Pluralism
The "Problem" of Minorities

Jennifer Jackson-Preece

> The general tendency of the post-war movements for the promotion of
> human rights has been to subsume the problem of . . . minorities under
> the broader problem of ensuring basic individual rights to all human
> beings, without reference to membership in ethnic groups. The leading
> assumption has been that members of . . . minorities do not need, are not
> entitled to, or cannot be granted rights of a special character. The doc-
> trine of human rights has been put forward as a substitute for the con-
> cept of minority rights, with the strong implication that minorities
> whose members enjoy individual equality of treatment cannot legiti-
> mately demand facilities for the maintenance of their ethnic particu-
> larism.
>
> —*Inis Claude*[1]

HUMAN RIGHTS AND PLURAL SOCIETIES

The idea of human rights is predicated on the notion that every individual
human being, by virtue of his or her humanity, should have the freedom to
define, pursue, and realize his or her conception of the good life. In other
words, every man and woman, regardless of which sovereign jurisdiction
they happen to inhabit, should enjoy the circumstances to be a fully autonomous individual. From this fundamental conviction arises a whole series of
rights designed to ensure that such basic conditions of liberty exist for all
members of humankind. That has important implications for international
relations.

49

Ethnocultural pluralism is a common feature of many states. (According to one estimate, the contemporary states system is composed of just under two hundred states that contain over five thousand ethnic groups.[2]) Arguably because human beings have a predisposition to create diverse communal attachments, to associate with their own people at their own time in their own place, they want to enjoy and exercise this freedom to form and join their own group. Moreover, the fact that such diverse identities and associations continue to exist despite political efforts to alter or eradicate them would seem to suggest that very many individuals consider these ethnocultural expressions to be an essential component of their conception of the good life. Yet, despite this evidence, both liberal philosophy and international practice directed at human rights have historically been ill disposed to the minority problems that very often arise in situations of ethnocultural pluralism. Why? Because individual rights-based political thought and action was a fundamental component of the political transformation from the divine right of kings to popular sovereignty and representative government. This connection between what we now refer to as "human rights" and "democracy" led to a series of assumptions that ultimately rendered the idea of "minority rights" highly problematic within the liberal tradition, as will be discussed more fully in the next section. To put it simply, minority rights as distinct from equal citizenship guarantees came to be associated with political instability, disorder, and conflict; from this perspective, recognizing minority rights would put at risk the social consensus on which peace, order, and representative government was built. As a result, problems associated with ethnocultural identities, associations, or expressions have tended to be either ignored by liberals or addressed only through general guarantees of freedom of expression, association, and equality. For this same reason, the international human rights system created after 1945 has, until very recently, largely ignored the dilemmas experienced by members of minority groups as distinct from the majority population within states.

This chapter will examine both the initial failures to address minority rights in the post-1945 human rights discourse and recent initiatives to rectify this shortcoming. In so doing, it will argue that cultural pluralism is an essential feature and important value of the human condition. For this reason, pluralism ought to be actively promoted rather than merely tolerated within the liberal human rights discourse since it is only in situations of social pluralism that freedom can be fully realized. Achieving genuine autonomy for all humankind will therefore require not only respect for individual liberties but also special guarantees for ethnocultural minorities in addition to the already-recognized equal rights provisions currently included in multilateral human rights agreements.

THE "PROBLEM" OF PLURALISM

Historically, the idea of rights emerged in the context of Western social and political thought of the seventeenth and eighteenth centuries. At this time, the idea that every man had his appointed status and function in a preestablished order was breaking down in the face of an advancing individualism expressing itself theologically in Protestantism, economically in mercantile capitalism, and politically and philosophically in the theory of natural rights and the social contract. The new theory was intended not as a justification but as a criticism of the existing order; its tone was radical, and in its ultimate employment, it was revolutionary.[3]

In other words, as noted earlier, rights-based political thought and action were fundamental components of the political transformation from the divine right of kings to popular sovereignty and representative government. For this reason, the fundamental rights and freedoms of the liberal tradition beginning with the American Declaration of Independence and the French Declaration of the Rights of Man were generally understood to be a means of protecting "the people" from tyranny by the sovereign prince or government.

It is at this point in the history of political ideas that ethnocultural pluralism becomes problematic. Who are the people in whom sovereignty, and indeed liberty, ultimately resides? The people are the nation, and the state exists as an expression of the national will. "The principle of all sovereignty rests essentially in the nation. No body and no individual may exercise authority which does not emanate from the nation expressly" (article 3, 1789 Declaration of the Rights of Man and of the Citizen). Moreover, "for a nation thus abused to arise unanimously and to resist their prince, even to the dethroning of him, is not criminal but a reasonable way of vindicating their liberties and just rights."[4] This is the critical point at which the idea of political community as the ultimate source of both authority and individual liberty enters the liberal tradition, and natural rights become confused with citizenship rights and democracy. Rousseau's conception of the social contract is predicated on the belief that in surrendering his or her will to the general will, the individual does not lose freedom but instead gains it as a member of an independent political community. Popular sovereignty and representative government put this conviction into practice; from this perspective, special minority rights beyond those of equal citizenship are perceived as threats to the survival of the overarching political community and the fundamental freedom it gives rise to. We see that today in the deep controversy in France, which penetrated to the heart of the French government, over the question of granting some modest autonomy to Corsica.

As the nineteenth century progressed, this new political thinking spread to areas outside Western Europe and North America. The idea of the nation as a political or civic community and its concomitant notion of national identity became increasingly infused with ethnocultural characteristics, thereby rendering the position of ethnocultural minorities even more difficult. In Central, Southern, and Eastern Europe, the new revolutionaries were confronted by multilingual and multicultural empires that continued to base their rule on ancient dynastic rights arising from marriage, succession, purchase, conquest, and so forth, with little regard for either constitutions or representative institutions. How, then, could the "will of the people" be expressed and developed in circumstances where territories were far flung and scattered, central administration was weak, and civic institutions were largely absent? The answer was, of course, to develop an alternative basis on which to mobilize popular support and action: language and culture rather than political or civic community.

This emphasis on language and culture gave a new dynamism to the original Anglo-French idea of the nation-state grounded on popular sovereignty: Whereas previously states made nations, henceforth nations would make— and break—states. The amalgamation of smaller territories (e.g., Venice, Florence, Milan, etc.) inhabited by the same linguistic and cultural group into a single sovereign, territorial unit (e.g., Italy)—or, conversely, the partition of larger territories in which different linguistic and cultural groups intermingled under the same sovereign authority (e.g., the Hapsburg and Ottoman Empires) into smaller political units with more homogeneous ethnocultural populations (as in the case of Greece, Serbia, Montenegro, Macedonia, Romania, and Bulgaria) would preoccupy international relations from 1848 to 1919. The politicization of ethnicity and culture introduced a whole new dynamic to relations within and between states; it gave rise to a new principle of international legitimacy—national self-determination—that demands that the state and the ethnonation should coincide. This principle was only prepared to recognize one kind of state—the nation-state—whose boundaries were no longer determined by "the courses of rivers, the direction of mountains, or the chances of war, but according to races or rather [ethno] nations."[5]

Initially, this new idea was understood to be a natural corollary of both individual liberty and popular sovereignty—the fundamental values in defense of which the American and French Revolutions ostensibly had been fought. As John Stuart Mill wrote in his 1861 treatise *On Representative Government*:

> Where the sentiment of nationality exists in any force, there is a prima facie case for uniting all the members of the nationality under the same government, a government to themselves apart. This is merely saying that the question of government ought to be decided by the governed. One hardly knows what any

division of the human race should be free to do, if not to determine with which of the various collective bodies of human beings they choose to associate themselves.

[However, Mill went on to add that] When a people are ripe for free institutions, there is a still more vital consideration Free institutions are next to impossible in a country made up of different nationalities.[6]

Liberals like Mill considered ethnocultural pluralism a serious political problem because it appeared to undermine the social consensus and shared political values on which representative institutions were based. The despotism commonly associated with the multilingual, multicultural Hapsburg and Ottoman Empires was construed as further evidence—should any be needed—that liberalism could not easily be achieved in ethnoculturally plural societies. Thus, it is only to be expected that Mill and Western liberals like him, viewed liberty and national self-determination as natural allies in the fight against despotism and dynastic rule. The various national movements demanded the union of ethnonations divided by dynastic empire and the independence of other ethnonations suppressed within dynastic empire: Western liberals expected, or at least hoped, that the new nation-states achieved in this way would practice representative government and guarantee the rights of the individual.

Unfortunately, history has demonstrated time and again that once ethnocultural homogeneity is accepted as the ideal basis of political organization, the individual liberty of members of minority groups becomes precarious. In such circumstances, the state "tends to act as if it is a single and unitary nation." If, in fact, it is not this, it must "endeavour to make the facts correspond to the ideal," regardless of the rights and liberties of those among its citizens who do not belong to the majority ethnic group.[7] At the same time, the reverse is also true: Every ethnonation or fraction thereof that is not an independent nation-state must strive to become one. In this way, individual ethnic, cultural, and linguistic identities become objects of political manipulation. The individual no longer determines his or her nation; instead, the nation determines the individual. National self-determination quickly becomes national determinism.

Just as the state domestically came to view ethnocultural pluralism as potentially destructive of its territorial integrity and political cohesion, so, too, did the society of states increasingly associate such diversity with international instability and conflict. Historically, the problem of pluralism has evoked two international responses designed to eliminate it: (1) the manipulation of either borders to match peoples or peoples to match borders with a view to creating uniform ethnocultural populations within states, or (2) individual human rights to equality and nondiscrimination with the tacit acceptance of domestic assimilationist measures designed to create homogeneity in culture, language, and values within existing jurisdictions.

First, international efforts to create uniformity within states have led to both internationally sanctioned population transfers and boundary revision in the hope of achieving a better fit between juridical territories and ethnonational populations. Population transfers sanctioned by international agreement occurred on several occasions during the twentieth century.[8] For example, minority exchanges between Greece and Turkey and to a lesser extent also between Greece and Bulgaria following World War I were provided for in the 1919 Treaty of Neuilly and 1923 Treaty of Lausanne. Similarly, the transfer of ethnic Germans back to Germany from across Central and Eastern Europe after World War II was authorized by the 1945 Potsdam Protocol.[9] Boundary revision to create ethnoculturally homogeneous states was attempted by the victorious great powers of 1919. Both of these approaches assume there is some optimal division of territory that will succeed in giving every ethnonation its own homogeneous state. Experience, however, has proven that any solution to the problem of pluralism, which attempts to peacefully secure a fit between ethnocultural groups and boundaries—population transfers and border revision—is in reality no solution at all. This approach ultimately fails because the ideal of every ethnonation in its own homogeneous state is in practice unobtainable without the use of considerable force and resultant human suffering.

Second, the problem of pluralism has been addressed by redefining it in terms of individual discrimination and equality, thereby provoking international requirements for existing states to remove any legal or political barriers of individual membership in a minority by guaranteeing equality of civil and political rights to all its citizens regardless of their ethnonational identity in accordance with prevailing liberal practices. Such international stipulations, though laudable in and of themselves, are nevertheless well suited to a political belief in the value of uniformity since they are fully compatible with domestic programs aimed at assimilating individual members of minorities into the dominant linguistic and cultural group. For example, if equality is defined as sameness, then stipulating that all children must be taught in the same (majority) language does not violate equal rights provisions. Equality coupled with assimilation was supported by the United States and other major Western (liberal) powers after World War II because of both the failure of the League of Nations minority system[10] to prevent ethnic conflict in Europe and the prospect of decolonization in Asia and Africa, where ethnocultural pluralism was even greater and thus potentially even more destabilizing. Consequently, the new international order established after 1945 included a system of universal individual human rights but not one of special minority rights, as will be discussed in the next section.

As a result of these various approaches to the problem of pluralism, not all ethnocultural minorities are in the same position relative to the majority.[11] Some ethnocultural minorities want to be incorporated within the majority but are separated from it against their will—*minorities by force.* In these cases, the majority deliberately differentiates between itself and members of the minority by, for example, calling attention to ascriptive differences in terms of race, ethnicity, language, religion, and so forth, and uses these characteristics as the basis for oppression designed to perpetuate the separation of the two communities. This sort of oppressive treatment was the experience of many Jewish communities in Central and Eastern Europe between the two world wars; of African Americans in the southern United States prior to the 1960s; and indeed of black South Africans during the era of apartheid, who were in a nondominant (thus "minority") position with respect to the white ruling elite. In such circumstances, equal rights and protection from discrimination are necessary to ensure the individual autonomy of minority members. Liberalism in general, and the international human rights regime in particular, has made substantial achievements in this area over the past fifty years.

Other ethnocultural minorities want to preserve their distinctiveness as unique ethnic, cultural, religious, or linguistic communities within the territory of the state but are instead subject to majority campaigns of assimilation, expulsion, or, at the most extreme, genocide[12]—*minorities by will.* Unwanted assimilation is a common experience of minorities during nation-building campaigns in the name of the majority national community (e.g., Catalans and Basques in Spain; Welsh, Irish, and Scots in the United Kingdom; Flemings in Belgium; Moslems in Bulgaria; Hungarians and Roma in Romania and Slovakia; Tibetans in China, etc.). Expulsion, too, has been frequently used by states to overcome the problems associated with troublesome minority by will communities; post-1945 examples include the expulsion of ethnic Germans from Central and Eastern Europe between 1945 and 1948, the population movements accompanying the partition of India and Pakistan in 1947, the Palestinian expulsions accompanying the creation of the state of Israel in 1948, the expulsion of Asians from Uganda in the early 1970s, the exodus of Moslems from Bulgaria in the 1980s, and the various acts of ethnic cleansing associated with the breakup of Yugoslavia in the 1990s. In situations in which the minority in question is territorially concentrated, assimilation and expulsion are very often underscored by a fear of secession or irredentism that tends both to exacerbate minority/majority tensions and to give an added sense of urgency and sometimes also violence to these state measures. The ultimate act of violent elimination of a minority is, of course, genocide as can be evidenced not only in the Holocaust but also more recently in Cambodia, Rwanda, and Bosnia. In such circumstances, equal rights and protection from discrimination are not by themselves sufficient to ensure the individual autonomy of minority members. In addition, special guarantees designed to preserve and promote minority identities and communities are necessary to ensure all individuals have the freedom to make the cultural expressions and associations they genuinely value. Liberalism in general, and the international human rights regime in particular, has made only limited progress in this area over the past fifty years. Consequently, this is one of the areas in which recent interest and future action must be concentrated to fulfill the goal of human rights—namely, to ensure that every individual human being has the freedom to define, pursue, and realize his or her conception of the good life.

HUMAN RIGHTS AND PLURALISM AFTER 1945

The new international system created after 1945—and with it the various United Nations and regional human rights texts—was formulated largely "without consideration of the questions of principle" that arise from the existence of ethnocultural minorities in a "world dominated by the concept of the national state as the . . . unit of political organization."[13] This is hardly surprising given that the international actors that created this system were none other than states and therefore deeply suspicious of would-be rival claimants to their authority, territory, or population. The idea of statehood, including the related concepts of popular sovereignty and self-determination, is not easily reconciled to that ethnocultural pluralism that minority rights would perpetuate. Accordingly, the only minority grievances considered legitimate were those involving discrimination by the majority such that individual equal rights guarantees were seen as the appropriate response. Any minority claims to special treatment as a distinctive community were viewed as tantamount to secessionist demands and thus could and, in the interests of international peace and stability, should be ignored. Consequently, minority claims for special rights in cultural, educational, religious, and linguistic matters over and above those of equal citizenship were noticeably absent from those treaties that created the post-1945 human rights system.

The Universal Declaration of Human Rights (1948) makes no mention of special minority rights but instead endorses the principles of equality and nondiscrimination. Among its various clauses, those referring to freedom of thought and religion (article 18), freedom of expression (article 19), freedom of peaceful assembly and association (article 20), and the right to freely participate in the cultural life of the community (article 27) do have relevance to the circumstances of minorities. However, these clauses do not grant the rights to culture, language, and education, which (some) minorities enjoyed (briefly) under the earlier League of Nations minority system.[14] While article 27 is directed at the preservation of cultural communities, the clause is vague as to whether cultural community in this context includes minority cultures or simply the dominant culture. This ambiguity has enabled states to argue that participation in the dominant culture is all this article guarantees; therefore, assimilationist policies directed against minorities have not been prevented by it.

Interestingly, the *travaux preparatoires* indicate that the initial draft of the Universal Declaration did include a guarantee that in all countries inhabited by a substantial number of persons of a race, language, or religion other than those of the majority, "minorities shall have the right to establish and maintain, out of an equitable proportion of public funds . . . their schools, cultural institutions, and to use their language before courts, organs of the state and in the press and public assembly."[15]

Yet, as the draft proposal went from one committee to the next, it was edited and finally removed altogether; once again, recognizing diversity was construed as inviting instability.

Instead, on the same day that the General Assembly passed the Universal Declaration of Human Rights, it also passed Resolution 217 C (III) entitled "The Fate of Minorities." In this resolution, the General Assembly acknowledged that it "could not remain indifferent to the fate of minorities" but, because it was difficult to adopt a "uniform solution" to this "complex and delicate issue" that has "special aspects" in each state in which it arises, decided "not to deal with the question" and instead to refer it to the UNCHR and Sub-commission for the Prevention of Discrimination and Protection of Minorities for further study.[16] Yet even this limited mandate was considered too controversial given the hostility of many member states toward minority provisions. As the subcommission's own rapporteur admitted, from the passing of this resolution until 1989, both the UNCHR and the subcommission failed to address the issue of special minority protection.[17]

Consequently, during the years from 1945 to 1989, only one UN convention incorporated a specific minority rights clause[18]: the International Covenant on Civil and Political Rights (ICCPR) (1966), whose article 27—originally proposed by the subcommission in 1950—stipulates that in those states in which ethnic, religious, or linguistic minorities exist, persons belonging to such minorities shall not be denied the right, in community with other members of their group, to enjoy their own culture, to profess and practice their own religion, or to use their own language.[19]

This provision gives state signatories the freedom to determine whether ethnic groups in their jurisdictions constitute such minorities by will. Needless to say, very many states that possessed minorities effectively avoided their international obligations in this regard by redefining these groups under a different rubric, be it "immigrant," "aboriginal," or whatever.

This general antipathy toward those guarantees that would have recognized and in so doing perpetuated minorities within existing states is also apparent in the activities of most regional organizations between 1945 and 1989. For example, colonial successor states in Latin America, Africa, and

Asia generally assumed that the absence of minority rights was more conducive to state success defined in terms of territorial integrity and internal political stability than would be the reverse. Thus, while the American Convention on Human Rights (1969) reiterates almost all of the rights included in the ICCPR, it does not include any reference whatsoever to minority rights along the lines of article 27. This absence of explicit minority provisions is also apparent in the Additional Protocol to the American Convention on Human Rights in the Area of Economic, Social and Cultural Rights ("Protocol of San Salvador") (1988). Similarly, while the African Charter on Human and People's Rights (1981) incorporates a people's right to self-determination, in practice "people" has been identified with the already-existing African states and not the various tribal groups within them. Likewise, although the Association of Commonwealth States repeatedly emphasized its commitment to individual human rights and racial equality, it said virtually nothing specific to the circumstances of minorities by will and their desire for protection against unwanted policies of assimilation or oppression. For example, the 1971 (Singapore) Declaration of Commonwealth Principles affirms "equal rights for all citizens regardless of race, colour, creed or political belief" and recognizes "racial prejudice as a dangerous sickness." However, "self-determination" is mentioned only in the context of "non-racialism" and opposition to "all forms of colonial domination." There is no reference at all to minority rights as distinct from equal citizenship. While the 1979 Lusaka Declaration of the Commonwealth on Racism and Racial Prejudice acknowledges that "everyone is free to retain pluralism in his or her culture and lifestyle," this statement is made only in the context of such pluralism being no justification for "the perpetuation of racial prejudice or racially discriminatory practices." Again, there is no mention of what actions, if any, a state ought to take to promote a pluralism of culture and lifestyles within its jurisdiction or whether these might include provisions that would help perpetuate minorities by will.

Even within Europe, where international minority rights had been recognized under the League of Nations system, there was no revival of special minority guarantees between 1945 and 1989 due to the widespread fear that this might rekindle old ethnic conflicts. For example, the Council of Europe (COE)—which during this time created what is arguably the most successful regional human rights system in the world—was nonetheless extremely hesitant to pursue a specific minority rights protocol to the European Convention on Human Rights (ECHR) (1950).[20] Instead, it maintained a publicly avowed position that special minority rights were at best "not very convincing" and at worse "aggravated existing tensions and difficulties."[21] Moreover, minority issues were "not deemed to be of extreme urgency" because of a widespread belief that protection against discrimination adequately protected all legitimate minority interests.[22]

Although the Helsinki Final Act (which established the Conference for Security and Cooperation in Europe) specifically mentions minorities in three different parts of the document—the Declaration on Principles, Principle VII, and the section entitled Cooperation in Humanitarian and Other Fields—the content of the provisions is confined to antidiscrimination measures and allowed states a wide latitude in interpreting the kinds of actions that could and could not be undertaken with regard to "minorities." Moreover, this initial interest in minority issues was not sustained in the various "CSCE Follow-up Meetings" that took place between 1975 and 1989. Instead, these meetings were dominated by a concern for the violation of individual human rights—particularly those civil and political liberties associated with the movement toward human rights and democracy in communist states.[23] So once again, "legitimate" minority interests did not include any rights in cultural, educational, religious, and linguistic matters over and above those of equal citizenship.

In sum, the circumstances of minorities by will were deliberately ignored by international actors during the Cold War due to the widespread conviction that the continued existence of such groups posed a threat to the territorial integrity and social cohesion of existing states and thus also to order and stability within the states system. The only legitimate minority grievances were those experienced by minorities by force, and so international human rights texts from this period give considerable emphasis to equal rights and antidiscrimination provisions but are virtually "silent" with regard to the special rights over and above equal citizenship that minorities by will believe are necessary to preserve and promote their distinct identities and ways of life.

This international attitude toward minorities by will had a number of consequences. It led to the conclusion that such minority matters were not properly subjects of international organizations or multilateral agreements. Instead, and not surprisingly, these issues were understood to be the preserve of the sovereign state in which they occurred. Without international stipulations to the contrary, very many states chose to "resolve" their minority problems not through minority rights conducive to a climate of constructive pluralism but instead through policies of assimilation or oppression. Unfortunately, as we have recently discovered, the long-term consequences of such policies are very often fundamentally destabilizing for the state affected. Instead of producing a shared identity, the unintended result of assimilation is oftentimes a growing minority/majority distrust and antipathy. Similarly, instead of perpetuating the current regime and its underlying ethnocultural power relations, oppression can provoke violent intercommunal conflicts of the sort recently witnessed, for example, in Rwanda and former Yugoslavia. Ironically, the Cold War stances with regard to minorities by will not only failed to protect the interests of these minority communities but very often also failed to preserve the internal stability of the states in which they, however tenuously, existed.

MINORITY RIGHTS AND PLURALISM AFTER 1989

Since 1989, the previous international response to pluralism within states (territorial inviolability coupled with individual equality guarantees) has come under growing criticism, not least owing to the increasing incidence of ethnic conflict around the globe. Televised images of the human suffering caused by ethnic conflict have shocked the conscience of international public opinion, at least in the West, and precipitated public demands for international action on minority issues. This public pressure has resulted in a greater willingness on the part of Western states to interfere in the domestic jurisdictions of nondemocracies, and so minority rights have increasingly featured in their attempts to foster democratic development in nondemocratic states, particularly (though not exclusively) in Eastern Europe. Significantly, whereas previously democratic assumptions tended to discredit minority claims for special rights in addition to those of equal citizenship, recently the idea of democracy has itself been reevaluated, and indeed redefined, by liberals who have come to recognize the need for a social consensus that is more than just "majoritarian." At the same time, the demonstrated peace and security risks associated with ethnic conflict have made it easier for international society to acknowledge minorities since the old fear that such action might precipitate ethnic violence has now become a moot point. As a result of these new perspectives, international actors are now beginning to come to the conclusion that the only way to successfully resolve the "problem" of pluralism is to create circumstances in which minorities and majorities can flourish side by side. Such constructive pluralism would seem to require at least minimal minority rights in cultural, educational, religious, and linguistic matters over and above those of equal citizenship.

If international minority rights guarantees are intended to ensure that all individual human beings have the freedom to define, pursue, and realize their conception of the good life, then the content of these provisions ought to reflect the circumstances of both minorities by force and minorities by will. Failure to do so will unavoidably result in the continued oppression or disadvantage of members of particular minority communities. For example, it would be inefficacious to grant minorities by force autonomy guarantees as such provisions would simply perpetuate the unwanted ghettoization by the majority (hence the creation of black "homelands" by the apartheid regime in South Africa, which were notoriously justified as "self-government" provisions). Similarly, it would be inefficacious to grant minorities by will *only* equal rights and antidiscrimination protection (i.e., without additional autonomy provisions) as these can be, and historically have been, used as instruments of unwanted assimilation by the majority. The new human rights agenda is thus seeking to augment the earlier provisions for individual equality and antidiscrimination measures with guarantees designed to preserve and promote minority languages, cultures, identities, and ways of life within states. In so doing, it is once again developing in conjunction with the liberal tradition out of which it emerged, which has in recent years also begun to incorporate a greater awareness of the social circumstances confronted by members of disadvantaged groups.

A major development in global standards on minority rights took place in 1992 when the UN Declaration on the Rights of Persons Belonging to National or Ethnic, Religious and Linguistic Minorities was officially proclaimed by the General Assembly. This declaration was noteworthy in the history of international human rights since it was the first such instrument devoted exclusively to minority concerns. The preamble and nine articles in part reiterated those rights already recognized in article 27 of the ICCPR. Persons belonging to minorities were recognized as having rights to existence, identity, and the enjoyment of culture, religion, language, social affairs, the economy, and public life. Special minority rights to participate in relevant national and regional decisions, to establish and maintain associations, and to have contact both within and across international frontiers supplemented these basic provisions. Moreover, the 1992 formulation reinforced a certain collective element by acknowledging that these rights could be exercised individually as well as in community with other members of the group. It also went on to remedy the earlier 1966 failure to specify state measures aimed at the promotion of minority rights. Henceforth, states were required to adopt provisions for minority language instruction and the promotion of knowledge concerning minority cultures and languages among the majority population. At the same time, minority concerns were to be taken into consideration in both domestic programs and international cooperation.

At the same time, the 1992 declaration reiterated the traditional international stance, which held that minority rights were not intended as vehicles to further minority secession or irredentism. Article 8 was therefore concerned not with the rights of minorities but with the sovereign rights of states including their sovereign equality, territorial integrity, and political independence. Indeed, the text was replete with vague or equivocal wording such as "encourage conditions," "appropriate measures," "where appropriate," "where possible," "where required," and "in a manner not incompatible with national legislation." These phrases continued to give state signatories a degree of maneuver sufficient to avoid or at least to limit those new minority rights obligations they considered most detrimental to their sovereign powers and prerogatives. In other words, sovereignty has by no means been abandoned; it remains the cornerstone of the international system, at least for the foreseeable future. Similarly, rewriting or redrawing sovereign jurisdictions, except by constitutional means and with the consent of all concerned, will not be recognized or encouraged.

What has begun to change, and arguably what needs to be further developed, is the substantive sovereignty (or good governance) practiced within frontiers. Despite its various shortcomings, the Declaration on the Rights of Persons Belonging to National, or Ethnic, Religious, and Linguistic Minorities—with its global applicability—constitutes a basis for international thinking on minority questions that is developing in this direction. Other international organizations might agree on something better than this basic code of state conduct toward minorities, but they cannot go beneath it and expect to justify their policies and actions on the issue. More than this, the UN declaration was a major acknowledgment that minority matters—including those of relevance to minorities by will—were once more legitimate subjects of international relations and not solely the concern of those states in which they occurred.

Following on from this United Nations initiative, European regional organizations have now also recognized the need for multilateral minority rights standard setting and enforcement. The Organization for Security and Cooperation in Europe (OSCE) has been concerned with formulating codes of state conduct toward minorities both as a way of minimizing ethnic conflicts and as a way of preventing the oppression of individual members of ethnocultural minority communities. The OSCE therefore incorporated statements of minority rights in all of those official documents, which formed the basis of the organization's activities since 1989. These included the main OSCE human rights standard-setting text of this period, the Copenhagen Document (1990), as well as the Charter of Paris for a New Europe (1990), the Geneva Report on National Minorities (1991), the Moscow Document (1991), the Helsinki Document (1992), and the Budapest Document (1994). Moreover, in December 1992, the OSCE created the office of High Commissioner for National Minorities (HCNM) to assist in member states' implementation of international minority standards and to help resolve ethnic conflicts.

At the same time, the condition of minorities was also examined by the COE as a potential obstacle to the democratic development of former communist states in the region and as an economic and social problem in those states that were on the receiving end of minority migrations. Various COE bodies including the Parliamentary Assembly, the European Commission for Democracy through Law, the Steering Committee of Human Rights, and the Committee of Ministers examined minority rights proposals between 1990 and 1995. The member states of the COE decided at their Vienna Summit Meeting on October 9, 1993, to adopt both a minorities protocol to the ECHR that would be open to ECHR signatories and a separate convention on minorities which would be open to both members and nonmembers of the COE. The decision to adopt a Convention on National Minorities was implemented in 1995, but little progress has been made thus far with regard to the additional protocol. This failure results from both ideological differences among member states as regards the suitability of individual versus collective minority rights formulations and a widespread fear that transferring minority responsibility to the European Court of Human Rights in Strasbourg would judicialize an issue over which many European states are determined to retain domestic political control.

While most OSCE and COE provisions for minority rights augment the post-1945 human rights regime and the global minimum standard outlined in the 1992 UN Declaration on Minorities, the 1990s European regional response to this problem also reveals both an important reappraisal of League of Nations linguistic and cultural guarantees and a possible extension of the right to self-determination of peoples. The COE's Charter for Regional or Minority Languages (1992), for example, contained far more extensive provisions for the use of minority languages than did the UN Declaration on Minorities. Six general categories of activity were recognized—education, judicial, and administrative authorities; the media; cultural activities and facilities; economic and social life; and transfrontier exchanges. Its provisions were therefore an important continuation of earlier League initiatives in this area—ideas, which had been largely forgotten or ignored during the Cold War. Unfortunately, the charter's enforcement mechanisms allowed for a certain number of opt-outs by state signatories.[24] As a result, its actual impact on minority circumstances may be more limited than the content of the provisions might otherwise indicate.

Similarly, the right to freedom from assimilation and forced population transfer was also an innovative European response to ethnic conflict. Explicit prohibitions against these sorts of government practices were not incorporated into the main body of any human rights agreement prior to 1990. There was a precedent in international agreements for sanctions against separation in its most violent or extreme form—namely, extermination or genocide. Genocide was prohibited in the Convention on the Prevention and Punishment of the Crime of Genocide (1948). Similarly, the UNESCO Declaration on Race and Racial Prejudice (1978) stated that all individuals had the right to be different, to consider themselves as different, and to be regarded as such. Importantly, this 1978 text affords evidence of a movement toward the prohibition of forced assimilation and population transfer in international thinking on minorities and related matters. Its preamble notes that racism is manifested through unjust practices among which are the forced assimilation of members of disadvantaged groups. However, no precedent existed for the explicit prohibition of forms of assimilation intended to alter an individual's language, culture, and ultimately his or her ethnic or national identity or to forcibly transfer an individual from one locale to another on the basis of ethnic or national identity.

The Copenhagen Document went beyond the international status quo in this regard when it stated in Section IV (32) that "persons belonging to national minorities have the right freely to express, preserve and develop their ethnic cultural, linguistic or religious identity . . . free of any attempts at assimilation against their will." Similarly, the Convention on the Protection of National Minorities specified that states shall refrain from both "practices aimed at the assimilation of persons belonging to minorities against their will" and "from measures which modify the proportions of the population in areas inhabited by persons belonging to national minorities."

In suggesting various forms of autonomy for national minorities, the European minority rights texts appeared to be refining the right to self-determination by advocating self-government within existing states where a national minority's outright independence cannot be realized. In the Copenhagen Document, reference was made in Section IV (35) to "appropriate local or autonomous administrations corresponding to the specific historical and territorial circumstances of . . . national minorities." The draft national minorities protocol put forward by the Parliamentary Assembly of the COE in 1993 would have taken this development still further. Article 11 of this proposal recognized the right of persons belonging to minorities to have at their disposal appropriate local or autonomous authorities or a special status matching the specific historical and territorial situation. Were these or similar measures to be adopted, the relationship between sovereignty, self-determination, and democracy would begin to change in certain key respects. Such changes would make these core principles far more amenable to the circumstances of those minorities by will that possess the normative characteristics (national identity and historic territory) currently recognized as the basis for membership within the society of states and yet, for various reasons, do not possess sovereignty. In as much as the collective right to self-determination has historically been understood within the liberal tradition as the fulfilment of individual autonomy, the extension of this right to national minorities and perhaps also indigenous peoples would ensure that all humans—including members of these groups—have the equal liberty to refine, pursue, and realize their conception of the good life in association with other members of their chosen national community.

Unfortunately, such suggestions remain highly controversial; many states continue to equate empowering national minority communities through the concession of self-government with undermining existing governmental institutions. As a result, all suggestions of autonomy for such minority groups specifically acknowledge the state's right to determine how or even whether autonomy will be implemented. So, for example, the Copenhagen Document identified autonomy as only one of the possible means to achieve the promotion of national minority identities and acknowledged that all such measures must be in accordance with the policies of the state concerned. Likewise, the Parliamentary Assembly's proposed draft national minorities protocol also deferred to the domestic legislation in its characterization of minority autonomy. At least the inherited political beliefs (and prejudices) of the nineteenth century are now being challenged within European organizations; that, in itself, is a significant development.

Certainly, there is evidence of an emerging European consensus on minority rights that is far more amenable to ethnocultural pluralism. The various minority rights standard-setting texts adopted by the COE and OSCE during the mid-1990s have now been reaffirmed in the provisions of the North Atlantic Treaty Organization's (NATO's) Partnership for Peace (1994) program with former states of the Soviet Bloc, the European Union's (EU's) Pact on Stability in Europe (1995), and various EU provisions stipulating accession criteria. There has thus come about a thorough interweaving of COE, OSCE, NATO, and EU provisions regarding security and minority rights. All of these major European organizations now appear to be operating in tandem using common minority rights criteria based on the standard-setting activities of the OSCE and COE. In this sense, then, one can reasonably speak of an emerging post–Cold War European minority rights system that reflects a new found respect for ethnocultural pluralism.

However, regional organizations in other parts of the globe have yet to address in any significant way the issues raised by minority by will communities and what, if any, rights they might legitimately claim to maintain their distinct language, culture, identity, and way of life. For example, both the Commonwealth's 1991 Harare Declaration and the 1995 Millbrook Action Program make special reference to "equal rights for all citizens," "racial prejudice and intolerance," and "problems of migration and refugees" but say nothing with respect to minorities by will and their desire for, among others, minority language rights and freedom from forced assimilation. The Proposed American Declaration on the Rights of Indigenous Peoples (1997) extends recognition to both indigenous peoples and "peoples whose social, cultural and economic conditions distinguish them from the majority" but adds the requirement that such peoples must have a status that is regulated "wholly or in part by their own customs, or traditions or by special law and regulations." In practice, this provision would give states the power to selectively determine which nonindigenous groups qualify for recognition and protection. African and Asian organizations are similarly reticent on this pressing issue—and that ongoing silence is a fundamental and indeed deliberate evasion of and equivocation on the serious problems currently confronting minority groups in many states.

Why does it persist? Because states in these regions continue to view ethnocultural diversity as a problem best solved not through constructive pluralism but instead through policies of assimilation or oppression. These views not only are well established historically but were also to a significant extent written into the rules of the existing international system; as a result, modifying them is not an easy task. Similarly, majorities—where they exist—seem to have an inherent tendency to give their own beliefs and opinions institutional force; making majorities more tolerant of difference or dissent is something that cannot be achieved overnight—and certainly not without government support. These fundamental difficulties are further compounded within quasi-states, failed states, collapsed states, internally illegitimate governments, and so forth. How can minority or any other human rights policies be implemented when there are no legitimate, functioning government structures? In other words, constructive pluralism requires as a *precondition* a minimum degree of good governance.

CONCLUSION: HUMAN RIGHTS AND CULTURAL PLURALISM

The problems posed by minorities have taken on a renewed importance in international and domestic politics; according to one study, seventy-nine of the eighty-two conflicts worldwide between 1989 and 1992 were linked to ethnocultural minority/majority differences within states.[25] Consequently, the relationship between minority rights and international stability is being reevaluated. In light of recent events in former Yugoslavia, Rwanda, and the former Soviet Union, it is becoming increasingly apparent that a failure to address the special rights of minorities may in the long term provoke precisely that sort of instability (intercommunal conflict, demands for secession or irredentism, mass refugee flows across frontiers, etc.) that "silence" on this issue had sought to avoid. So whereas in the past ethnocultural pluralism within states was recognized as an aberration to be ignored, suppressed, and where necessary eradicated, it is now slowly being accepted as the norm. Along with this emerging shift in attitude has come a dawning realization that constructive pluralism is to be preferred over both assimilation and confrontation. As a result, minority rights provisions are prominent in recent Western-led initiatives to foster democratic development in nondemocratic states.

Constructive pluralism—which is broadly comparable to the multiculturalism espoused by liberal theorists such as Isaiah Berlin, Will Kymlicka, Joseph Raz, and Judith Shklar[26]—acknowledges that pluralism within states is the consequence of a political desire for territorial inviolability in the context of a normal human propensity for communal attachments that makes sociological pluralism in ethnocultural terms a usual and even desirable state of affairs. It is precisely this aspect of human nature that gives rise to families, tribes, ethnicities, and indeed nation-states. In other words, we exist as social beings and not isolated individuals. Moreover, our fundamental human desire for a language, culture, and value system that is an expression of ourselves means that political attempts to forcibly suppress or alter these hallmarks of identity are unavoidably destructive of both human freedom and creativity. The guiding principle of this way of thinking about minority rights, to echo liberal theorist Judith Shklar, is that "social diversity is something that any liberal should rejoice in and seek to promote, because it is in diversity alone that freedom can be realized."[27] Accordingly, special minority rights guarantees over and above those of equal citizenship are something every human rights organization ought to recognize.

The constructive pluralism ethos does not consider pluralism to be a prima facie threat to the integrity of the state. Instead its central premise is that minorities who are recognized and supported by the state are far less likely to challenge its authority or threaten its territorial integrity. International multilateral minority rights guarantees thereby aim to prevent ethnic conflict by encouraging domestic circumstances in which the language, culture, religion, and way of life of *all* ethnocultural communities can be preserved and promoted within existing borders in the interest of the individual autonomy of their members. Majorities are required to respect minorities' desire to preserve their way of life, while at the same time the minority is required to respect the majority's right to do the same; and on this basis, unilateral minority efforts to secede from the existing state are precluded. However, negotiated political settlements between groups compatible with democratic practices are encouraged—and where these opt for the creation of new states (as in the so-called velvet divorce whereby Czechoslovakia was replaced by Slovakia and the Czech Republic), international society would, of course, respect the wishes of the parties concerned. Such minority rights practices thus disclose a prior consideration for both democratic principles and the territorial status quo: the principle of self-determination is set in the context of respect for existing territorial boundaries, and international action is primarily directed at preventing violence within existing states rather than encouraging the recognition of new states except where this is an outcome of bona fide democratic negotiation.

Consequently, the proponents of constructive pluralism seek to justify not only government toleration but also positive government action to promote ethnocultural pluralism and to affirm the dignity, esteem, and mutual respect of all citizens whatever their ethnocultural identities. For this reason, special minority rights in addition to equal citizenship that will help preserve and promote minority ethnocultural identities within existing states are now starting to be recognized. Such rights include the freedom to speak a minority language in certain circumstances, the right to be educated in this language, the right to use minority language place names and surnames, the right to form minority associations and build minority schools and community centers, and so forth. Provisions of this kind are evident in the UN Declaration on the Rights of Persons Belonging to Minorities, in the COE's Charter for Regional or Minority Languages and Convention on National Minorities, and in various OSCE documents such as the Copenhagen Document and the Helsinki Document.

In the future, certain minority groups may themselves be deemed to possess rights as communities. Minorities by will that possess that normative characteristic—namely, national identity within a historic territory—that is recognized as the basis for international legitimacy and yet, for various reasons, do not possess their own sovereign state (e.g., Hungarians in Romania, Basques in Spain, Quebecois in Canada, etc.) are potential claimants for collective autonomy guarantees. Such groups are often labeled "national minorities" to distinguish them from other ethnocultural minorities (e.g., immigrants, migrant workers, or refugees) that are not in a position to make such normative claims. National minorities may eventually be given rights to self-government in those regions where they predominate or to an appropriate share of public revenues in order to build and maintain schools, churches, and other community institutions. Recent COE and OSCE recommendations in favor of minority autonomy disclose some movement in this direction.

Such group guarantees for national minorities should properly be understood as an extension of the already-recognized collective right to self-determination of peoples rather than as a departure from the declarative model of individual human rights outlined by Jack Donnelly in his chapter in this book. There is a historical precedent for such arrangements—namely, the League of Nations System of Minority Guarantees—that was understood to originate from the norm of self-determination and not declarative human rights, which, of course, it predated. Moreover, the fundamental value at stake in these endeavors remains that essential liberal concern for the autonomy of the individual and his or her ability to define, pursue, and realize his or her conception of the good life. Thus, groups must respect the liberty of their members including those who freely choose to dissent from majority opinions or ways of life. This line of reasoning currently applies to those traditional bearers of the collective right to self-determination of peoples—namely, states—and so one can only assume that it would also apply to other groups (i.e., national minorities or indigenous peoples) that might acquire collective rights under this principle. Thus, a collective right to internal self-determination for national minorities (and perhaps also indigenous peoples) should be compatible with the declarative model of individual human rights as currently practiced in international relations.

In sum, the new human rights agenda ought to include initiatives that reflect the growing realization that cultural pluralism is an essential feature of humanity and a necessary precondition for individual liberty. Traditional civil and political liberties should be revised to better accommodate cultural pluralism. Since culture is by definition an aspect of "community," individual rights formulations should, where appropriate, incorporate or at least acknowledge a collective component but with the proviso that the individual liberty of dissenters must always be respected. Special minority guarantees have long been recognized within the domestic constitutions and political traditions of many states (e.g., Belgium, Canada, Fiji, Malaysia). Multilateral initiatives of this kind are now being implemented within the United Nations and European regional organizations. It is hoped these organizations (with the support of states like those mentioned earlier) will continue to develop pluralist norms and that other regional human rights bodies will follow their example.

It must, however, be recognized that pursuing constructive pluralism within international organizations whose members are states is likely to be highly problematic. The history of minority rights since 1945 suggests that many states that possess minorities (particularly though not exclusively those in Africa, Asia, and Latin America) are likely to view any such international requirements as unacceptable incursions in their sovereign affairs. More than this, until such time as local authorities satisfy minimal levels of good governance, domestic compliance with international minority rights (and indeed human rights more generally) will be difficult to achieve. These issues are very serious practical problems and should not be underestimated—but nor should they be used as an excuse for international organizations to adopt a "wait and see" mentality. For change, however incremental, to occur, international actors must begin to take the initiative in defining and implementing the new human rights agenda.

NOTES

1. Inis Claude, *National Minorities: An International Problem* (Cambridge, Mass.: Harvard University Press, 1955), 211.

2. Ted Robert Gurr, *Minorities at Risk: A Global View of Ethnopolitical Conflict* (Washington, D.C.: Institute of Peace Press, 1993), 1.

3. S. I. Benn and R. S. Peters, *The Principles of Political Thought* (New York: Collier, 1959), 110.

4. Bernard Bailyn, *The Ideological Origins of the American Revolution* (Cambridge, Mass.: Belknap, 1992), 93.

5. Alfred Cobban, *The Nation-State and National Self-Determination* (New York: Thomas Crowall, 1970), 109.

6. John Stuart Mill, *Utilitarianism, On Liberty, Considerations on Representative Government* (London: Everyman, 1999), 392–93.

7. Cobban, *Nation-State*, 109.

8. See Jennifer Jackson-Preece, "Ethnic Cleansing as an Instrument of Nation-State Creation: Changing State Practices and Evolving Legal Norms," *Human Rights Quarterly* 20, no. 4 (1998): 817–43.

9. The post–World War II movement of German minorities began as an attack of "ethnic cleansing" and was only formalized at Potsdam, when the Allied Powers tried (without much success) to humanize the process. See M. Marrus, *The Unwanted* (Oxford: Oxford University Press, 1985), and *Der Spiegel Special: Die Deutschen nach der Stunde Null* (1995), no. 4.

10. The League of Nations Minority System bound those new or reconstituted Central and East European states of the interwar period, 1919–1939, to grant certain rights in addition to equal citizenship to the minority communities within their jurisdictions as a means of preserving the post–World War I territorial settlement. See Jennifer Jackson-Preece, *National Minorities and the European Nation-States System* (Oxford: Clarendon, 1998), chap. 5.

11. It should be pointed out that the characterization of a given group as a minority by force or minority by will reflects the conditions prevailing at a particular moment in history and should not therefore be interpreted as applying for all time. In other words, over time it is quite conceivable for a group possessing the characteristics of a minority by force to acquire the attributes of a minority by will and vice versa. Jean Laponce first employed this distinction in *The Protection of Minorities* (Los Angeles: University of California Press, 1960).

12. Expulsion and genocide are not limited to minority by will circumstances, although I would argue that such actions are more frequently directed at minorities by will than at minorities by force precisely because the former are more likely to be viewed as potential rivals by the majority in control of the state (i.e., secession and irredentism are generally associated with minorities by will and not minorities by force).

13. Claude, *National Minorities*, 113.

14. The League of Nations Minority System applied only to the new or reconstituted states of Central and Eastern Europe, the Aaland Islands, and Iraq. Moreover, the historical evidence suggests that the guarantees it recognized were never intended for universal application but only as a specific and possibly limited response to a series of problems arising in particular states.

15. United Nations, E/CN.4/Sub.2/384/Add.2, 44.

16. United Nations, E/CN.4/Sub.2/41.

17. United Nations, E/CN.4/Sub.2/1989/43, 4.

18. Three other UN conventions are in varying degrees relevant to national minorities: the 1948 Convention on the Prevention and Punishment of the Crime of Genocide, the 1957 ILO Convention Concerning Indigenous and Tribal Populations, and the UNESCO Convention against Discrimination in Education.

19. United Nations, ICCPR, article 27.

20. Nevertheless, outside the auspices of the COE, certain of its member states did enter into minority agreements to resolve outstanding minority by will questions.

For example, the De Gasperi–Gruber Agreement of 1946 between Austria and Italy gave various rights to the German-speaking minority by Bolzano and Trento. The Italian government undertook, among other things, to provide primary and secondary education in German to members of these national minority communities and to ensure parity of German and Italian in the public administration. Similarly, a 1955 agreement between Denmark and the Federal Republic of Germany guaranteed the German minority in Denmark and the Danish minority in Germany equality before the law; the right to establish educational institutions; the right to maintain cross-border religious, cultural, and professional relations; the right to an appropriate share of public broadcasting facilities; and the use of Danish or German in the law courts and public offices of either state. In addition, the Austrian State Treaty of 1955 recognized Slovene and Croatian as official languages alongside German in Carinthia, Burgenland, and Styria and gave minority language education rights to these communities. Finally, the 1954 Special Statute for the Territory of Trieste gave a number of special privileges to the Slovene and Croatian minorities in the Italian administered zone, most especially as regards minority language education.

21. Council of Europe, Document 1002 of 1959.

22. Council of Europe, Document 1299 of 1961.

23. Vojtech Mastny, *The Helsinki Process and the Re-integration of Europe 1986–1991: Analysis and Documentation* (London: Pinter, 1992), 11–21.

24. Each party undertakes to apply a minimum of thirty-five paragraphs or subparagraphs from the section of the charter that lists various measures to promote the use of regional or minority language; of these thirty-five, at least three paragraphs must refer to educational provisions, another three to cultural activities and facilities, and one each to judicial authorities, administrative authorities, the media, and economic and social life.

25. "Towards a Constructive Pluralism," www.unesco.org/culture/culturalpluralism, 1.

26. See, for example, Isaiah Berlin, *The Crooked Timber of Humanity* (London: Murray, 1990); W. Kymlicka, *Multicultural Citizenship* (Oxford: Oxford University Press, 1995); Joseph Raz, *The Morality of Freedom* (Oxford: Oxford University Press, 1986); Judith Shklar, *Legalism* (Cambridge, Mass.: Harvard University Press, 1986).

27. Shklar, *Legalism*, 5.

4

Indigenous Rights

Hurst Hannum

It is impossible to quantify the number of indigenous, native, or tribal peoples in the world, but they are present in every region. Some estimates range as high as 10 percent of the world's total population,[1] but, whatever the number, indigenous peoples constitute a significant cultural and demographic factor in many states. They are perhaps most visible—and have become most politically active—in the Americas, where they number at least thirty million people.[2]

The European settlement of the Western Hemisphere and resulting displacement and marginalization of the peoples living on the continent at the time have become a classic example of the colonization of indigenous peoples, but comparable situations exist in the rest of the world. The colonization of Australia and New Zealand by Europeans fits the pattern found in the Western Hemisphere, although it is more difficult to determine which groups in Africa, Asia, and Europe are indigenous (as opposed to ethnic or national minorities), since the lines between who is or is not "indigenous" are often blurred.

These definitional issues are discussed further later, but it may be sufficient as an introductory statement to suggest that indigenous peoples are those who (1) identify themselves as indigenous; (2) exhibit historical continuity with preinvasion or precolonial societies, particularly in terms of culture and governmental/social institutions; and (3) continue to live primarily in a traditional manner, distinct from the dominant society that surrounds them, including practices such as communal ownership and use of land and resources and a spiritual attachment to the territory in which they live.

Indigenousness today does not necessarily depend on which group was in a given location first, since all civilizations came from somewhere else if one goes back far enough. But where a self-contained, nondominant group exhibits the social, cultural, and societal characteristics described earlier, the term *indigenous* will probably be appropriate.

Without descending hopelessly into terminological confusion, it also should be noted that many indigenous peoples refer to themselves as "nations," in the sense that that term was developed in eighteenth-century Europe. Many such indigenous nations in North America were viewed as sovereign governments by early colonists, and a number of North American Indian nations entered into treaties with governments such as Canada, France, Great Britain, and the United States.[3]

However, these treaties made little practical difference in mitigating the discrimination and land seizures to which Indians were subjected, and there is no identifiable difference in suffering or survival between "treaty" and "nontreaty" indigenous groups. While the existence of treaties has had significant domestic legal impact in recent years in some countries, their breach has been of no more concern to the international community than the breach of countless treaties among European states, many of which were created or destroyed by acts of so-called Great Powers, irrespective of treaty obligations.

Most indigenous and tribal peoples not only have been attacked militarily by invading settlers but have subsequently seen their culture and way of life systematically assaulted. Colonial powers and nineteenth-century states in the Americas attempted to conquer and exterminate hostile tribes, force the assimilation of more acculturated indigenous groups, erode traditional culture and landholdings, and expand private property at the expense of the collective or communal holdings of indigenous peoples.[4] Early European colonists in Latin America, for example, used indigenous labor first as slaves and subsequently as forced wage laborers. Religious missionaries often played a prominent role, frequently intervening to protect indigenous populations from abuse and lobbying for more effective protective measures. At the same time, however, missionaries saw their own role as one of "civilizing" and "converting" the "heathen" natives and showed relatively little concern for preserving indigenous culture.[5]

Similar encounters occurred between more technologically or militarily advanced groups in Asia and Africa, which overran or surrounded nomadic, tribal, and other smaller groups who subsequently were encompassed in empires or states without their consent. Today, population pressures and modern communications and technology continue to close in on all but the most isolated indigenous communities.

Indigenous rights, unlike the rights of religious and other minorities, were not recognized as a separate issue of international concern until relatively recently. Even more starkly than minority rights, as noted in chapter 2 by

Jack Donnelly, indigenous rights pose a dilemma for states in which rights are believed to inhere in individuals, rather than groups. While it is true that nondiscrimination and equality rights (in addition to many other human rights) may be applied to indigenous individuals as such, the historical situation of indigenous peoples, their geographic concentration, their attachment to particular territories, and the fact that their institutions of self-government have largely survived make recognition of true group rights necessary, if the goal is to enable indigenous peoples to preserve their way of life. It is precisely the exercise of a meaningful degree of self-government—in addition to the protection of religious and cultural values—that indigenous groups seek to maintain and/or expand. Such self-government is an essential part of their heritage, unlike the primarily cultural or linguistic concerns of many minorities.[6]

Thus, from the earliest efforts of indigenous nations to gain admission to the League of Nations, the demands of indigenous peoples for government-to-government recognition have been quite different from the concern of minorities to preserve their culture, language, and traditions. It is a truism within UN discussions that minorities do not enjoy the right of self-determination, while (as discussed later) the relationship between indigenous peoples and self-determination is still being defined.

In addition to the discriminatory and paternalistic way in which they have been generally treated by states, both indigenous groups themselves and the domestic legal regimes under which they live are extraordinarily diverse. In some states, indigenous peoples are accorded a special status that may grant them certain rights not available to other groups of citizens but that also may impose disadvantages on their full participation in society. In other states, indigenous citizens are treated like all other citizens, at least in theory. Whatever the theoretical rights granted to indigenous individuals or communities, however, the reality has consistently been one of discrimination, poverty, and powerlessness.

MAJOR ISSUES

Prior to the gradual development of international human rights norms in the second half of the twentieth century, the human rights of indigenous peoples were accorded no greater attention than the human rights of any other segment of a state's population. Murder, slavelike working conditions, land seizures, interference with family life, and discrimination became cognizable as human rights violations in appropriate international forums, but it was not until the 1980s that new international norms began to be developed to address the specific situation of indigenous peoples.[7]

Development of these norms was sporadic, uncoordinated, and often overlapping, and a quasi-chronological approach is the best means of offering a sense of how indigenous rights have (or have not) come to be seen as a unique subset of human rights. Before summarizing those developments, however, we will first turn to three of the most problematic issues associated with indigenous rights, which have at their heart the appropriateness of recognizing the rights of groups, as opposed to the rights of individuals. These are the related questions of defining indigenous peoples, determining to what extent they enjoy the right of self-determination, and identifying which aspects of indigenous rights are rightly viewed as having a collective dimension.

Definition

After years of occasionally heated debate, the UN Sub-commission Working Group on Indigenous Populations decided not to include a definition of "indigenous peoples" in its draft declaration.[8] It was felt that any definition was bound to be controversial and would be attacked by those who felt it included too many groups, as well as by those who thought that it was overly restrictive. The controversy would likely detract from the more important goal of drawing attention to and articulating the rights that indigenous peoples needed in order to protect and develop their cultures.

Definitions are important only if significant consequences are to be drawn from falling within or outside their parameters. However, given the expansive set of rights identified in both the UN and the Organization of American States (OAS) draft declarations discussed later (as compared to the rights of minorities recognized in comparable UN and European instruments), it will probably be in the interests of many groups that wish to expand their political and economic power to deem themselves "indigenous." At the same time, of course, many states would prefer to see "the indigenous problem" limited to the Western Hemisphere, Australia, and New Zealand, where all would agree that Indians, Maori, and Aboriginals constitute classic examples of indigenous peoples and their suffering.

From the perspective of the European colonialist, all of the native populations in the Americas, Africa, and Asia could have been considered indigenous, although that designation obviously carried with it connotations of primitive or uncivilized or inferior. But where the Europeans did not settle and achieve numerical as well as political dominance (as they did, for the most part, in the Americas), against whom should Africans and Asians assert their rights as indigenous peoples? Whatever human rights problems may exist on those continents, it seems difficult to consider groups now in power as any less indigenous or native to the country than less powerful groups, which also found themselves within new colonial-based states.

This problem was partially overcome by the International Labor Organi-

zation (ILO) when it decided to address the situation not only of "indigenous" but also of "tribal" peoples—those, for instance, who would be
identified by India and Pakistan as "scheduled tribes" or who are sometimes
referred to as "hill tribes" elsewhere in Asia.[9] The focus was placed on the
characteristics of these groups and their relationship to the dominant society,
not on the question of who displaced whom in the earlier days of empire.
This approach also corresponds to an informal understanding among many
Africans and Asians that it is appropriate to include within the "indigenous"
category small, often isolated, ethnic groups or nomadic communities that
have remained separate from the mainstream society of the state.

Under article 1 of ILO Convention No. 169, adopted in 1989, indigenous
peoples are "those who are regarded as indigenous on account of their
descent from the population which inhabited the country . . . at the time of
conquest or colonisation or the establishment of present state boundaries
and who, irrespective of their legal status, retain some or all of their own
social, economic, cultural and political institutions." The convention also
applies to "[t]ribal peoples . . . whose social, cultural and economic conditions distinguish them from other sections of the national community, and
whose status is regulated wholly or partially by their own customs or traditions or by special laws or regulations."

As a matter of legal interpretation, the latter definition is difficult to distinguish from that of any ethnic group, unless one assumes that use of the
word *tribal* itself connotes a certain kind of (undefined) society. How does
one distinguish between those "whose social, cultural and economic conditions distinguish them from other sections of the national community, and
whose status is regulated wholly or partially by their own customs or traditions" and groups that, in other contexts, might be termed ethnic, religious,
linguistic, or national minorities?

The draft declaration on indigenous rights adopted by the OAS Inter-
American Commission on Human Rights[10] now follows the ILO approach:
It applies to undefined "indigenous peoples,"[11] as well as to "peoples"
defined identically to "tribal peoples" in ILO Convention No. 169.[12]

The key to a meaningful interpretation of these provisions may lie in the
broad differences in "social, cultural, and economic conditions" that exist
between indigenous/tribal and other peoples. These distinctions are different
from and, one might argue, additional to the differences of language, religion, ethnicity, or nationality that characterize minorities. German speakers
in South Tyrol, for example, are clearly a minority group, based on language
and nationality, but their social, cultural, and economic status is not much
different from that of Italians. The same could not be said about the Twa in
Rwanda, the Hmong in Vietnam, or the Yanomami in Brazil, whose lifestyles
are very distinct from the societies that surround them.

Geographic isolation or separateness also seems to characterize indigenous/tribal peoples, although nowhere is this criterion specified in any of the texts or proposed definitions. Land and territory are considered vital to the culture of most indigenous groups, and possession or use of a defined territory is a necessary minimum requirement for indigenous peoples to exercise many of the rights set forth in the various instruments. (Of course, many national and other minorities also inhabit reasonably well-defined territories, although they are often not the sole occupiers.)

Related to geographic separateness is the fact that indigenous peoples have a much better-developed set of traditional political institutions than do most minorities. Indeed, the powers identified in the UN and OAS drafts, as well as in ILO Convention No. 169, would be difficult to exercise without the existence of an indigenous government capable of taking decisions on behalf of the community as a whole. Indigenous peoples have been self-governing for centuries, in a way that cannot be said to be true for even national minorities.

At the end of the day, however, just as formal definitions of *minority* have generally been avoided in international texts, it seems appropriate—and perhaps even necessary—to leave the concept of "indigenousness" somewhat vague. So long as the concept is based on social, economic, cultural, and political characteristics rather than on historical patterns of migration and settlement, a workable definition should emerge over time.

Self-Determination

A great number of recent articles and books address the issue of self-determination, including its applicability to indigenous peoples, and it is impossible to do more than sketch the outlines of the debate here.[13]

In brief, indigenous peoples assert as a matter of logic that they are "peoples" within the internationally understood definition of that term and that therefore they benefit from the international norm stating that "all peoples have the right of self-determination."[14] Any other interpretation, they submit, unfairly discriminates against them by creating two categories of "peoples," those who have the right to self-determination and those who do not. The draft UN declaration on indigenous rights adopts this approach, simply reiterating the language of the human rights covenants.[15]

There are two problems with this argument. The first problem is that, while there may be agreement that the right to self-determination exists, there is no internationally accepted definition of the "peoples" who possess the right. The colonial "peoples" who had the right to independence were not ethnically distinct groups but rather included the entire population that inhabited a particular colonial territory.[16] The second problem is that the application of a right as essential as the right of self-determination should not depend on definitional conclusions that has more to do with semantics than with the reality of those they purport to encompass. The status, desires, needs, and rights of indigenous communities do not change depending on their designation as groups, communities, populations, peoples, or nations, and simplistic efforts to pretend that categorization as a "people" ends the debate are doomed to failure.

On the other side, many states object to any reference to an indigenous right to self-determination, because they, too, misinterpret the right as an absolute right that attaches unconditionally to any group identified as a "people." The misunderstanding is compounded by states' frequent equation of a right to self-determination with a right to secession or independence, a correlation that may have been true during the process of decolonization but that has not been accepted either before or since. A simple reference to the former Yugoslavia should suffice: The world community recognized the right of all those living within the territories of the six Yugoslav republics to become independent upon the dissolution of the federation, not the right of any ethnically defined "people" to proclaim their independence. This territorial, as opposed to ethnic, imperative was reinforced by the refusal to recognize similar rights for the largely Albanian province of Kosovo, because it was a province rather than a republic under Yugoslav law.

The concerns of states are addressed in both ILO Convention No. 169 and the draft OAS declaration by inclusion of a caveat that designation of indigenous groups as peoples "shall not be construed as having any implication with respect to any other rights that might be attached to that term in international law,"[17] a position opposed by most indigenous organizations.

Most indigenous groups (although there are exceptions) have stated clearly that they have no desire to secede formally from the states within whose boundaries they are located. What they do desire is a large degree of self-government, including the right to veto or reject incompatible state laws, while remaining within the internationally recognized boundaries of the state.

There will obviously be a great deal of debate over how much self-government is appropriate for indigenous peoples, who vary widely in population and culture, and how to balance the interests of indigenous peoples with the legitimate interests of other citizens of the state. However, that balance should not turn on inclusion or exclusion of "self-determination" from the catalogue of indigenous rights. The more specific articulation of what the right to self-government or self-determination might mean, as found in article 31 of the draft UN declaration and article 15 of the draft OAS declaration,[18] is likely to be more helpful in guiding consensual divisions of authority between indigenous and state governments than mere invocation of the right to self-determination. At the same time, states should not fear that mention of self-determination inevitably presages the state's disintegration.

Collective Rights

The issue of collective versus individual rights has bedeviled nearly every international discussion of the rights of minorities, indigenous peoples, and other groups, as discussed in chapters 2 and 3. The UN covenants on human rights, the 1992 UN Declaration on minority rights,[19] and the various European instruments on minorities[20] carefully refer to the rights "of persons belonging to" minorities. In contrast, neither ILO Convention No. 169 nor the draft UN or OAS declarations on indigenous rights hesitate to recognize collective rights.

Several articles in the UN draft specifically proclaim "collective and individual" rights for indigenous peoples and their members, and the OAS draft recognizes that "[i]ndigenous peoples have the collective rights that are indispensable to the enjoyment of the individual human rights of their members. Accordingly the states recognize *inter alia* the right of the indigenous peoples to collective action, to their cultures, to profess and practice their spiritual beliefs, and to use their languages."[21] The concept of collective rights also is implicit in the OAS declaration's recognition of indigenous rights to autonomy and self-government (article 15), maintenance of customary law (article 16), ownership and control over land and intellectual property (articles 18 and 20), approval of national development plans (article 21), and the observance of treaties (article 22).

The fear of some states, notably the United States, appears to be that recognizing the rights of indigenous groups *qua* groups will grant to those groups potentially dangerous authority over their members. While this potential does, of course, exist, indigenous lobbyists agreed during the drafting of the UN declaration that they would abide by "internationally recognized human rights standards" in the course of developing their institutional structures and "juridical customs, traditions, procedures and practices."[22] More important, as is the case with federal or other autonomous units within a state, the state itself will retain the right and responsibility to protect the human rights of individual citizens, be they indigenous or not.

Of course, recognizing group rights is not new. Although couched in individualistic terms, freedom of religion, assembly, association, and other rights are inherently communal in their exercise. States (and international human rights norms) permit private religious organizations to determine their own membership and to discriminate based on gender and belief. Corporations and other institutions have rights and responsibilities distinct from those of their individual shareholders or members.

Indigenous peoples seek the right to determine their own political, economic, and social policies, and, as even Donnelly recognizes, in order for them to do so, one must recognize meaningful collective rights for indigenous governments, not just individual rights that can be exercised collectively. It is also to be expected that indigenous interpretations of human rights norms may vary from those that would be followed by highly urbanized states, just as what constitutes a "fair trial" or an "adequate standard of living" depends on conditions in a particular society. To borrow a phrase from European human rights jurisprudence, both states and indigenous governments should enjoy a "margin of appreciation" that allows them to adopt their own policies and balance individual rights against societal needs, and there is no reason to expect that indigenous peoples will be less concerned about achieving the appropriate balance.

THE INTERNATIONAL CONTEXT

We now turn to a brief summary of the manner in which indigenous rights have been and are being addressed by various international organizations, without which one cannot understand the place of indigenous issues within the more general plan of human rights. The first section summarizes the ways in which non-indigenous-specific human rights bodies have addressed human rights issues raised by indigenous peoples. The second section summarizes the major normative and institutional innovations of direct interest to indigenous peoples that have been created or are currently under consideration.

International Action on Human Rights Violations against Indigenous Peoples

As is true for other human rights, the corpus of the law of indigenous rights has developed rather haphazardly, depending on the political realities of various forums. Although these forums suffer from all of the well-known deficiencies of international mechanisms to promote and protect human rights, they do offer precedents for identifying at least the minimum content of some indigenous rights. They also provide examples of why the further development and implementation of indigenous rights remain essential.

United Nations

The human rights of indigenous peoples have been addressed in wide variety of UN human rights forums, and the present chapter cannot survey them all. The following subsections therefore address the most directly relevant bodies in which indigenous rights per se have been considered.

Human Rights Committee   The Human Rights Committee is charged with supervision of the International Covenant on Civil and Political Rights, which over 140 states have ratified. Although the covenant does not include any specific reference to indigenous rights, the committee has interpreted a number of communications brought to its attention by means of individual petition under the Optional Protocol to the Covenant[23] as raising issues within the scope of article 27, which deals with the rights of minorities.[24]

In an early case, *Lovelace v. Canada*,[25] the committee upheld the right of an Indian woman to live on her tribe's reservation, despite a law that would have denied her this right because she had married a non-Indian man. The committee found that she would otherwise be prevented from enjoying her culture, in community with the other members of her tribe, as guaranteed under article 27.

The committee reached a superficially opposite result in the case of *Kitok v. Sweden*,[26] where it upheld Sweden's denial of Kitok's right to engage in reindeer herding, even though Kitok was ethnically a Saami, based on Kitok's ancestral village's refusal to grant him membership. Under Swedish law, the village had the right to restrict reindeer herding in order to ensure its economic viability, since reindeer herding is an essential part of Saami culture. Although it expressed "grave doubts" about Swedish legislation that permitted an individual member of an ethnic minority to be denied the right to engage in an economic activity that is an essential element of the minority's culture, the committee in effect concluded that the right of the Saami to restrict reindeer herding as a means of preserving their culture outweighed Kitok's individual right.[27]

In *Ominayak v. Canada*,[28] the committee concluded in rather sweeping language that "historical inequities" and "certain more recent developments [i.e., granting oil, gas, and timber leases] threaten the way of life and culture of the Lubicon Lake Band [an indigenous community] and constitute a violation of article 27 so long as they continue." However, it then immediately expressed its approval of a proposal by Canada to "rectify the situation" by offering a combination of other land and compensation to members of the Lubicon Lake Band, to compensate for damage caused by the leases. Two years later, the committee rejected a claim by another Canadian tribe that Canada's failure to allow the tribe to participate directly in discussions over reform of Canada's constitution violated the tribe's rights to political participation.[29]

Indigenous peoples have attempted to raise the issue of their right to self-determination, under article 1 of the covenant, in a number of cases. However, the committee has consistently held that article 1 is beyond the scope of its jurisdiction under the Optional Protocol,[30] although it has discussed self-determination in the context of its review of periodic state reports.

Sub-commission Working Group on Indigenous Populations   Created in 1982, the Working Group on Indigenous Populations of the (then) UN Subcommission on Prevention of Discrimination and Protection of Minorities has been the single most significant forum in which indigenous issues are considered by the United Nations. Its oversight mandate extends only to "review[ing] developments pertaining to the promotion and protection" of the human rights of indigenous peoples, and the Working Group has no authority to investigate or determine individual complaints. Nonetheless, it has become, in effect, a public forum in which both specific and general indigenous grievances can be raised.

Uniquely at the time of its creation, the Working Group is open to participation not only by states and nongovernmental organizations formally recognized by the United Nations[31] but also to indigenous peoples and their representatives. As a result, the Working Group's annual two-week sessions in Geneva are usually attended by five hundred to one thousand indigenous people, which in turn have created an effective lobbying force for indigenous issues. A number of state delegations also participate in the sessions, and a fruitful dialogue has been initiated, at least occasionally, between indigenous groups and the countries in which they live.

The Working Group's initial mandate also extended to monitoring "the evolution of international standards" concerning indigenous rights. This led to drafting the declaration on indigenous rights discussed later. Proposals for a "permanent forum" for indigenous peoples at the United Nations also were first made at the Working Group.

Permanent Forum on Indigenous Issues   As noted, indigenous participation in the United Nations via the Sub-commission's Working Group has been extensive since the early 1980s, and indigenous representatives greatly influenced the text of the draft declaration adopted by the working group in 1993. For many years, however, indigenous peoples have sought greater institutional recognition, more appropriate to their view that they should participate in some aspects of the UN's work on a par with governments. By the mid-1990s, this desire had coalesced around proposals for a "permanent indigenous forum" to be created within the UN system that would be empowered to address the entire range of indigenous interests.

While general consensus was soon reached on the need to create some form of a new body, serious disagreements persisted as to that body's mandate, membership, and position within the UN hierarchy.[32] The maximalist indigenous position called for a body at the level of the Economic and Social Council, with equal representation for indigenous peoples and states; indigenous peoples would choose the former themselves. The mandate of the forum would be as broad as possible, including the power to adopt policy decisions and resolve conflicts between indigenous peoples and states.

Some states supported merely extending the scope of the existing subcommission working group, but most accepted that an indigenous forum could serve as an advisory body, perhaps subsidiary to the Commission on Human Rights, whose authority would not extend to conflict resolution but would otherwise encompass fairly broad powers of giving advice and recommendations. Considerably different opinions were put forward as to the membership and the means of selecting members of the forum; most governments were uncomfortable with the idea of indigenous representatives who would be considered to be at the same level as state representatives.

The Commission on Human Rights formally proposed creation of a "Permanent Forum on Indigenous Issues" in April 2000.[33] The forum will be a subsidiary organ of the Economic and Social Council (ECOSOC), reporting directly to it, with a mandate to advise ECOSOC, including providing recommendations, on indigenous issues within the mandate of ECOSOC itself that relate to "economic and social development, culture, the environment, education, health and human rights."[34] Avoiding the issue of indigenous parity with states, the forum is to be composed of sixteen individual experts, eight to be nominated by governments and elected by ECOSOC and eight to be appointed by the (governmental) president of ECOSOC "on the basis of broad consultations with indigenous organizations taking into account the diversity and geographical distribution of the indigenous people of the world, as well as the principles of transparency, representativity [*sic*] and equal opportunity."[35]

The indigenous forum, whose first session was held in May 2002, will thus exist on a par with other functional commissions of ECOSOC, such as the Commission on Human Rights and Commission on the Status of Women, although its members will serve as individual experts rather than government (or indigenous) representatives. Its effectiveness will no doubt depend on the political skills and reputation of its members, as well as on the content of its proposals. In any event, creation of the Permanent Forum on Indigenous Issues is a significant success for indigenous lobbyists, confirming that indigenous issues in all their aspects are a legitimate concern of the UN system.

Organization of American States

The OAS, within the jurisdiction of whose members many of the world's indigenous peoples are found, took little formal notice of the plight of Indians within the hemisphere until the 1990s. The one exception to this lack of formal action was the creation of the Inter-American Indian Institute in 1940. The institute is now a specialized agency of the OAS; it acts as a standing committee to organize periodic Inter-American Indian Congresses (which are considered organs of the OAS) and also provides advisory services and technical services to OAS member states.[36] However, it was not until 1985 that indigenous people were able to attend the institute's periodic congresses without invitations from their national governments.

The mandate of the Inter-American Commission on Human Rights extends to all OAS member states, but the commission has had no special authority or obligation to concern itself with the rights of indigenous peoples. It is only through individual complaints to the commission and its occasional reports on the human rights situations in particular countries that a few specific indigenous situations have been examined.[37]

Faced with a number of individual petitions concerning indigenous people in the late 1960s and early 1970s, the commission in 1972 did adopt a resolution on "special protection for indigenous populations." The resolution states that the protection of indigenous populations is a "sacred commitment" of OAS member states and calls on states, in particular, to train and monitor public officials so that they will deal with indigenous people appropriately.[38] Unfortunately, until 1995 the resolution and recommendation adopted the following year remained the only general statement on indigenous rights adopted by the commission, and they appear to have had little practical impact.

Although the commission has discussed indigenous rights in the context of several reports on human rights situations in particular countries, until the late 1990s it had reached written conclusions dealing specifically with indigenous rights in only five cases.[39] In the first three cases, concerning the Guahibo in Colombia,[40] the Aché in Paraguay,[41] and the Yanomami in Brazil,[42] the commission adopted rather cursory statements or resolutions, finding violations in the last two cases. In the Yanomami case, the commission did imply that indigenous peoples might be guaranteed additional rights specific to their needs, when it noted that "international law in its present state, and as it is found clearly expressed in Article 27 of the International Covenant on Civil and Political Rights, recognizes the right of ethnic groups to special protection on [*sic*] their use of their own language, for the practice of their own religion, and, in general, for all those characteristics necessary for the preservation of their cultural identity."[43] However, the commission's conclusions rested on the narrower language of the American Declaration on the Rights and Duties of Man rather than creating new indigenous-specific rights.

The fourth case, concerning the Miskito Indians in Nicaragua, resulted in a major report and deserves fuller discussion.[44] Although the proximate cause of the complaint was violence in Nicaragua that led to the forced relocation of a large number of Miskito Indians, the case became much more complex due to divisions among the original complainants and expansion of the complaint to include broader issues of indigenous rights to autonomy and self-determination. The Sandinista government of Nicaragua, which was engaged in a civil war with the U.S.-backed *contras* at the time, participated actively in the commission's proceedings and invited it to conduct an on-site investigation into the complaints.

After numerous unsuccessful attempts to negotiate a friendly settlement, the commission concluded that there had been violations of the Miskitos' rights to life and liberty, but it also found that some of the forced relocations were justified as permissible derogations from normal human rights guarantees, in light of the military situation in Nicaragua at the time. Of greater interest is the commission's treatment of Miskito claims (1) that they had inherent rights to the lands they had traditionally occupied and (2) that they enjoyed additional political rights because of their status as indigenous peoples, in particular the right to self-determination.

With respect to land rights, the Nicaraguan government categorically rejected the argument that the Miskitos had rights any different from those accorded to all other citizens of Nicaragua and observed that "[t]erritorial unity stands above any other consideration and is not subject to discussion of any kind."[45] Stating that it was "not in a position to decide on the strict legal validity of the claim of the Indian communities to their ancestral lands,"[46] the commission simply concluded with a recommendation that a "just solution" be found that would meet "both the aspirations of the Indians and the requisites of territorial unity" of Nicaragua.[47]

The commission adopted a similar position of encouraging compromise with respect to the broader political claims put forward by the Miskitos, although its legal conclusions were somewhat more precise. After first noting that the American Convention on Human Rights prohibits discrimination but contains no specific provision related to "ethnic groups" (the commission's term for the Miskitos), the commission proceeded to analyze article 27 of the Covenant on Civil and Political Rights, to which Nicaragua was also a party.[48] After finding that the covenant guaranteed to minorities the rights to use their own language, practice their own religion, and enjoy their own culture, the commission went on to consider "whether or not ethnic groups also have additional rights [beyond those set forth in article 27], particularly the rights to self-determination or political autonomy."[49] Its conclusion remains one of the only statements to date by a quasi-judicial or judicial international human rights body to address directly the question of indigenous self-determination:

> The present status of international law [in 1984] does recognize observance of the principle of self-determination of peoples, which it considers to be the right of a people to independently choose their form of political organization and to freely establish the means it deems appropriate to bring about their economic, social and cultural development. This does not mean, however, that it recognizes the right to self-determination of any ethnic group as such.[50]

Citing, *inter alia*, UN General Assembly resolutions 1514 of December 14, 1960,[51] and 2625 of October 13, 1970,[52] the commission concluded that the right to self-determination could never justify disrupting the territorial integrity of a sovereign state.

Clearly uncomfortable with the conservative reading of international law it had just given, however, the commission went on to note that the absence of any legal right to autonomy or self-determination did not grant to Nicaragua "an unrestricted right to impose complete assimilation on those Indians."[53]

> Although the current status of international law does not allow the view that the ethnic groups of the Atlantic zone of Nicaragua have a right to political autonomy and self-determination, special legal protection is recognized for the use of their language, the observance of their religion, and in general, all those aspects related to the preservation of their cultural identity. To this should be added the aspects linked to productive organization, which includes, among other things, the issue of the ancestral and communal lands. . . . [I]t is fundamental to establish new conditions for coexistence between the ethnic minorities and the Government of Nicaragua, in order to settle historic antagonisms and the serious difficulties present today.[54]

Finally, a fifth case, the Mayagan (Sumo) Awas Tingni Community Case, challenged logging operations on indigenous territory in Nicaragua by a South Korean contractor, which had been agreed to by the government but without consultation with the Awas Tingni community. The commission adopted a report on the case in 1998, and the case was subsequently forwarded to the Inter-American Court of Human Rights.

The court's August 2001 judgment[55] upheld the rights of the Awas Tingni community and has become one of the most influential international decisions concerning indigenous peoples. It first found that Nicaragua had violated the right to judicial protection contained in article 25 of the American Convention on Human Rights by failing "to create an effective mechanism for delimitation and titling of the property of the members of the Awas Tingni Mayagna Community, in accordance with the customary law, values, customs and mores of that Community," based on the state's own laws and constitution.[56] The court went on to find that the right to private property, set forth in article 21 of the convention, protects "the rights of members of the indigenous communities within the framework of communal property, which is also recognized by the Constitution of Nicaragua. . . . Indigenous groups, by the fact of their very existence, have the right to live freely in their own territory; the close ties of indigenous people with the land must be recognized and understood as the fundamental basis of their cultures, their spiritual life, their integrity, and their economic survival."[57] Thus, by failing to demarcate indigenous land and by granting concessions to third parties to exploit resources on that land, Nicaragua was held also to have violated article 21 of the convention.

It remains to be seen whether the court's broad language will be extended to include situations in which the state has not itself recognized indigenous land rights, as was the case in Nicaragua, but its pronouncements certainly recognize indigenous rights to a much greater extent than had been held previously by any international tribunal.

Given the attacks on indigenous peoples that continue to occur in many American countries, it is surprising that the commission has only rarely addressed indigenous issues in the context of its general reports on the human rights situation in various states.[58] Of course, indigenous peoples are often victims of human rights violations that affect society at large, particularly peasants, but the specific situations of indigenous peoples had been considered in only a few reports until recently.[59]

The commission did find that the Maya-Quiche in Guatemala suffered from "centuries-old prejudice"[60] against them that was manifested in nearly every facet of Guatemalan political, economic, and cultural life. Despite recognition of indigenous culture, dress, and language in the Guatemalan constitution, the commission found inequality and de facto discrimination to be widespread:

> The reality—which the Government openly acknowledges—shows that Guatemala's indigenous people cannot exercise the same rights and do not have the same opportunities that the ladino population or the people of European descent enjoy. . . .
>
> Those who retain characteristics that identify them as Mayas—language, community structure, dress, religious practices—are not only excluded from positions of power and prestige in the nation, but in general are scorned by politicians, conservatives, liberals or Marxists.
>
> The overall policy of the State has been aimed at keeping them [indigenous people] out of jobs and ignoring their "backward" traditions, to allow some of the more "civilized" to become ladinos, and to brutally "mow down any who pose a direct challenge to Creole or Ladino dominance."[61]

As noted earlier, the Inter-American Court of Human Rights delivered its first judgment in a case relating primarily to indigenous rights in 2000, but it addressed indigenous issues indirectly in two earlier cases. The Chunimá case concerned alleged murders of indigenous rights activists in Guatemala, although it did not raise issues specific to indigenous peoples.[62] In the Aloeboetoe case, the court considered traditional tribal law in determining the amount of compensation to be paid by the Suriname government to the victims' families.[63]

Normative Developments[64]

International Labor Organization

Following concern with the plight of indigenous workers and a series of studies that began early as the 1920s, in 1957 the International Labor Organization (ILO) adopted Convention (No. 107) Concerning the Protection and Integration of Indigenous and Other Tribal and Semi-tribal Populations in Independent Countries.[65] Although from today's perspective the convention is paternalistic and clearly envisaged assimilation as its ultimate goal, it also contained important provisions on nondiscrimination, recognition of the right of collective and individual indigenous land ownership, prohibition of forced integration, respect for indigenous customary laws, and the right to be compensated for land taken by the government.

Thirty years later, in part due to pressures from nongovernmental organizations and indigenous groups themselves, the ILO replaced Convention No. 107 with a nonassimilationist and nonintegrationist text, Convention (No. 169) Concerning Indigenous and Tribal Peoples in Independent Countries.[66] Although many indigenous representatives at the time criticized the convention as not recognizing sufficiently broad indigenous political rights, the convention does require consultation with indigenous peoples whenever laws or administrative regulations directly affecting them are considered.[67] Governments are to adopt "special measures" to safeguard indigenous interests, with the consent of the affected people, and are to recognize and protect the "social, cultural, religious and spiritual values and practices" of indigenous peoples.[68] Indigenous peoples "shall have the right to decide their own priorities for the process of development as it affects their lives, beliefs, institutions and spiritual well-being and the lands they occupy or otherwise use, and to exercise control, to the extent possible, over their own economic, social and cultural development."[69]

With respect to the crucial issue of land, governments are to recognize the "rights of ownership and possession . . . over the lands, which they [indigenous peoples] traditionally occupy . . . [and] to safeguard the right of the peoples concerned to use lands not exclusively occupied by them, but to which they have traditionally had access for their subsistence and traditional activities."[70] While the rights of indigenous peoples to natural resources are to be "specially safeguarded," governments are permitted to own or exploit those resources, subject only to consultation with the peoples concerned.[71] Finally, a number of articles deal with, *inter alia*, recruitment and conditions of employment, vocational training, health, education, and cross-border contacts.

Although Convention No. 169 had been ratified by only fourteen states as of mid-2000, ten of those states were in Latin America; the Inter-American Indian Institute was among the intergovernmental organizations that participated in the convention's drafting. The convention is subject to the regular process of ILO supervision,[72] and it remains the most important legally binding international instrument on indigenous rights.

United Nations

As discussed earlier, the Working Group on Indigenous Populations of the UN Sub-commission on the Promotion and Protection of Human Rights (known until 1998 as the Sub-commission on Prevention of Discrimination and Protection of Minorities) has been actively reviewing the situation of indigenous peoples around the world since 1982. After eight years of discussions, in which hundreds of indigenous individuals and NGOs participated regularly, the Working Group adopted a draft Declaration on the Rights of Indigenous Peoples in 1993.[73] Due to the unprecedented level of influence and participation by indigenous people themselves, the Working Group's text largely reflects positions taken by indigenous organizations (although one should not always assume unanimity on the part of indigenous groups).

Since its approval by the subcommission, the draft has languished in an open-ended working group of the subcommission's parent body, the UN Commission on Human Rights. Although a few states participated in the early debates of the Working Group, it has only been at the level of the full commission that most state representatives began to express their positions on the draft declaration.[74] As one might expect, some of their positions vary considerably from those supported by indigenous representatives, although there seems to be general agreement on the desirability of drafting a declaration that eventually will be adopted by the UN General Assembly. Unfortunately, the attitude of some indigenous representatives that the subcommission draft should be adopted on a "take-it-or-leave-it" basis has not contributed to serious dialogue, and some states are more than willing to delay the process indefinitely rather than compromise.

The UN draft differs in several important respects from that adopted later by the OAS, discussed later, although the thrust of both documents is to articulate a relatively broad set of indigenous rights. Generally speaking, the UN provisions are couched in relatively vague (or even confusing) language, but they seek to maximize indigenous control over land, the environment, development, and their own political and social structures. The UN draft also deals with several issues omitted from the OAS draft, such as self-determination and dispute resolution between indigenous communities and states.

The provisions on land rights are quite strong, giving indigenous peoples the right "to own, develop, control and use the lands and territories . . . which they have traditionally owned or otherwise occupied or used."[75] Article 27 provides for the restitution of or compensation for indigenous lands taken without "full and informed" consent, and article 30 allows indigenous peoples to prohibit any development project that might adversely affect their territories.

Indigenous peoples have the right to determine their own citizenship[76] and maintain "their institutional structures and their distinctive juridical customs . . . in accordance with internationally recognized human rights standards."[77] Article 20 further provides that states must obtain the consent of indigenous peoples before adopting and implementing any "legislative or administrative measures that may affect them."

Finally, a number of provisions calls on states to take "effective measures" to guarantee the rights set forth in the declaration, such as the right of indigenous peoples under article 22 to "special measures for the immediate, effective and continuing improvement of their economic and social conditions, including in the areas of employment, vocational training and retraining, housing, sanitation, health and social security."

In addition to a more careful phrasing of some of the provisions, the most contentious issues in the UN draft are those outlined at the beginning of this chapter (i.e., self-determination, a definition of "indigenous," and collective rights). The fate of the draft is likely to depend upon whether a sufficient degree of consensus, if not unanimity, can be reached on these major issues.

Organization of American States

The original mandate of the Inter-American Commission on Human Rights gave it no reason to focus on indigenous issues in the Americas. However, the OAS has not been immune to the increasingly effective lobbying carried out by indigenous organizations and human rights NGOs, and the norm-setting activities of the UN and ILO no doubt contributed to the OAS's willingness to address indigenous issues.

The Inter-American Commission first proposed that it begin drafting a legal instrument defining indigenous rights in 1989, the year in which the ILO adopted Convention No. 169. A subsequent meeting of experts held at the Inter-American Indian Institute in 1991 concluded that a declaration would be the most appropriate form for the instrument, and the commission subsequently solicited opinions from OAS member states on the future instrument.[78]

After further internal discussions, the commission adopted an initial draft in September 1995, which was again sent to OAS governments for their comments.[79] The most recent draft, based on comments received from governments, indigenous groups, and others, was adopted in February 1997.[80] Timetables for final adoption have been continually pushed back, although it is now hoped that a final declaration might be adopted by the OAS General Assembly in 2002 or 2003.

The commission's draft declaration was adopted after the UN draft discussed earlier, and, at least in the early phases, the drafting process was less influenced by indigenous organizations. This summary focuses on areas of difference between the OAS and UN drafts, some of which may be bridged as the deliberative processes in both forums goes forward. The most important political and philosophical statements in the OAS declaration are perhaps those found in articles 7 and 8:

> Indigenous peoples have the right to their cultural integrity, and their historical and archeological heritage, which are important both for their survival as well as for the identity of their members.[81]
>
> The states shall recognize and respect indigenous ways of life, customs, traditions, forms of social, economic and political organization, institutions, practices, beliefs and values, use of dress, and languages.[82]
>
> Indigenous peoples have the right to indigenous languages, philosophy and outlook as a component of national and universal culture, and as such, [states] shall respect them and facilitate their dissemination.[83]

The declaration goes on to address more specifically issues of language, education, religion, family, health, and the environment. Like the UN draft, the OAS declaration imposes numerous affirmative obligations on states to promote or facilitate the exercise of the rights by indigenous peoples, as opposed to the more typical "negative" formulation of other human rights instruments.

Article 11, which is concerned with family relations, addresses the sensitive issue of the adoption of indigenous children. Unlike the UN draft declaration, which prohibits the removal of indigenous children from their families and communities "under any pretext,"[84] the OAS draft only requires that courts and other institutions give consideration to the views of the indigenous individuals, families, and communities concerned.[85]

Section Four, on "organizational and political rights," is perhaps most notable for what it omits: any specific reference to the right of self-determination. However, as discussed earlier, article 15(1) does follow the language of common article 1 of the two UN covenants on human rights, by stating that indigenous peoples have the right "to freely determine their political status and freely pursue their economic, social, spiritual and cultural development." Article 25 implicitly recognizes the principle of the territorial integrity of states, stating that "[n]othing in this instrument shall be construed as granting any rights to ignore boundaries between states."

Complementing the right to self-government is the right of indigenous peoples to participate "in all decision-making, at all levels, with regard to matters that might affect their rights, lives and destiny."[86] This right to participate does not grant to indigenous peoples a general right of veto over national policies, but it does ensure that their voices will be heard.

Customary indigenous law is to be deemed "part of the states' legal system" and should be applied in all matters arising within indigenous communities.[87] State courts also are directed to observe indigenous law and custom in proceedings concerning indigenous peoples or their interests.[88] Article 17 runs counter to the general trend of the declaration to empower separate indigenous institutions, in that it calls on states to facilitate inclusion of indigenous institutions and traditional practices in states' "organizational structures" and provides that state institutions "relevant to and serving indigenous peoples" should be designed so as to promote indigenous identity and values.

Seizures of land by settlers or by the state are at the center of most attacks on indigenous cultures and ways of life. At the same time, of course, developing countries faced with widespread poverty and an expanding population are likely to covet land that may be only sparsely populated by indigenous peoples, as well as the potential natural resources contained within such regions.

Section Five of the OAS declaration addresses these issues of land rights, as well as intellectual property, development, and special measures to protect indigenous workers. Indigenous rights to land and territories include (1) legal recognition of the various forms of collective ownership and use of territory by indigenous peoples, (2) ownership of lands and territories "historically occupied" by indigenous peoples, (3) use of territories to which indigenous peoples "have historically had access for their traditional activities and livelihood," and (4) the inalienability of these indigenous ownership and usufruct rights.[89]

Timber, oil, gold, and other mineral resources have proved to be almost irresistible attractions to indebted governments, individual peasants, wealthy landowners, and transnational corporations, and the exploitation of natural resources in areas traditionally inhabited or used by indigenous peoples has often led to explosive clashes between indigenous peoples and either settlers or government forces. Although the resources themselves may not have been important to traditional indigenous cultures, their exploitation inevitably results in substantial disruption of indigenous cultural and economic life. At the same time, many Latin American constitutions or laws reserve ownership over all subsoil resources within the national territory to the state, whether the land itself is in public or private hands.

The OAS draft attempts a compromise between the land rights of indigenous peoples and the exploitation of natural resources by the state. It first declares the basic principle that "[i]ndigenous peoples have the right to an effective legal framework for the protection of their rights with respect to the natural resources on their lands."[90] However, the succeeding paragraph appears to allow the state to exploit these resources, so long as indigenous peoples are consulted and so long as they participate in the benefits of exploitation, including receiving compensation for any damage caused.[91] These provisions should be read in conjunction with those concerning the environment, which provide that indigenous peoples "have the right to conserve, restore and protect their environment, and the productive capacity of their lands, territories and resources."[92]

Provisions on an indigenous right to development seem to tilt the balance back toward indigenous peoples themselves, whose development priorities are to prevail "even where they are different from those adopted by the national government or by other segments of society."[93] Unless "exceptional circumstances" exist, no development plan affecting indigenous peoples may be adopted without their "free and informed consent."[94]

This brief summary is necessarily incomplete and somewhat cursory. The language of the OAS draft is more moderate and its goals somewhat more modest than those found in the UN draft declaration. Although it might be expected that an OAS declaration on indigenous rights, as a regional instrument, could be more specific and more expansive than a global instrument, the present draft is, in fact, less detailed than the UN draft.

CONCLUSION

This chapter has adopted a legalistic approach to the issue of indigenous rights, because debates over whether indigenous people should enjoy special rights and just what those rights should be have largely occurred in the legal-political framework of the United Nations and other international organizations. In the short span of twenty years, consensus seems to have been reached on an answer to at least the first question, in that there is widespread support for including indigenous peoples among those vulnerable groups whose human rights deserve special attention. This has been due, in large part, to the relatively sophisticated and persistent efforts of the indigenous peoples themselves, aided by human rights NGOs and a few friendly governments.

However, adoption of a declaration or creation of a new UN organ does not guarantee that rights will be respected. The real test for indigenous rights will come when the international community attempts to hold governments accountable for the political obligations they assume under the UN and OAS declarations. Indeed, implementation of existing norms that protect the human rights of indigenous peoples is sorely lacking in many states, and the first challenge of the twenty-first century will be simply to enforce "ordinary" prohibitions against the murder, discrimination, and intimidation of which indigenous people are so often victims.

Many of the indigenous-specific rights articulated in the UN and OAS drafts, particularly those concerned with political and economic autonomy, must be balanced against competing government interests and, in some instances, the competing rights of others. At the same time, however, few rights are absolute, and balancing individual (or group) rights against the power of government is a task that should be familiar to international human rights bodies.

This chapter does not attempt to resolve the philosophical clashes over individual versus collective rights or majority versus minority rights. However, the legitimacy that the concept of indigenous rights is acquiring, as well as the articulation of the specific content of those rights, are important steps toward guaranteeing that the relationship between indigenous peoples and the states that surround them is based on greater equality and mutual respect in this century than has been the case in the preceding five centuries. Disagreement over the precise extent of indigenous rights will no doubt continue, but their existence can no longer be questioned.

NOTES

1. Jason Clay, "Looking Back to Go Forward: Predicting and Preventing Human Rights Violations," in *State of the Peoples*, ed. Marc S. Miller (Boston: Beacon, 1993), 67.

2. *Annual Report of the Inter-American Commission on Human Rights 1988– 1989*, 247. (The commission's annual reports are hereinafter cited as *"IACHR Annual Report"*).

3. See generally UN Sub-commission on the Promotion and Protection of Human Rights, study on treaties, agreements and other constructive agreements between states and indigenous populations (Miguel Alfonso Martinez, special rapporteur), UN Doc. E/CN.4/Sub.2/1999/20 (1999). For an indigenous view of the early relationship between Native Americans and the European settlers, see Oren Lyons and John Mohawk, eds., *Exiled in the Land of the Free: Democracy, Indian Nations, and the U.S. Constitution* (Santa Fe, N.M.: Clear Light, 1992).

4. It is, of course, impossible to generalize about an entire category of people, but the attacks on Indian and tribal peoples throughout the world are well known. Much of the impetus for international action on indigenous issues was provided by a massive UN study prepared in the 1980s, *Study of the Problem of Discrimination against Indigenous Populations* (José R. Martinez Cobo, special rapporteur), UN Doc. E/CN.4/Sub.2/1986/7 & Adds. 1–4 (1986) (hereinafter cited as UN Indigenous Study). Among many other broad surveys, reference might be made to Independent Commission on International Humanitarian Issues, *Indigenous Peoples: A Global Quest for Justice* (London: Zed, 1987), and the various reports published by nongovernmental organizations such as Survival International (London), Cultural Survival (Cambridge, Mass.), International Work Group for Indigenous Affairs (Copenhagen), Indian Law Resource Center (Washington, D.C.), Center for World Indigenous Studies (Olympia, Wash.), and Minority Rights Group (London).

5. For a discussion of the philosophical justifications for the conquest of the Americas, see Robert A. Williams Jr., *The American Indian in Western Legal Thought: The Discourses of Conquest* (New York: Oxford University Press, 1990). A

discussion of the historical legal context is found in S. James Anaya, *Indigenous Peoples in International Law* (Oxford: Oxford University Press, 1996), 9–38.

6. Of course, as discussed by Jackson-Preece, many minorities would like to exercise a greater degree of self-government than they now enjoy. However, this desire is primarily prospective, as opposed to reflecting political and/or economic power that minorities formerly enjoyed but subsequently lost.

7. In some ways, this attention to indigenous issues was simply part of a growing international movement to identify vulnerable groups whose human rights needed special protection. For example, special conventions or declarations have been adopted since the 1970s on refugees, women, children, minorities, migrant workers, prisoners and other detainees, religious intolerance, and racial discrimination.

8. The UN draft declaration is discussed more fully later in this chapter.

9. This approach is reflected in the titles of ILO Convention (No. 107) Concerning the Protection and Integration of Indigenous and Other Tribal and Semi-tribal Populations in Independent Countries, signed June 26, 1957, entered into force June 2, 1959, 328 U.N.T.S. 247, and ILO Convention (No. 169) Concerning Indigenous and Tribal Peoples in Independent Countries, adopted June 27, 1989, entered into force September 5, 1991.

10. Proposed American Declaration on the Rights of Indigenous Peoples, approved by the IACHR on February 26, 1997, OAS Doc. OEA/Ser.L/V/II.95, Doc. 6 (1997) (hereinafter "OAS Draft Declaration").

11. Article 1(2) provides simply, "Self-identification as indigenous shall be regarded as a fundamental criterion for determining the peoples to which the provisions of this Declaration apply."

12. This reversed the approach adopted in the first (1995) draft, *infra* note, which would have been limited to the particular circumstances of the Americas and defined indigenous peoples as "those who embody historical continuity with societies, which existed prior to the conquest and settlement of their territories by Europeans."

13. For contrasting views, compare, for example, Anaya, *Indigenous Peoples in International Law*, 75–125; Russel L. Barsh, "The Challenge of Indigenous Self-Determination," *University of Michigan Journal of Legal References* 277 (1993): 26; Lea Brilmayer, "Secession and Self-Determination: A Territorial Interpretation," *Yale Journal of International Law* 177 (1991): 16; Antonio Cassese, *Self-Determination of Peoples: A Legal Reappraisal* (Cambridge: Cambridge University Press, 1995); Hurst Hannum, "Rethinking Self-Determination," *Virginia Journal of International Law* 1 (1993): 34; Maivân Clech Lâm, "The Legal Value of Self-Determination: Vision or Inconvenience?" in *People or Peoples: Equality, Autonomy and Self-Determination* (Montreal: International Centre for Human Rights and Democratic Development, 1996), 79–142; Dean Suagee, "Self-Determination for Indigenous Peoples at the Dawn of the Solar Age," *University of Michigan Journal of Legal Reference* 671 (1992): 25; and Donna Lee Van Cott, "Prospects for Self-Determination of Indigenous Peoples in Latin America: Questions of Law and Practice," *Global Governance* 43, no. 1 (1996): 2.

14. The only formal international treaties that include this statement are the two international covenants on human rights, although the principle has been repeated in many UN General Assembly resolutions and other international instruments and is by now universally considered to be a norm of customary international law.

15. See article 3. The text of the UN draft, hereinafter cited as UN Draft Declaration, is found in UN Doc. E/CN.4/Sub.2/1993/29, Annex I (1993), and is reprinted in 34 *International Legal Materials* 541 (1995).

16. See Hannum, "Rethinking Self-Determination," 11–39.

17. See article 1 of ILO Convention No. 169, and article 1 (3) of the OAS declaration.

18. Article 31 sets out, "as a specific form of exercising their right to self-determination," indigenous rights to "autonomy or self-government in matters relating to their internal and local affairs, including culture, religion, education, information, media, health, housing, employment, social welfare, economic activities, land and resources management, environment and entry by non-members, as well as ways and means for financing these autonomous functions." The OAS draft contains similar language.

19. Declaration on the Rights of Persons Belonging to National or Ethnic, Religious or Linguistic Minorities, G.A. Res. 47/135, December 18, 1992.

20. See, for example, Framework Convention for the Protection of National Minorities, signed February 1, 1995, entered into force February 1, 1998, Europe; T.S. No. 157.

21. OAS Draft Declaration, article 2(2).

22. UN Draft Declaration, article 33.

23. For a discussion of the petition mechanism under the Covenant, see Sián Lewis-Anthony, "Treaty-Based Procedures for Making Human Rights Complaints within the UN System," in *Guide to International Human Rights Practice*, ed. Hurst Hannum (Ardsley, N.Y.: Transnational, 1999), 41–50.

24. Article 27 reads, in its entirety, "In those States in which ethnic, religious or linguistic minorities exist, persons belonging to such minorities shall not be denied the right, in community with the other members of their group, to enjoy their own culture, to profess and practise their own religion, or to use their own language."

25. Communication R.6/24, Report of the Human Rights Committee, UN Doc. A/36/40, Annex 18 (1977), 166.

26. Communication No. 197/1985, Report of the Human Rights Committee, UN Doc. A/43/40, Annex 7(G) (1988), 207.

27. The committee's decision was no doubt influenced by the fact that Kitok was, in practice, permitted by the village to graze and farm his reindeer on communal lands, even though he did not have a legal right to do so.

28. Communication No. 267/1984, Report of the Human Rights Committee, UN Doc. A/45/40, vol. 2, Annex 9(A) (1990), 1.

29. *Mikmaq People v. Canada*, Communication No. 205/1986, Report of the Human Rights Committee, UN Doc. A/47/40, Annex 9(A) (1992), 213.

30. See Human Rights Committee, General Comment No. 23(50) (Art. 27), UN Doc. CCPR/C/21/Rev.1/Add.5 (1994), para. 3.1.

31. Consultative status has been granted to over one thousand national and international organizations, with a wide variety of interests. Their status and activities are governed by ECOSOC Res. 1996/31 (1996), amending ECOSOC Res. 1296 (XLIV) (1968).

32. See generally the reports of two open-ended working groups established by

the UN Commission on Human Rights to consider this issue, in UN Docs. E/CN.4/ 1999/83 (1999) and E/CN.4/2000/86 (2000).

33. Res. 2000/87 of April 28, 2000.

34. Res. 2000/87 of April 28, 2000, op. para. 2.

35. Res. 2000/87 of April 28, 2000, op. para. 1.

36. See UN Indigenous Study, 140–45; Inter-American Commission on Human Rights, *Inter-American Yearbook on Human Rights 1969–1970* (Washington, D.C.: OAS, 1976), 73–83.

37. See generally Dinah L. Shelton, "The Inter-American Human Rights System," in *Guide to International Human Rights Practice*, ed. Hannum, 121–34.

38. See *IACHR Annual Report 1972*, 63–65. This and the 1973 recommendations regarding indigenous populations are summarized in Inter-American Commission on Human Rights, *Ten Years of Activities 1971–1981* (Washington, D.C.: OAS, 1982), 328–29.

39. For a survey and analysis of these early cases, see Shelton H. Davis, *Land Rights and Indigenous Peoples: The Role of the Inter-American Commission on Human Rights* (Cambridge, Mass.: Cultural Survival, 1988); also see Hurst Hannum, "The Protection of Indigenous Rights in the Inter-American System," in *The Inter-American System of Human Rights*, ed. David J. Harris and Stephen Livingston (Oxford: Clarendon, 1998).

40. Case No. 1690 (Colombia), *IACHR Annual Report 1973*, 21–22.

41. Case 1802 (Paraguay), *IACHR Annual Report 1977*, 36–37.

42. Case No. 7615 (Brazil), *IACHR Annual Report 1984–1985*, 24–34.

43. Case No. 7615 (Brazil), *IACHR Annual Report 1984–1985*, 31. This is a somewhat broader articulation of article 27 than is found in the text itself, which is set forth in note.

44. *Report on the Situation of Human Rights of a Segment of the Nicaraguan Population of Miskito Origin*, OAS Docs. OEA/Ser.L/V/II.62, doc. 10 rev. 3 (1983) and OEA/Ser.L/V/II.62, doc. 26 (1984) (hereinafter "Miskito Report").

45. Miskito Report, 126.

46. Miskito Report, 127.

47. Miskito Report.

48. The examination of the covenant was justified by referring to article 29(b) of the American Convention, which directs the commission to interpret the convention in a way that does not restrict rights recognized by virtue of any other convention to which a state may be a party.

49. Miskito Report, 78.

50. Miskito Report, 78–79.

51. Declaration on the Granting of Independence to Colonial Countries and Peoples.

52. Declaration on Principles of International Law concerning Friendly Relations and Co-operation among States in accordance with the Charter of the United Nations.

53. Miskito Report, 81.

54. Miskito Report, 81–82.

55. *Mayagna (Sumo) Awas Tingni Community v. Nicaragua*, Judgment of August 31, 2001, Ser. C No. 79.

56. *Mayagna (Sumo) Awas Tingni Community v. Nicaragua*, para. 138.

57. *Mayagna (Sumo) Awas Tingni Community v. Nicaragua*, paras. 148, 149.

58. The commission's increasing interest in indigenous issues is illustrated by its recent publication of a report on *The Human Rights Situation of the Indigenous People in the Americas*, OAS Doc. OEA/Ser.L/V/II.108, doc. 62 (2000), which summarizes both the earlier cases discussed in this chapter and several more recent cases examined by the commission.

59. Among the reports that have discussed indigenous issues in some detail, see the commission's three reports on the situation of human rights in Colombia, OAS Docs. OEA/Ser.L/V/II.53, Doc. 22 (1981), 208–17; OEA/Ser.L/V/II.84, Doc. 39 rev. (1993), 229–37; and OEA/Ser.L/V/II.xx (1999), Chap. X. Also see *Third Report on the Situation of Human Rights in Guatemala*, OAS Doc. OEA/Ser.L/V/II.66 (Oct. 1985); *Report on the Situation of Human Rights in Mexico*, OAS Doc. OEA/Ser.L/V/II.100, Doc. 7 rev. 1 (1998), Chap. VII; and *Second Report on the Situation of Human Rights in Peru*, OAS Doc. OEA/Ser.L/V/II.106, Doc. 59 rev. (2000), Chap. X. A recent press release indicated that the commission is currently examining some forty cases pertaining to indigenous peoples; see IACHR, Press Release No. 23/01 (September 28, 2001).

60. IACHR, *Fourth Report on the Situation of Human Rights in Guatemala*, OAS Doc. OEA/Ser.L/5/II.83, Doc. 16 rev. (1993), 36.

61. IACHR, *Fourth Report on the Situation of Human Rights in Guatemala*, 33–34 (citation omitted).

62. See Chunimá Case (Emergency Provisional Measures), July 15, 1991, Order of the President of the Inter-American Court of Human Rights, reprinted in *1991 Inter-American Year Book on Human Rights*, 1104. The case was settled without a final judgment having been adopted.

63. See Aloeboetoe Case (Reparations), Inter-American Court of Human Rights, Ser. C, No. 15 (1993). This aspect of the case is briefly summarized in Jo M. Pasqualucci, "The Inter-American Human Rights System: Establishing Precedents and Procedure in Human Rights Law," *University of Miami Inter-American Law Review* 297, nos. 329–31 (1995): 26.

64. Discussions of the development of indigenous rights internationally may be found in, for example, Anaya, *Indigenous Peoples in International Law*, 39–71; Russel L. Barsh, "Indigenous Peoples in the 1990s: From Object to Subject of International Law?" 7 *Harvard Human Rights Journal* 33 (1994); Howard R. Berman, "Perspectives on American Indian Sovereignty and International Law, 1600 to 1776," in *Exiled in the Land of the Free: Democracy, Indian Nations, and the U.S. Constitution*, ed. Oren Lyons and John Mohawk (Santa Fe, N.M.: Clear Light, 1992), 125–88; Hurst Hannum, *Autonomy, Sovereignty, and Self-Determination: The Accommodation of Conflicting Rights* (Philadelphia: University of Pennsylvania Press, 1996), 74–103, 501; Siegfried Wiessner, "Rights and Status of Indigenous Peoples: A Global Comparative and International Legal Analysis," 12 *Harvard Human Rights Journal* 57 (1999); UN Indigenous Study, and the annual reports of the Working Group on Indigenous Populations of the UN Sub-commission on Promotion and Protection of Human Rights.

65. *Supra* note 9.

66. *Supra* note 9.
67. ILO Convention No. 169, supra note 9, article 6(1)(a).
68. ILO Convention No. 169, article 5(a).
69. ILO Convention No. 169, article 7(1).
70. ILO Convention No. 169, article 14(1).
71. ILO Convention No. 169, article 15.
72. See generally Lee Swepston, "Human Rights Complaint Procedures of the International Labor Organization," in *Guide to International Human Rights Practice*, ed. Hannum, 85–101.
73. ILO Convention No. 169, *supra* note 9.
74. Both the subcommission and its working groups are composed of experts elected by the commission, who serve in their individual capacities and not as state representatives.
75. UN Draft Declaration, article 26.
76. UN Draft Declaration, article 32.
77. UN Draft Declaration, article 33.
78. A fairly extensive summary of the responses received (from eleven governments and twenty indigenous organizations) is included in the commission's *1992–93 Annual Report*, OAS Doc. OEA/Ser.L/V/II.83, Doc. 14, corr. 1 (1993), 263–310. A useful summary of subsequent proposals may be found in a "working document" prepared by the chair of the OAS working group on the declaration, OAS Doc. OEA/Ser.K/XVI, GT/DADIN/doc.53/02 (2002).
79. Draft Inter-American Declaration on the Rights of Indigenous Peoples, O.A.S. Doc. OEA/Ser.L/V/II.90, doc. 9 rev. 1, reprinted in *IACHR Annual Report 1995*, 207–18.
80. OAS Draft Declaration.
81. OAS Draft Declaration, article 7(1).
82. OAS Draft Declaration, article 7(3).
83. OAS Draft Declaration, article 8(1).
84. UN Draft Declaration, article 6.
85. OAS Draft Declaration, article 11(2).
86. OAS Draft Declaration, article 15(2).
87. OAS Draft Declaration, article 16(1) and (2).
88. OAS Draft Declaration, article 16(3).
89. OAS Draft Declaration, article 18(1)–(3).
90. OAS Draft Declaration, article 18(4).
91. OAS Draft Declaration, article 18(5).
92. OAS Draft Declaration, article 13(3).
93. OAS Draft Declaration, article 21(1).
94. OAS Draft Declaration, article 21(2).

5

Protecting the Human Rights of Women

Eva Brems

A feminist perspective on international human rights law and politics emerged during the last decade of the twentieth century. Feminism was relatively late in confronting international human rights but, from all evidence, is here to stay. Radhika Coomaraswamy, the UN special rapporteur on violence against women, calls it a "revolution": "[W]omen's rights have been catapulted onto the human rights agenda with a speed and determination that has rarely been matched in international law."[1] The United Nations World Conference on Human Rights, held in Vienna in 1993, was a major turning point. Women's groups from around the world with multiple agendas sharpened their skills of coalition making and lobbying and experienced the strength of their combined forces.[2] Earlier efforts, particularly the series of UN conferences on the advancement of women that had started in 1975, were part of a period of gestation; Vienna marked the birth of an international women's human rights movement.[3]

Feminist critiques have for some time been applied to crucial areas of domestic law. Many of the analytical and methodological tools developed in the domestic context are now being applied to international human rights law. In this chapter, I examine how feminist claims are transforming international human rights and suggest where this growing impact may lead. Three different approaches to the protection of women's rights will be addressed. The first is based on what might be called the "sameness" of women and men, while the other two take women's "specificity" as a starting point, one leading to a claim for special human rights for women and the other to a claim for the feminist transformation of human rights for all.

There is a certain chronological order in this presentation in that the "sameness" approach historically came first, and the idea of a feminist transformation of human rights is relatively recent. Yet the three approaches are not intended to reflect the viewpoints of specific persons or groups but rather should be seen as theoretical models, or analytical tools, to facilitate discussion of different ways in which women's human rights can be approached. In the real world, hardly anyone promotes a purely "sameness" approach. What is known as "liberal feminism" comes closest, yet it includes some elements of a "specificity" approach. Moreover, most proponents of a specificity model support both certain proposals for special women's rights, and certain "feminist transformations" of human rights. We are faced not so much with a choice among three models as with a choice between different combinations of measures linked to the three approaches.

All three approaches are as relevant today as they are for the future. However, this chapter will focus most strongly on feminist transformations of international human rights. This is justified in the first place because of the future-oriented perspective of this book: the impact of feminist transformations of human rights is only starting to be felt, and their potential for the future is far-reaching. Moreover, within the specificity approach, this chapter will promote the transformative approach more than special women's rights, because it fits best in a conception of universality based on all-inclusiveness. Finally, the claim for the recognition of women's specificity in international human rights cannot be considered in isolation since identity-based claims are being launched by others, notably minorities, indigenous peoples, and representatives of non-Western societies. Though similar to the feminist demands in form and in their underlying rationale, these other claims are often at odds with feminist views when it comes to their substance. Managing multiple specificities is another huge challenge for international human rights in the next fifty years.

SAMENESS

In the simplest of terms, both women and men are human, which means that in many respects they are the same and they want to be treated in the same way. The principle of the universality of human rights[4] and the ensuing rule of nondiscrimination in the enjoyment of human rights are meant to assure such equal treatment.[5] When human rights first appeared on the international scene, with the Universal Declaration of Human Rights (UDHR) in 1948, they had a strong emphasis on natural law. The idea of universality was based on that of an essential "human" nature. It was believed that human rights captured the common denominator of all human beings and that all the values and concerns they embody, from political participation over property to labor standards, were somehow inherent in all humans, independent of social class, culture, or gender; that they expressed a common human dignity. An important consequence was the assumption that the formulation of these rights—as, for instance, in the UDHR—was neutral with regard to such factors as culture or gender. Hence the ambition to apply the same rights, in the same way, to everybody regardless of their gender, class, and so forth. The ideal of equality of the sexes was that of formal, gender-blind equality.

Formal equality of the sexes was a huge challenge in 1948, a time when, in many states, women had only recently obtained the right to vote.[6] Formal equality only gradually became a reality, and it is still not realized today. Discrimination against women in all areas of life is widespread. The number of laws still on the books that formally and explicitly discriminate against women is extensive. According to the Sudanese Personal Law for Muslims Act, enacted in 1991, for example, a woman needs a male guardian to contract her own marriage. During marriage, she is required to obey her husband, and while her husband can divorce her at will, she can divorce him only on certain grounds and after a court procedure.[7] In South Africa, women married under customary law are considered minors and cannot enter into any legal contract without the consent of their husbands or guardians.[8] And in Saudi Arabia, women are not allowed to drive cars.[9]

Even where the laws protecting women against discrimination exist, the practice is often one in which the rules are flagrantly violated on a daily basis. Recently Human Rights Watch reported how abuses against women have been carried out frequently and with virtual impunity in states such as Russia, South Africa, Pakistan, and Jordan that largely failed to fulfill their obligations to provide protection.[10] In the United States, Human Rights Watch identified violence by custodians against women in prisons[11] and in Bosnia, discrimination against women with regard to loans and training programs in reconstruction programs.[12] The organization also accused the Mexican government of not protecting the rights of pregnant women that are guaranteed under domestic legislation but violated by transnational corporations in the export-processing sector.[13]

As these examples show, the sameness approach toward women's human rights remains highly relevant. Such discriminatory practices deny the sameness of women and men on the basis of patriarchal constructions of difference, which do not necessarily view women as inferior but are almost inevitably distortions brought on by the interpretation of the specificity of women by men (i.e., by outsiders in a dominant position). Activists for women's rights thus need to continue to focus on eliminating patriarchal constructions of difference and on achieving formal equality before the law through the abolition of discriminatory laws and the enforcement of antidiscrimination legislation.[14] This type of feminist activism rests within mainstream human rights rules and institutions and has been called the "doctrinal" or "institutional" approach[15] or, in an analogy with feminist approaches to domestic law, "liberal feminism."[16] It may seem too limited to many living in Western countries where its goals have largely been reached, but it is a necessary step, which can make an enormous difference in the lives of women.

Another consequence of the sameness of women and men is that women experience many of the same human rights violations as men. If a political party or a religious sect is outlawed, female and male members are equally affected. If a village is burned down and the crops are destroyed, all its inhabitants suffer. There is no need for different rules for men and women, nor is there any need for different control mechanisms. Yet in those situations as well, a women's perspective on human rights may make sense simply because women are often not aware of their entitlement. There is a need to make women more aware of their rights in many societies and provide them with access to human rights discourse and remedies.[17]

SPECIFICITY

Biological differences between men and women lead to different personal experiences, as do role patterns in the family and in the broader society. Beyond these differences, some feminists also claim that there are inherent psychological differences between the sexes.[18] At the same time, men have dominated the history of international human rights since the Universal Declaration. Today, the natural law approach to human rights no longer prevails. The concept of "human nature" is under fire, and considerable dispute persists about whether a neutral perspective is possible at all. We realize now that however well intentioned the drafters of the declaration, their attempt to assume a common human nature inevitably resulted in a projection of their own experiences, needs, and values onto the rest of humanity. Despite the participation of Eleanor Roosevelt, those were predominantly the experiences, needs, and values of well-off white Western men. The same holds true for developments in human rights theory and practice since 1948.

As social groups emerge from domination, they become aware of this distortion within international human rights, and they advance claims to correct it. After the end of the Cold War, human rights jumped to the forefront of international relations, and their power substantially increased. Emancipation movements, such as the women's movement, became aware of the increased potential of international human rights to realize their agendas. As a result, the claims to correct the biases of international human rights have become louder, in particular those from the women's movement and those from non-Western societies. Those claims are based on a different conception of universality and equality. They start from a realization that neutrality and objectivity are, practically speaking, impossible and, as a consequence, formal equality is not sufficient when there are relevant differences, such as there are between men and women.

From that perspective, equality can no longer be realized by eliminating all context-related factors but rather by deliberately taking some such factors into account. If human rights are to be universal in the sense that they apply in an equal manner to all women and all men, they must take some gender-based differences into account instead of stressing their irrelevance. This is not necessarily at odds with the earlier view of universality and equality, which purports to eliminate differences. The difference to be eliminated in that first conception is difference as constructed by dominant outsiders, *in casu* by men. The difference to be recognized in this second view, however, is difference as experienced by the insiders. In this case: by women themselves.

The main focus of this chapter is on the adaptation of international human rights law to the specific needs and experiences of women. Although the specificity approach may obviously be linked to a strand of feminism known as "cultural feminism,"[19] it should not be interpreted as taking sides in the feminist debate between "sameness" and "difference." Particularly when discussing the future of international women's human rights over the next several decades, the emphasis on specificity simply offers a more fruitful approach.

The theoretical framework within which these issues will be addressed is that of "inclusive universality."[20] Inclusive universality is based on the inclusion of all people in the human rights framework. It accepts the critique that the pretended neutrality of human rights is inherently biased and, as a result, insists that formal applicability of standards is not enough to guarantee general inclusion in human rights protection. It recognizes that people who do not correspond to the implicit reference point of human rights (the human being in its male and Western manifestation) experience a form of exclusion because their needs, concerns, and values are not taken into account to the same extent as those of Western men. Inclusive universality proposes to correct this situation by accommodating particularist claims from those who are excluded.

With regard to women, this means listening to what women have to say about how the present system of international human rights does not sufficiently protect them, does not correspond to their needs, and does not reflect their priorities. There is now a strong and well-organized women's movement advancing such arguments and making very concrete proposals for changes to standards, organizations, mechanisms, and policies. If human rights are to be universal, they should respond to these claims, for several reasons. In the first place, from a democratic perspective, inclusion requires participation. If human rights are the rights of all humans, all humans must have a say in defining what they are and how they are used. This means that women should be present when human rights standards are formulated and when agendas are set. They should be there in fact, and they should be there in the sense that they are being fully taken into account with all their gender-specific concerns.

Human rights should also respond to the claims of women (or others who have been excluded) for pragmatic reasons. The connection between human rights standards and practice, on the one hand, and the life experiences of people, on the other, is crucial. Human rights make no sense unless they are relevant to the experience of people. They only work if the people activate them; they strongly rely on an active civil society. Women make up at least half of the human population. If a significant group of women feel disconnected from human rights, this undermines not only their significance as "human" rights but also their effectiveness.

The history of human rights can be read as a story of increasing inclusion. Both the form and substance of human rights evolve with the inclusion of groups that have suffered discrimination in the past. Only after women accede to the status of full human beings in the eyes of the community[21] do they have a voice in determining what human rights should be about. The emancipation of working people led to the expansion of human rights into the field of socioeconomic claims, and the emancipation of colonized peoples led to a wider recognition of the right to self-determination and the introduction of the notion of a right to development.[22] Likewise, women are determined to put their stamp on international human rights. How can women's specificity be accommodated within international human rights law? In general, two different methods are possible.

The first method involves "flexibility" or differentiation of human rights standards, depending on the context (the relevant specificities). Either new standards are created specifically for the members of the excluded group, or a margin of variation is left within general standards so that the needs and values of different groups can be taken into account. With regard to women, the creation of special "women's human rights" is the main expression of "flexibility." The second involves the "transformation" of human rights standards, with general norms or institutions being changed in response to the particularist claims of those who have been excluded. In many respects, the transformation of general human rights standards in response to the claims of women holds the most promise for the future.

Thus, within the "specificity approach," a distinction is made between an approach that uses a "flexibility" technique, and one that uses a "transformation" technique. The former is focused on creating special rights and mechanisms for women. The latter attempts to change the general rights standards and mechanisms, so that the improvements that are inspired by women's special concerns are moved to the center and can be enjoyed by all.

The three approaches to women's human rights—sameness, flexibility, and transformation—reflect the three types of claims that may be addressed to rights discourse from the perspective of identity politics, as analyzed by Higgins. The sameness approach reflects the complaint of groups "that they are inappropriately defined as different."[23] The flexibility approach deals with the complaint of groups "that their distinctiveness is inappropriately ignored or disrespected by the majority."[24] Finally, the transformation approach is the most radical, expressing "an alternative Universalist vision that challenges the foundational commitments of the majority."[25] Yet however radical some of the arguments may be, they remain "internal to our human rights framework in that they accept the aspirations of the existing scheme at a general level but argue that those aspirations have been improperly defined in some cases and inadequately met in others."[26]

FLEXIBILITY: HUMAN RIGHTS FOR WOMEN

It is logical that the initial response to feminist demands for the inclusion of women's specificity in international human rights should have been to add specific human rights for women. For one thing, additions to human rights standards and institutions targeted at those excluded are more readily interpreted as a response to that group than are modifications of a general nature. "When women complain, let's do something for them" is the straightforward reasoning of the flexibility approach. The visibility of the addition and its symbolic value are nearly as important as its impact in the real world. Second, the creation of specific women's human rights standards and institutions leaves the mainstream system intact. When claims for important changes have to be met, adding something new is a much less drastic intervention than questioning and reshaping what already exists. Hence the flexibility approach is, at once, less drastic and more visible than the transformation approach.

In many ways, the international movement for the advancement of women dates back to before World War II and was initiated quite apart from the human rights movement. In the 1920s, feminist activists from the Americas pressured their governments into creating the Inter-American Commission of Women (Commission Interamericana de Mujeres [CIM]).[27] The CIM drafted the Inter-American Convention on the Nationality of Women (1933) and promoted an Equal Rights Treaty (1928).[28] With the creation of the Organization of American States (OAS) in 1948, the CIM became an autonomous specialized commission of the OAS. It drafted two more women's conventions in 1948: the Inter-American Convention on the Granting of Political Rights to Women and the Inter-American Convention on Granting Civil Rights to Women.[29] After shifting its efforts to problems of education and development, the CIM returned to the question of women's rights in the 1980s, with its work on the Inter-American Convention on the Prevention, Punishment, and Eradication of Violence against Women, adopted by the General Assembly of the OAS on June 9, 1994.[30]

The CIM was also influential in the creation of the United Nations Commission on the Status of Women (CSW) in 1946.[31] Until the early 1970s, the CSW was mainly oriented toward the promotion of equal rights for women,[32] drafting the Convention on the Political Rights of Women (1952), the Convention on the Nationality of Married Women (1957), the Convention on Consent to Marriage, Minimum Age for Marriage, and Registration of Marriages (1962), and a number of declarations.[33] The CSW also drafted the Convention on the Elimination of All Forms of Discrimination against Women (CEDAW, 1979), the most important expression of the "human rights for women" approach. The CEDAW has its own supervising body, the Committee for the Elimination of Discrimination against Women (CmEDAW).

Within the structure of the United Nations, the Division for the Advancement of Women (DAW) is the secretariat for both CSW and CmEDAW.[34] Other "bureaucratic spaces"[35] for women's issues within the UN include UNIFEM (United Nations Development Fund for Women) and INSTRAW (International Research and Training Institute for the Advancement of Women). There are also a number of International Labor Organization (ILO) conventions—in particular, convention no. 45 concerning the employment of women on underground work in mines of all kinds (1935), convention no. 89 concerning night work of women in industry (1948, revising a 1934 convention), convention no. 100 concerning equal remuneration for men and women workers for work of equal value (1951), convention no. 103 concerning maternity protection (1952, revising a 1919 convention), convention no. 111 concerning discrimination in respect of employment and occupation (1958), and convention no. 156 concerning equal opportunities and equal treatment for men and women workers with family responsibilities (1981).

What has thus been developed within the international system are specific instruments and institutions dealing with women's rights that are expressions of a "flexibility" approach to the issue of human rights for women. Yet within this approach, different attitudes can be distinguished toward the issue of gender. Several of the older instruments, for example, reflect a "sameness" approach. Texts such as the UN Convention on the Political Rights of Women (1952) and the ILO Equal Remuneration Convention (1951) are based on a concept of formal equality that elevates women to the same level of rights as men. Because they use a male reference point, however, such texts cannot (nor are they intended to) do justice to the specific needs and experiences of women. They are gender-specific in form but not in substance.

Other texts are based on women's specificity, yet they interpret it in a way that leads to the exclusion of some women. In line with traditional role patterns, these "protective" instruments[36] see women as especially vulnerable and in need of protection. For example, in the UN Declaration on the Protection of Women and Children in Emergency and Armed Conflict (1974), women are put on the same level as children. They are "the most vulnerable members of the population" (article 1), "defenceless" (article 2), and in general depicted as passive victims. In the ILO conventions on night work (1948) and on work in mining (1935), the patriarchal protection of women even leads to their exclusion from certain types of activities. While many women may agree with such views of femininity and many also may benefit from these provisions, others feel that this approach does not do justice to them as persons capable of making their own choices.

In the more recent texts, the goal is to include an array of women's perspectives that is as complete as possible. In the first place, they try to address the ways in which the experience of human rights violations, whether suffered by men or women, is influenced by gender. For example, denial of the right to food or adequate housing in a society where women bear the primary responsibility in these fields affects women differently than men.[37] Another typical situation occurs when women are subjected to arbitrary violence—for example, in detention, where this frequently takes the form of sexual assault.[38] A fortiori, these texts also address violations in which gender is a determining factor, such as relating to the sexuality of women or their reproductive capacity.

Texts on women's rights that adopt this approach have been labeled "corrective" instruments[39] and include conventions that address trafficking in women, the UN Convention on Consent to Marriage, Minimum Age for Marriage, and Registration of Marriages (1962), the UN Declaration on the Elimination of Violence against Women (1993), and the Inter-American Convention on the same subject (1994). The latter texts particularly reflect the perspective of women by extending protection against violence that is committed in the private sphere and violence that results from cultural factors.

The CEDAW contains elements of all three approaches. As largely an anti-discrimination convention, it has a strong sameness component as many provisions give women "equal rights with men." Other provisions have a protective character, in particular with regard to women's reproductive function (articles 11[1][f] and [2][d]). And there is a strong corrective element in the provisions that deal with issues in which women are not treated equally: political and public life (articles 7–8), nationality (article 9), education (article 10), employment (article 11), health care (article 12), economic and social life (article 13), legal status (article 15), and marriage and family relations (article 16). The document also devotes an article to the specific problems of rural women (article 14) and another to trafficking in women and prostitution (article 6). In these areas, the CEDAW imposes specific obligations on states, which would not necessarily be read under gender-neutral provisions. For example, in the field of education, states are required to eliminate stereotyped concepts of the roles of men and women (article 10[c]) and to reduce female student dropout rates (article 10[f]), and in the field of employment, specific measures are required to prevent discrimination against women on the grounds of marriage and maternity (article 11[2]). Moreover, the concept of equality in the CEDAW goes beyond formal equality. It recognizes affirmative action measures (article 4), extends protection to all aspects of life (article 1), and stresses the need to modify discriminatory cultural patterns (article 5).

In recent years, especially since the UN world conferences of Vienna (human rights, 1993) and Beijing (women, 1995), the idea of special instruments has, nevertheless, lost the support of many women. Specialization has come to be seen as marginalization[40] or ghettoization[41] with the existence of specific treaties leading to a neglect of women under the mainstream human rights regime.[42] At the same time, mechanisms created under specific treaties are underfunded and lack strong enforcement.[43] The concerns of women, it is argued, should be at the center of human rights, not on their periphery, and gender-specific violations should be addressed through the mainstream instruments, using the mainstream supervisory mechanisms.

For the future, there may be good arguments to limit the creation of new specialized instruments. Yet it would be foolish to totally reject those that exist. The CEDAW, in particular, has much potential that has not yet been fully used and should not be abandoned, especially the Optional Protocol, which was opened for signature on December 10, 1999,[44] and entered into force on December 22, 2000. This protocol has the potential to dramatically strengthen the role of the CmEDAW. It provides a complaint procedure for individuals and groups and a process of inquiry into grave or systematic abuses. The absence of an individual complaint procedure was a major deficiency in the original CEDAW,[45] and with its inclusion, the convention deserves a new chance in the coming decades.[46]

TRANSFORMATION: WOMEN'S RIGHTS ARE HUMAN RIGHTS

The argument for "mainstreaming" calls for the full integration of women's rights into the international regime so that the problems that women face are taken into account whenever human rights are on the agenda. For example, monitoring gender-specific issues should not be left to the CmEDAW but should be taken up also by other supervising committees such as those established under the International Covenant on Civil and Political Rights (ICCPR), the International Covenant on Economic, Social, and Cultural Rights (ICESCR), the Torture Convention, and the CRC.[47] Thus far, the situation has varied with the Committee on Economic, Social and Cultural Rights and the Committee on the Rights of the Child being most responsive, and the Committee on the Elimination of Racial Discrimination and the Committee against Torture the least.[48] "Mainstreaming" also means that the perspectives of women can bring about a transformation of the system of protection,[49] with "a reappraisal of and a qualitative change in the relevant institutions, laws, and procedures."[50] Charlotte Bunch has noted that the transformative approach is increasingly the choice of women who are now actively working on human rights.[51]

Both the flexibility model and the transformation model propose changes in human rights norms and institutions, or at least in the way norms are interpreted and applied in response to women's specific gender experiences. Both assert that the human rights regime developed in a male-dominated environment and that insufficient female input explains some gaps in the system that need to be remedied. The difference between them is in the scope of the remedy. The flexibility model proposes to complete the human rights system with specific "women's" norms or institutions. It rests on the supposition that the gaps discovered through women's gender experience are relevant only for women, and it tailors the cure to that diagnosis. The transformation model, on the other hand, attributes a more universal value to women's claims, arguing that they reflect general deficiencies in the human rights regime, applicable as much to men as to women. There may be different reasons why men have not raised such issues: because they suffer less from those deficiencies or in fewer numbers or because those who have suffered have not been in a position to bring about change. In the transformation model, changes in rights brought on by women apply equally to both men and women. A good example is the right to parental leave that generally emerges from the hardship that women have in combining a career with a family. Women usually take the initiative in ensuring the right of parental leave, but men experience the problem of the double burden as well, and where the right to parental leave exists, many men are happy to make use of it, even though more women do so.

There are two strong arguments for preferring a transformation approach to a flexibility approach in advancing the human rights of women. First, the transformation approach is more inclusive and shows more respect for difference. How seriously will the claims of women be taken if they are applicable to women alone? Real participation implies the power to change the general parameters, the power to contribute to the definition of what human rights are about, not only for women but also for all. If it is true that, thus far, human rights reflect a male bias,[52] then the inclusion of women must lead to questioning some of the concrete features of human rights that manifest this bias. Charlesworth rightly states that "unless the experiences of women contribute directly to the mainstream international legal order . . . , international human rights law loses its claim to universal applicability: it should be more accurately characterized as international men's rights law."[53]

Human rights "are not static, nor are they the property of any one group."[54] Just as other excluded groups, women are claiming human rights and, "in the process, expanding the meaning of rights to incorporate their own hopes and needs."[55] As noted earlier, the struggle for inclusion of the working classes in human rights resulted in the addition of a whole category of economic and social rights. Similarly, the struggle for inclusion of non-Western people(s) reenforced the right to self-determination and led to the formulation of the right to development. In a similar vein, women want to achieve fuller inclusion in international human rights through transformation of the norms and institutions of the regime. The assertion that "women's rights are human rights" expresses both a demand to be included "in the project of human rights and a radical redefinition of what that project entails."[56]

Second, the integration of a women's perspective in international human rights should not lead to new types of exclusion. A flexibility approach runs the risk of excluding men from new types of human rights protection. Today much of the critical thinking about law and politics comes from one or another specific perspective such as race or gender. However, innovative solutions proposed on the basis of such analysis may often be as pertinent outside as well as within that specific context. The principle of universality of international human rights requires that additional human rights protection, from wherever it emerges, apply to all human beings.

In the context of gender specificity, it must in particular be borne in mind that gender itself is a construction. Seen as a whole, the differences between men and women are only one side of the picture, and the nature and the importance of these differences are relative in time and space. For example, the idea of breaching the public/private divide correctly assumes that, as a rule, the private sphere is more important to women than the public sphere. Yet at the same time this is not a situation most feminists want to preserve. For many, an equal presence of men and women in both spheres is the goal. Some men already live more fully in the private sphere than some women, and it is hardly justifiable to limit the protection against violations in the private sphere to women. Yet that is precisely what is happening, as such protection is provided for only in gender specific texts such as CEDAW and the UN Declaration on the Elimination of Violence against Women.[57]

Some transformations also have a wider impact than what might be projected by those who promote them from a particularist perspective. Consider the same example of the breach of the public/private divide. In international human rights law, the accountability of private actors for human rights violations is central to such widely divergent issues as the application of human rights standards to the behavior of companies and the prosecution of war criminals. There is a broad potential for coalition making and for extending the benefits of a breakthrough on one issue to others.

EXAMPLES OF THE TRANSFORMATION APPROACH BREACHING THE PUBLIC/PRIVATE DIVIDE

The process of transformation approaches the international human rights regime from the perspective of women, but it provides that men should equally benefit. This is evident in the effort to breach the public/private divide, which is already an important theme in feminist critiques of domestic law and a main demand of feminists that could transform international human rights. Even though the rights of both men and women are violated within family life, the private character of the home environment is used as an excuse by public authorities to escape their responsibilities to prevent and remedy this harm. Feminists, nevertheless, claim that the harm done to women at home or at work is political, not personal, as it contributes to maintaining relations of "power, domination, and privilege between men and women in society."[58]

In international law, the "private sphere" can be seen as an even wider area, extending to all relations among private persons, in contrast to their relations with public authorities. Traditionally, international law is binding only on states, so that only acts committed by government officials could be labeled human rights violations. Where judicial or quasi-judicial control mechanisms accompany human rights treaties, normally complaints about violations can only be addressed against states, as those are the signatories of the treaty. Yet contemporary doctrine and case law increasingly accept the responsibility of states to prevent and remedy human rights violations committed among private persons.

In the case law of the European Court of Human Rights (ECtHR), this is part of the "positive obligations" of states to protect human rights.[59] For example, in a 1998 judgment, the court held the United Kingdom responsible for a violation of article 3 of the European Convention (prohibition of torture and inhuman or degrading treatment or punishment), because a British jury had found a man who was sued for physically abusing his stepson not guilty. The court stated that article 3 "requires States to take measures designed to ensure that individuals within their jurisdiction are not subjected to torture or inhuman or degrading treatment or punishment, including such ill-treatment administered by private individuals."[60] This was confirmed and extended a 2001 judgment, which added that "these measures should provide effective protection, in particular, of children and other vulnerable persons and include reasonable steps to prevent ill-treatment of which the authorities had or ought to have had knowledge."[61] In this case, the British authorities were held responsible for a violation of article 3 because they had failed to remove children from an abusive family environment and hence to protect them from serious long-term neglect and abuse. On the basis of this case law, it is clear that in Europe, states are obligated to provide sufficient protection against domestic violence.

The Inter-American Court of Human Rights also recognizes that states have a duty to prevent or punish human rights violations committed by private individuals.[62] The deliberations in the UN Human Rights Committee seem to be going in the same direction.[63] Hence, from a legal point of view, there are no obstacles to holding states accountable for violations of women's rights in the private sphere. Nor should there be any scruples among human rights activists about campaigning against issues such as domestic violence. For that matter, some of the most vigorous human rights campaigns have addressed abuses such as slavery and racism that also occur at the hands of private actors.[64]

The attention of activists is currently focused on violations within the family and on cultural rules or practices that are at odds with human rights. Most efforts have gone into the campaign about violence against women[65] and in particular for the recognition of domestic violence as a human rights issue.[66] In 1992, the CmEDAW issued General Recommendation No. 19, interpreting violence as a form of discrimination under CEDAW and holding states "responsible also for private acts if they fail to act with due diligence to prevent violations of rights or to investigate and punish acts of violence and for providing compensation."[67] Moreover, violence against women in the private sphere is included both in the 1993 Declaration on Violence against Women and in the mandate of the special rapporteur on violence against women, appointed in 1994.

Thus, important progress has been made, although action is still fixed on holding states accountable under international law for violations committed by private actors. Yet the possibility of holding private actors directly accountable should not be excluded.[68] Direct accountability before international tribunals is presently limited to international crimes. Yet domestic courts regularly hold individuals accountable for human rights violations on the basis of constitutional provisions or directly applicable human rights treaties. Outside the judicial sphere, there are even more possibilities. Nongovernmental organizations (NGOs), for example, may campaign against private perpetrators. In one case, Amnesty International decided in 1997 to initiate pilot projects to campaign against private violators, several of the projects dealing with women's rights.[69]

UPGRADING ECONOMIC
AND SOCIAL RIGHTS

Feminist activists also argue that more importance be given to economic and social rights, because they consider the social and economic spheres as more central to women's advancement than the public, political forums where civil and political rights are exercised.[70] In spite of the rhetorical consensus on the indivisibility and interdependence of all human rights,[71] economic and social rights still occupy a second-rank position within the general human rights picture. They are generally considered to lack direct effect and justiciability. Governments, international organizations, and even NGOs systematically neglect economic and social rights in their human rights agendas. In its statement to the 1993 World Conference on Human Rights, the Committee on Economic, Social and Cultural Rights emphasized that

> [t]he shocking reality . . . is that States and the international community as a whole continue to tolerate all too often breaches of economic, social and cultural rights which, if they occurred in relation to civil and political rights, would provoke expressions of horror and outrage and would lead to concerted calls for immediate remedial action. In effect, despite the rhetoric, violations of civil and political rights continue to be treated as though they were far more serious, and more patently intolerable, than massive and direct denials of economic, social and cultural rights.[72]

While there is considerable merit to the argument that economic and social rights are more critical to the advancement of women than civil and political liberties, the relation between sets of rights is no less complex. When basic human rights to food, housing, and good health are concerned, grave violations, in particular in developing countries, generally affect women more harshly than men. Work-related human rights are also oriented toward paid labor, neglecting the work that women perform at home and in the fields that families own and cultivate.[73] In this regard, upgrading economic and social rights is but a necessary step that needs to be complemented by a reorientation[74] that reflects the overall experience of women. There is an obvious relevance here to the discussion of bridging the public/private divide in that economic and social rights are overly oriented toward activities in the public sphere, neglecting the work that goes on inside the home. Moreover, women living in poverty point out the need to recognize the interconnectedness of all categories of rights in practice: for them it is impossible to see the exercise of civil and political freedoms outside the context of the structural causes[75] of their poverty, which denies them human dignity and leaves them vulnerable to violent abuse.[76]

EMERGING STANDARDS

Integrating the needs and experiences of women can affect general human rights standards either through new formulations or through innovative interpretations of existing standards. Together, according to Coomaraswamy, they constitute a "fourth generation" of human rights[77] that is emerging in such areas as reproductive rights, sexual violence, the right of asylum, and rights connecting to slavery and slavery-like practices. These are examples of a transformative approach rather than a flexibility approach, because the situations they bring within the focus of human rights attention do not exclusively concern women, and the normative changes thus inspired concern general standards, applicable to both men and women.

Reproductive Rights[78]

Reproduction is an area in which many states intervene when they pursue nationalist, economic, religious, or other interests to control population growth through pronatalist or antinatalist policies. These invariably focus on regulating the reproductive capacities of individuals.[79] These policies affect both women and men, yet women are most directly concerned. Over the years, women's movements have increasingly focused on reproduction as a human right, an issue that was first brought to the international scene at the International Conference on Human Rights in Teheran in 1968. In its Final Act, the conference recognized that "parents have a basic human right to determine freely and responsibly the number and spacing of their children."[80]

This language was significantly expanded in the World Population Plan of Action adopted in Bucharest in 1974: "All couples and individuals have the basic right to decide freely and responsibly the number and spacing of their children and to have the information, education and means to do so; the responsibility of couples and individuals in the exercise of this right takes into account the needs of their living and future children, and their responsibilities towards the community."[81] In 1979, under article 16(1)(e), CEDAW recognized the same right in a legally binding fashion: "States Parties . . . shall ensure, on a basis of equality of men and women . . . the same rights to decide freely and responsibly on the number and spacing of their children and to have access to the information, education and means to enable them to exercise these rights." Other CEDAW articles are also relevant to reproductive rights.[82]

A major breakthrough came with the 1994 Cairo Population Conference, where the international women's health movement, greatly expanded since the 1970s and 1980s, became a major player.[83] The Cairo Programme of Action contains a chapter on reproductive rights and reproductive health. Reproductive health is a comprehensive concept[84] that includes the "full spectrum of health needs associated with women's reproductive and sexual activities"[85] and that embraces reproductive rights. On that subject, paragraph 7.3 provides that

> reproductive rights embrace certain human rights that are already recognized in national laws, international human rights documents and other consensus documents. These rights rest on the recognition of the basic right of all couples and individuals to decide freely and responsibly the number, spacing and timing of their children and to have the information and means to do so, and the right to attain the highest standard of sexual and reproductive health. It also includes their right to make decisions concerning reproduction free of discrimination, coercion and violence, as expressed in human rights documents.

The 1995 Beijing Declaration and Programme of Action, adopted at the Fourth United Nations World Conference on Women, reconfirms the Cairo definitions of reproductive health and reproductive rights,[86] adding a specific emphasis on the rights of women: "The human rights of women include their right to have control over and decide freely and responsibly on matters related to their sexuality, including sexual and reproductive health, free of coercion, discrimination and violence" (para. 96); also, "the neglect of women's reproductive rights severely limits their opportunities in public and private life, including opportunities for education and economic and political empowerment. The ability of women to control their own fertility forms an important basis for the enjoyment of other rights" (para. 97).

The CEDAW provisions aside, reproductive human rights have not yet been included in other legally binding documents. Nonetheless, the Cairo and Beijing Declarations, both based on a broad worldwide consensus, provide strong authority to guide the interpretation of existing human rights, including the right to health and the right to privacy (which encompasses sexual and reproductive freedom).[87] Further developments in this area could lead to the recognition of "sexual rights" that are broader than reproductive rights but failed to gain general acceptance at the Cairo and Beijing conferences.[88] The enjoyment of reproductive rights is, moreover, continuously influenced by medical advances, so much so that radical feminists already accuse reproductive technology of subjecting women to patriarchal control.[89] Strengthening reproductive rights is a way of guaranteeing that whatever developments may occur, the dignity, equality, and freedom of individuals—both men and women—remain central.

Sexual Violence

One of the most basic protections offered by human rights is that against state-inflicted violence. Whenever violence is inflicted on individuals—for example, by soldiers during a war or by police during detention—sexual violence is frequently included, in particular (but not only) against women. Yet international law has been slow in recognizing the seriousness of this type of violence. Rape by state officials has only recently been recognized as torture, among others by the Inter-American Commission on Human Rights,[90] the United Nations special rapporteur on torture,[91] and the European Court on Human Rights.[92]

The general outrage brought on by the horrendous spread of rape during the war in the former Yugoslavia served as a catalyst for the development of international law in this area. The Vienna Declaration had condemned "the systematic rape of women in war situations" among other massive violations of human rights (para. 28) and now the statute of the International Tribunal for the former Yugoslavia[93] includes rape as a crime against humanity[94] (article 5[g]). A general requirement for crimes against humanity, however, is that they must be part of a widespread or systematic attack against a civilian population. A similar provision is included in the statute of the International Tribunal for Rwanda[95] (article 3[g]). In the Rome Statute of the International Criminal Court, this is expanded;[96] not only is rape indictable as a crime against humanity, but so are "sexual slavery, enforced prostitution, forced pregnancy, enforced sterilization, or any other form of sexual violence of comparable gravity," if it has the same systematic or widespread character (article 7[1][g]). At the same time, such acts are also indictable as war crimes[97] whenever they constitute a grave breach of the Geneva Conventions (article 8[2][b][xxii] and [e][vi]). The indictments and judgments of the Yugoslavia and Rwanda Tribunals have given particular attention to sexual violence.[98]

These new provisions signal a step forward from the Geneva Conventions, which have been criticized for interpreting sexual violence as an attack on women's honor and on the sanctity of motherhood, thus subordinating the violation of women's bodies to the humiliation of the group. In this, they had assumed a kind of "protective" attitude and failed to treat women as autonomous subjects.[99] This is an area of the law on which there is continuing reflection that may lead to other innovative standards or interpretations, such as establishing massive forced impregnation as genocide.[100]

In the broad area of human rights, outside of violence in time of war, moreover, the main question revolves around sexual violence in private relations. The public/private divide remains the main obstacle in designating sexual violence as a violation of human rights. If that can be surmounted, there is no reason why serious cases of domestic violence should not be qualified as torture. It has convincingly been demonstrated that in many cases, all the constitutive elements of torture are found and that from the victim's perspective, the experience is horribly similar.[101]

Right to Asylum

The right to asylum from persecution is a human right (article 14 UDHR). The international law in this regard is found in the 1951 Convention Relating to the Status of Refugees as modified by the 1967 Protocol Relating to the Status of Refugees. The convention defines a refugee as a person who, "owing to well-founded fear of being persecuted for reasons of race, religion, nationality, membership of a particular social group or political opinion, is outside the country of his nationality and is unable or, owing to such fear, is unwilling to avail himself of the protection of that country."

Under these provisions, persecution on the basis of gender is not grounds for asylum, an omission that has long been a serious issue for women's rights activists.[102] Gender-based persecution, they insist, is systematic and widespread and no less serious than persecution based on race or other criteria. Again, the public/private divide seems to be the main obstacle, as gender-based persecution is suffered mainly at the hands of private persons. Gradually it has nonetheless come to be recognized that gender-based persecution may be recognized by including groups of women under the category of "membership of a particular social group,"[103] and several countries have taken important steps in this direction.[104] Yet in the present state of international law, the right to asylum of women fleeing from such ordeals as forced marriage, massive rape, and genital mutilation depends on the goodwill and changing policies of a small number of states. Changes along these lines are slow and uncertain. In the long run, the only solution offering adequate protection to these women is the inclusion of gender as a category of persecution in the international texts.

Slavery

Even before the origin of international human rights law *sensu stricto*, the international law against slavery included separate rules against the traffic in women for prostitution.[105] Hence, early on, the term *slavery* was interpreted in such a way as to encompass situations in which mainly women were and are the victims. Moreover, as slavery as an institution was increasingly reduced, international norms evolved with provisions against slavery-like practices. In 1957, for example, the Economic and Social Council adopted the Supplementary Convention on the Abolition of Slavery, the Slave Trade, and Institutions and Practices Similar to Slavery, which included institutions and practices especially affecting women (e.g., the sale of a woman in marriage, the transfer of a wife by her husband, and the transfer of a wife through inheritance).[106]

Since the 1970s, a Working Group on Contemporary Forms of Slavery has been active in the United Nations, and its mandate has been expanded into many areas that concern women; these include the sale of children, the sexual mutilation of female children, the exploitation of prostitution of others, sex trafficking, sex tourism, the exploitation of migrant workers, the sexual exploitation of women during wartime, violence against women, and early marriages.[107] The definition of such practices under the rubric of "slavery" has an important symbolic and political effect since, together with torture, slavery is one of the central violations of human rights.

In the years to come, the question remains whether international legal standards will be more deliberately developed in terms of these expansive gender-sensitive definitions of slavery and slavery-like practices. Women's rights activists continue to lobby for such developments. For example, as current international antitrafficking law[108] is "premised on a definition in which trafficking is linked to forced prostitution,"[109] it is ill equipped to address such current examples as the "coerced recruitment and transportation of women . . . for a variety of other forced labour and slavery-like practices, such as forced domestic labour, factory labour, and commercial marriages."[110] For that matter, there is reason to abandon the strict connection between trafficking and slavery-like practices, as not all women who undergo trafficking are subjected to slavery-like practices, nor have all women who are subjected to these practices been trafficked.[111] The Global Alliance against Trafficking in Women, a coalition of NGOs, has made important proposals for new standards in this regard.[112]

Proposals for Additional Standards

There are other feminist proposals for new human rights standards, but these are farther from gaining general acceptance. One proposal is that international humanitarian law no longer focus on direct violence but rather also take into account the long-term effects of armed conflicts, which often disproportionately affect women.[113] Charlesworth, for example, argues that "conflict exacerbates the globally unequal position of women and men in many ways. We know," she continues, that "distinctive burdens [are] placed on women through food and medical shortages caused by conflict. When food is scarce, more women than men suffer from malnutrition, often because of cultural norms that require men and boys to eat before women and girls. Humanitarian relief for the victims of conflict regularly fails to reach women, as men are typically given responsibility for its distribution. Economic sanctions imposed before, during, or after armed conflict have had particular impact on women and girls, who are disproportionately represented among the poor. Although the effect of these practices falls heavily on women, they are not understood by international law to be human rights abuses that would engage either state or individual responsibility."[114]

Still another proposition is to expand the definition of genocide to include the generally culturally determined practice of female infanticide whether committed through direct killings or through neglect of female children (with their consequent death frequently due to malnutrition).[115] A completely different proposal is that of restricting the scope of the freedom of expression, so that it no longer protects pornography.[116] In this context it should be noted, however, that present international standards already allow for the restriction and even prohibition of pornography by national—or, for that matter, international—authorities. It seems that those who desire stricter measures in this area should aim their arrows not at international human rights standards but rather at political decision makers.

OTHER FEMINIST TRANSFORMATIONS OF HUMAN RIGHTS

The women's human rights movement is extremely diverse, encompassing groups and individuals campaigning for a wide range of different issues. One such issue is the *language* of human rights. Many women have trouble with the consistent use of male pronouns in almost all international human rights texts. The Convention on the Rights of the Child is an exception; wherever possible, it uses the gender-neutral "the child," and where the use of the possessive pronoun is necessary, it uses "his or her." The importance of language in gender equality has been analyzed in many different contexts, and the argument has been made that it operates at both a direct and a subtle level to exclude women by constructing and reinforcing their subordination.[117] The language in the Convention on the Rights of the Child is a model for future international texts.

Even more important is the representation of women in international bodies dealing with human rights issues. Equal representation is not only a matter of democratic participation but also a necessary requirement if the needs and experiences of women are to be incorporated into the activities of international organizations. Despite strong insistence from activists,[118] the representation of women in mainstream human rights bodies is still unacceptably low.

One big step further in the representation idea is Knopp's rather utopian proposal for direct representation of women as a group on the international scene. In many international forums, women are supposed to be represented by their state. Yet when the state is seen as a patriarchal construction, it is desirable to circumvent it. Knopp's proposal builds on the experience of the representation of unions and employers in the ILO and the increasing tendency for indigenous peoples to represent their interests directly in international agencies. In the same way, women might be directly represented and thus able to present their claims from their own experience.[119]

Another crucial matter involves integrating a woman's perspective into the methodologies used for investigating and enforcing human rights norms.[120] Gallagher finds that "when human rights abuses against women are identified, the wider context of the violation is almost invariably ignored. There is a subsequent failure to explore and acknowledge the root causes of violations against women and to develop effective responses."[121] This is an example, moreover, of how a remedy to enhance the rights of women may improve protection more generally. Methodologies developed within feminist studies may have broader applicability. Feminist analysis has been described as "contextual, experiential, and inductive. Whereas much social theory is hierarchical, abstract, and deductive, the feminist starting point is from actual human experience and the implications of that experience."[122] More generally, taking the experience of victims into account may lead to more effective methods for responding to all human rights violations.

Some feminists also criticize the *individualist* character of international human rights. They argue, on the one hand, that women have a *relational* world-view, which is not adequately expressed in terms of individual rights[123] and, on the other, that violations of a woman's human rights are, in many cases, structural problems which are also not accounted for.[124] This criticism, however, does not have to lead to an advocacy for group rights, especially since group rights under international law are largely conceived in terms of ethnic groups that often subordinate women.[125] The rights of women as a group have received some attention in domestic law in connection with issues like affirmative action, but they have rarely been recognized under international law. In the years to come, the collective dimension of women's rights may come to the forefront, for example, as a framework for addressing the root causes of gender discrimination. However, from an inclusive perspective, this would be a step in the wrong direction, as the same structural problems usually also affect men, and remedies created in response to women's group claims risk excluding them.[126] The final example is the claim for the inclusion of women's human rights, or at least the prohibition of gender discrimination, in the category of *jus cogens*.[127] This fits perfectly in the mainstreaming concept: women's human rights are to move from the periphery to the core of international human rights, and the core of the core consists of those human rights with *jus cogens* value. In substance, this claim is not absurd, either, as there is a clear parallel with the prohibition of racial discrimination, which is a *jus cogens* rule. The symbolic value of this transformation cannot be overestimated. Eliminating gender bias from the inner core of international human rights would be a major victory for women's human rights. However, as *jus cogens* per definition changes slowly, this is not to be expected in the short term.

MULTIPLE SPECIFICITIES

If human rights are to be all-inclusive, they should take into account the relevant differences between men and women. Yet caution is needed to avoid efforts designed to fully include women resulting in the exclusion of some of them.

When the "women's movement" reacts against the invisibility of women in the conception of "humans" in dominant human rights discourse, it puts forward an image of "woman" that inevitably reflects the experiences of the dominant group in that movement. Within the organized women's movement acting on the international scene, the most powerful lobbying and agenda setting is generally done by white Western women. Minority women and non-Western women have strongly criticized their invisibility in the dominant feminist discourse.[128] Mohanty has shown how Western feminist texts fail to capture an insider view of non-Western women's lives and create a "third world woman" as a singular monolithic subject.[129] Even in face-to-face encounters, Western feminists often fail to listen to their sisters from the South. Azizah al-Hibri relates that during the UN world conferences in the nineties, women from developing countries were frustrated to find that women from the West attempted to speak for all women:

> In Copenhagen, Third World women were told that their highest priorities related to the veil and clitoridectomy (female genital mutilation). In Cairo, they were told that their highest priorities related to contraception and abortion. In both cases, Third World women begged to differ. They repeatedly announced that their highest priorities were peace and development. They noted that they could not very well worry about other matters when their children were dying from thirst, hunger or war. . . . They will not seek to achieve their liberation by denigrating their religion or culture or by forcing upon their community's inappropriate priorities and demands. They will do it their own way.[130]

For many non-Western women, Western feminism focuses too narrowly on gender discrimination. As one writer emphasized:

> The point is that factors other than gender figure integrally in the oppression of Third World women and that, even regarding patriarchy, many Third World women labour under indigenous inequitable gender relationships exacerbated by Western patriarchy, racism, and exploitation. . . . Third World women can embrace the concept of gender identity, but must reject an ideology based solely on gender. . . . We must create a feminist movement which struggles against

those things which can clearly be shown to oppress women, whether based on race, sex, or class or resulting from imperialism.[131]

A certain degree of generalization is inherent in any group-based emancipation movement, and all generalizations are in some way exclusionist. Yet if generalization becomes essentialism, if internal diversity within the group is ignored, the exclusion becomes particularly serious. In the women's movement, this risk can be avoided if, in addition to the central theme of gender, other factors are taken into account. The contextualization of human rights in the pursuit of inclusive universality should, in principle, extend to all specificities that have been the basis for exclusion from the dominant model. For example, the claim of non-Western people to see the particularity of their economic situation and of their culture integrated in human rights is as strong as women's claim with regard to their gender specificity. Non-Western women find themselves at the crossroads of both sets of claims. Contemporary feminist discourse on international human rights recognizes the diversity of women around the world and embraces in principle the claims of women from the South for a stronger focus on development-related rights.[132] Still, in the overall picture of women's human rights claims, these claims remain underexposed. With regard to non-Western cultures and human rights, global feminism continues to fight traditional practices and rules subordinating women, yet an important shift is noticeable. Where "foreign" cultures and practices used to be regarded from an outsider perspective and were easily branded as patriarchal, today the insider voices of the women concerned are increasingly heeded.[133]

In principle, the above-discussed human rights claims of women and non-Western people are claims of groups, based on the communal features of their members that distinguish them from the dominant group. Yet, since the specificities of different groups are combined in individuals, the only way to avoid exclusion is to replace the group perspective with the perspective of the individuals concerned. Contrary to the abstract individuals on which the enlightenment conception of human rights relies, these should be contextualized individuals, with their relevant specificities. Hence, a consequence of inclusive universality in terms of method is that the perspective should be that of the (actual or potential) victim of human rights violations. This does not *a priori* exclude a conception of women's rights (or cultural rights for that matter) as group rights, but they must be conceived in function of the individual. As a result, on concrete issues involving a conflict between different specificities, the perspective of the individual(s) concerned is crucial. Some of the most problematic of these issues involve conflicts between the rights of women (as constructed by the dominant discourse) and cultural or religious rules or practices.

In the confrontation between human rights and culture, human rights activists easily assume that culture has to change. After all, human rights have a revolutionary nature: they are supposed to alter the outlook of a society. Feminism, being an assertive movement, rarely wants to compromise in that respect. Yet, at the same time, religion is protected as a human right in itself, and culture is increasingly coming to be seen in the same way. For that matter, women in traditional societies may give high value to their culture, including the practices that violate their rights. In any such case, it is the decision of the woman who is directly involved, the woman who is the "insider," that counts.

It is important to realize that Western feminist interpretations of a cultural practice may be totally disconnected from the experience of women who are "on the inside."[134] Moreover, even if they experience a practice as discriminatory or repressive, adult women are capable of balancing any pain they might suffer against the positive benefit they derive from participating in their own culture. The right to make their own choice has to be protected by international human rights.[135] This means that the human rights movement has to come out strongly in support of women's participation in the internal cultural debate about such rules and practices. If such debate results in changes that eliminate the oppressiveness of the rule or practice, a perfect solution is reached.[136] It also means that individual women's right to opt out[137] of certain practices or cultures has to be supported. The fact is that while forcing women to wear Islamic dress or to endure genital mutilation may be considered human rights violations, their right to choose to participate in such practices has to be respected. From an "insider" perspective, laws outlawing such practices can no more be supported than laws imposing them.

Going further, there is the issue of strategies and priorities. Female genital mutilation (FGM) is an example of an issue on which feminists have blundered immensely in the past. Without attempting to understand the perspective of the "insider," they have called it "torture" and "barbaric" and alienated and angered African women who may be opposed to the practice yet demand respect for their culture.[138] African women who have joined the fight against practices such as FGM should decide how to proceed and how to set priorities. For a Somali woman who would like FGM to disappear, for example, the more urgent issues may be food, housing, medical care, and education. It is also a matter of strategy. Respect for other cultures is not incompatible with campaigning against certain cultural practices. Yet this campaigning has to give culture its due and be directed from inside, at the grassroots level. Moreover, the reasons for opposing the practice must be close to the experiences of the women who are most concerned. In most cases it is advisable to leave feminist theories of patriarchy at home. Sometimes it may even be advisable to leave human rights discourse at home.

Again, the importance of the "insider" perspective is not only a matter of democratic participation but also a matter of pragmatism. Feminist analysis has long been developing methodologies to deal with the diversity of voices in women's rights discourse in both domestic and international settings[139] and with the complexity of real-life situations. In particular, feminist scholars have addressed not only the conflicting loyalties of women in traditional societies to gender equality, on the one hand, and cultural practices, on the other,[140] but also the multiplicity of oppressions suffered by poor women, minority women, and homosexual women.[141] More than most approaches, feminism should be able to overcome the dilemma between universality and diversity.[142] Among the many benefits of feminist analysis to be integrated in mainstream human rights, this capacity is crucial.

THE NEXT FIFTY YEARS

What developments can be expected over the next fifty years? Formal equality of women and men before the law (the "sameness" approach) is no longer contested yet still has to be realized over much of the world. It should be a realistic goal to eradicate all formal gender discrimination over the foreseeable future. At the same time, education and increasing activism should substantially enhance an awareness among women about their rights and an understanding on the part of men how the conditions under which women live regularly subject them to gross violations.

It is unlikely that many new "women's human rights" instruments will be created. Yet those already set up have some unexplored potential. In particular, CEDAW should prove more effective when the Optional Protocol enters into force. The individual complaint mechanism not only will benefit many individual women but will also lead to the development of a case law that will elaborate and strengthen international women's rights norms and that is likely to inspire domestic judges.

We can also anticipate that women will increasingly favor "transforming" human rights to respond to their special experience while remaining universally applicable. This is to be preferred over the "special rights" approach, because it shows more respect for women's diversity and because it does not exclude men from innovations in the field of human rights protection.

Recent transformations that have been taking shape will likely be strengthened. The public/private divide should no longer be considered a legal obstacle, yet the extension of human rights protection in the private sphere still needs to gain general recognition and acceptance. The standard-setting developments in the area of domestic violence are promising, yet it is unfortunate that they are restricted to women.

Moreover, it is likely that private perpetrators will increasingly be held responsible for human rights violations in international (criminal) tribunals, in domestic courts and in extrajudicial human rights campaigns. With regard to upgrading and reorienting economic and social rights, the women's movement has been less successful. In any event, the next few decades will be decisive for the question whether a human rights approach can solve economic and social problems. In the light of the expected strengthening of the position of non-Western activists within the women's movement, it is possible that feminists will build a coalition with others, including the third and fourth world movements and organized labor, in support of economic and social rights.

The new standards that have been developing in the areas of reproductive rights, sexual violence, asylum, and slavery-like practices are likely to be more solidly established in the near future. It is hoped that their benefits will be extended to men as well as women. Furthermore, improvements are also likely in the use of gender-sensitive language, the representation of women in human rights bodies, and the integration of a gender perspective in human rights methodologies. These improvements will in turn have an indirect positive effect on many other issues. Non-Western women from developing countries will certainly be more effective in international activities, arguing that issues of peace and economic development are critical to advancements in human rights and that those directly affected, the "insiders," have to resolve conflicts that arise between human rights and cultural practices, on their own terms rather than on any abstract notion of right and wrong. The future, as always, is difficult, if not impossible, to predict. Nonetheless, there is considerable hope that the forces of change already unleashed will greatly improve the lives of millions of women all over the world.

NOTES

1. Radhika Coomaraswamy, *Reinventing International Law: Women's Rights as Human Rights in the International Community* (Cambridge, Mass.: Human Rights Program, Harvard Law School, 1997), 9.

2. Coomaraswamy, *Reinventing International Law,* 14–16.

3. Manisha Desai, "From Vienna to Beijing: Women's Human Rights Activism and the Human Rights Community," in *Debating Human Rights: Critical Essays from the United States and Asia,* ed. Peter Van Ness (New York: Routledge, 1999), 187.

4. For example, article 2(1) Universal Declaration of Human Rights: "Everyone is entitled to all the rights and freedoms set forth in this declaration, without discrimination of any kind, such as race, colour, sex, language, religion, political or other opinion, national or social origin, property, birth or other status."

5. Equal treatment does not always mean "the same treatment." There are many different conceptions of equality and nondiscrimination, including those that recognize that equal treatment requires different treatment when there are relevant differences. A formulation such as that of article 2(1) UDHR can be read in that sense as

well. In the context of the present analysis, such conceptions fall under the "specificity" rubric. Under "sameness," a conception of equality is discussed which focuses on the common humanity of men and women, in the light of which the differences between them are considered irrelevant.

6. In Belgium, women got the right to vote that same year, in 1948. That was only a few years later than the women of France (1944) and Italy (1945). See Katarina Tomaševski, *Women and Human Rights* (London: Zed, 1993), 9.

7. Asma Mohamed Abdel Halim, "Challenges to the Application of International Women's Human Rights in the Sudan," in *Human Rights of Women: National and International Perspectives,* ed. Rebecca J. Cook (Philadelphia: University of Pennsylvania Press, 1994), 401–3.

8. Human Rights Watch, *World Report 2000* (New York: Author, 2000); www.hrw.org/wr2k.

9. The ban was based on tradition. In November 1990, women demonstrated for the right to drive, driving in convoy in the capital Riyadh. As a result, the Ministry of the Interior formally banned female drivers. Amnesty International, *Human Rights Are Women's Rights* (London: Author, 1994).

10. Human Rights Watch, *World Report 2000.*

11. Human Rights Watch, *World Report 2000.*

12. Human Rights Watch, *World Report 2000.*

13. Human Rights Watch, *World Report 2000.*

14. Feminist activism is frequently effective in this field. For example in Uganda, women's rights activists pushed their government to accept a new law granting women equal property rights. Human Rights Watch, *World Report 1999.*

15. Karen Engle, "International Human Rights and Feminism: When Discourses Meet," *Michigan Journal of International Law* 13 (Spring 1992) 531–64.

16. Kathleen Mahoney, "Theoretical Perspectives on Women's Human Rights and Strategies for Their Implementation," *Brooklyn Journal of International Law* 21 (1996): 802–8.

17. The problem of insufficient rights awareness also exists among men. Yet given women's subordinate position in most societies, raising women's rights awareness requires special attention.

18. See Carol Gilligan, *In a Different Voice: Psychological Theory and Women's Development* (Cambridge, Mass.: Harvard University Press, 1982).

19. Mahoney, "Theoretical Perspectives on Women's Human Rights," 808–14.

20. The concept of inclusive universality was developed to deal with non-Western particularist claims about human rights. See Eva Brems, "Human Rights: Universality and Diversity," Ph.D. diss., K.U. Leuven, 1999, to be published by Kluwer Law International.

21. See Cecilia Medina, "Toward a More Effective Guarantee of the Enjoyment of Human Rights by Women in the Inter-American System," in *Human Rights of Women. National and International Perspectives*, ed. Rebecca J. Cook (Philadelphia: University of Pennsylvania Press, 1994), 258.

22. See Andrew M. Deutz, "Gender and International Human Rights," *Fletcher Forum of World Affairs* (1993): 34.

23. Tracy E. Higgins, "Regarding Rights: An Essay Honoring the Fiftieth Anni-

versary of the Universal Declaration of Human Rights," *Columbia Human Rights Law Review* 30 (1999): 239.

24. Higgins, "Regarding Rights," 239.

25. Higgins, "Regarding Rights," 239.

26. Higgins, "Regarding Rights," 241.

27. Mary K. Meyer, "Negotiating International Norms: The Inter-American Commission of Women and the Convention on Violence against Women," in *Gender Politics in Global Governance*, ed. Mary K. Meyer and Elisabeth Prügl (Lanham, Md.: Rowman & Littlefield, 1999), 62–65.

28. This treaty consisted of just one article: "The contracting parties agree that with the ratification of this Treaty men and women have equal rights in the territories subject to their respective jurisdictions."

29. Meyer, "Negotiating," 64.

30. Meyer, "Negotiating," 65.

31. Meyer, "Negotiating," 64. First created as a subcommission, it was raised to the status of a commission of the Economic and Social Council in 1947. Elisabeth Prügl and Mary K. Meyer, "Gender Politics in Global Governance," in *Gender Politics in Global Governance*, ed. Mary K. Meyer and Elisabeth Prügl (Lanham, Md.: Rowman & Littlefield, 1999), 7.

32. In a second phase, the CSW focused on development. The CSW has been confronted with serious problems, including underfunding and lack of institutional weight. Toward the end of the 1980s, it converted to the idea of "mainstreaming" women's issues. See Laura Reanda, "The Commission on the Status of Women," in *The United Nations and Human Rights: A Critical Appraisal,* ed. Philip Alston (Oxford: Clarendon, 1992), 265–303.

33. Declaration on the Elimination of Discrimination against Women (1967), Declaration on the Protection of Women and Children in Emergency and Armed Conflict (1974), and Declaration on the Participation of Women in Promoting International Peace and Co-operation (1982, drafted by the Third Committee of the General Assembly, after an initial proposal was considered by the CSW).

34. Hillka Pietilä and Jeanne Vickers, *Making Women Matter: The Role of the United Nations* (London: Zed, 1994), 101.

35. Prügl and Meyer, "Gender Politics," 8.

36. Nathalie Kaufman Hevener, *International Law and the Status of Women* (Boulder, Colo.: Westview, 1983), 4.

37. Andrew Byrnes, "Toward More Effective Enforcement of Women's Human Rights through the Use of International Human Rights Law and Procedures," in *Human Rights of Women*, ed. Cook, 194.

38. Byrnes, "Toward More Effective Enforcement; Charlotte Bunch, "Transforming Human Rights from a Feminist Perspective," in *Women's Rights, Human Rights, International Feminist Perspectives*, ed. Julie Peters and Andrea Wolper (New York: Routledge, 1995), 12. I am by no means trying to deny the problem of sexual assault on men. The fact that many violations on the women's rights agenda are also undergone by men is precisely the reason why my own preference is that of a "transformation" approach; see *infra*.

39. Hevener, *International Law and the Status of Women*, 4.

40. Anne Gallagher, "Ending the Marginalization: Strategies for Incorporating Women into the United Nations Human Rights System," *Human Rights Quarterly* 19 (1997): 285.

41. Ursula A. O'Hare, "Realizing Human Rights for Women," *Human Rights* 21 *Quarterly* (1999): 368.

42. Hilary Charlesworth, "Transforming the United Men's Club: Feminist Futures for the United Nations," *Transnational Law & Contemporary Problems* 4 (1994): 446.

43. See Reanda, "The Commission on the Status of Women," 270; Anne F. Bayefsky, "General Approaches to the Domestic Application of Women's International Human Rights Law," in *Human Rights of Women*, ed. Cook, 352–53.

44. See Ursula A. O'Hare, "Ending the 'Ghettoisation': The Right of Individual Petition to the Women's Convention," *Web Journal of Current Legal Issues* (1997); webjcli.ncl.ac.uk/1997/issue5/o'hare5.html.

45. For example, Julie A. Minor, "An Analysis of Structural Weaknesses in the Convention on the Elimination of All Forms of Discrimination against Women," *Georgia Journal of International and Comparative Law* 24 (1994): 137–53.

46. The impact of an individual complaint mechanism is broader than the direct results in the cases that come before the commission. In particular, it allows the development of a case law, which can become an important guidance to the interpretation of women's rights in domestic law.

47. See Bunch, "Transforming Human Rights," 17; Andrew Byrnes, "Women, Feminism and International Human Rights Law—Methodological Myopia, Fundamental Flaws or Meaningful Marginalisation? Some Current Issues," *Australian Year Book of International Law* (1988–1989): 205–25; Byrnes, "Toward More Effective Enforcement."

48. Hilary Charlesworth, "The Mid-Life Crisis of the Universal Declaration of Human Rights," *Washington and Lee Law Review* 55 (1998): 791–92; Jane Connors, "General Human Rights Instruments and Their Relevance to Women," in *Advancing the Human Rights of Women: Using International Human Rights Standards in Domestic Legislation*, ed. Andrew Byrnes, Jane Connors, and Bik (Hong Kong: Commonwealth Secretariat, 1997), 31–35; Gallagher, "Ending the Marginalization," 294–309.

49. For example, Charlotte Bunch, "Organizing for Women's Human Rights Globally," in *Ours by Right: Women's Rights as Human Rights*, ed. Joanna Kerr (London: Zed, 1993), 145; Hilary Charlesworth, "Human Rights as Men's Rights," in *Women's Rights*, ed. Peters and Wolper, 111; Elisabeth Friedman, "Women's Human Rights: The Emergence of a Movement," in *Women's Rights*, ed. Peters and Wolper, 19; Julie Mertus and Pamela Goldberg, "A Perspective on Women and International Human Rights after the Vienna Declaration: The Inside/Outside Construct," *NYU Journal of International Law and Politics* 26: (1994): 231; O'Hare, "Realizing Human Rights," 400–2; Julie Peters and Andrea Wolper, "Introduction," in *Women's Rights*, ed. Peters and Wolper, 3; V. Spike Peterson and Jacqui True, "New Times and New Conversations" in *The "Man" Question in International Relations*, ed. Marysia Zalewski and Jane Parpart (Boulder, Colo.: Westview, 1998), 22.

50. Gallagher, "Ending the Marginalization," 288.

51. Charlotte Bunch, "Feminist Visions of Human Rights in the Twenty-First Century," in *Human Rights in the Twenty-first Century*, ed. Kathleen A. Mahoney and Paul Mahoney (Dordrecht: Martinus Nijhoff, 1993), 976.

52. Bunch, "Transforming Human Rights from a Feminist Perspective," 13.

53. Charlesworth, "Human Rights as Men's Rights," 105.

54. Bunch, "Transforming Human Rights from a Feminist Perspective," 13.

55. Bunch, "Transforming Human Rights from a Feminist Perspective," 13.

56. Christine Bell, "Women's Rights as Human Rights: Old Agendas in New Guises," in *Human Rights: An Agenda for the 21st Century*, ed. Angela Hegarty and Siobhan Leonard (London: Cavendish, 1999), 139.

57. Many other examples could be cited. See CEDAW's provisions on the specific problems of rural women (article 14) and on trafficking in women and prostitution (article 6), referred to earlier. Rural men also experience specific problems, and men are also the victims of trafficking and prostitution. To the extent that no general provisions exist with the same substance, this approach that formulates additional protective rules only to the benefit of women is at odds with the principle of inclusive universality.

58. Charlotte Bunch, "Women's Rights as Human Rights: Toward a Re-Vision of Human Rights," *Human Rights Quarterly* 12 (1990): 491.

59. The groundbreaking judgment in this context was *X and Y v. Netherlands*, ECtHR, March 26, 1985, Publications of the Court, Series A, No. 91. A mentally disabled girl of sixteen had been sexually abused while residing in a home for mentally disabled children. Her father lodged a complaint, yet no prosecution was initiated. Due to a gap in Dutch criminal legislation, it was not possible for the victim in this case to initiate the criminal procedure, as the girl lacked legal capacity, and no representation was possible. The ECtHR considered the abuse as a violation of article 8 ECHR (private life, including physical integrity) and held the state responsible for this violation, because it had failed to take adequate protective measures, in particular in its criminal legislation. This approach was later confirmed in other cases, and extended to other rights. Under article 11 ECHR (freedom of assembly), for example, states have a positive obligation to take measures so as to enable manifestations to take place without being hindered by physical violence of countermanifestants (ECtHR, *Ärzte für das Leben v. Austria*, June 21, 1988, Publications of the Court, Series A, No. 139).

60. ECtHR, *A v. United Kingdom*, September 23, 1998, Reports 1998-VI, § 22.

61. ECtHR, *Z and others v. United Kingdom*, May 10, 2001, § 73.

62. Inter-American Court of Human Rights, *Velasquez Rodriguez v. Honduras*, Ser. C, No. 4, Judgment of July 29, 1988 (1989), ILM 291.

63. O'Hare, "Realizing Human Rights," 396, citing the cases of *Mojica v. Dominican Republic*, *Human Rights Law Journal* 17 (1996): 18, and *Bautista v. Colombia*, *Human Rights Law Journal* 17 (1996): 19.

64. Bunch, "Transforming Human Rights from a Feminist Perspective," 14.

65. See Mertus and Goldberg, "A Perspective on Women and International Human Rights," 207–16; Jutta Joachim, "Shaping the Human Rights Agenda: The Case of Violence against Women," in *Gender Politics in Global Governance*, ed. Meyer and Prügl, 142–60. Violence against women, and its link to power relations, is

the central preoccupation of "radical feminism" (see Mahoney, "Theoretical Perspectives," 814–26). In the human rights sphere, the focus on violence has been taken over by feminists of different convictions, for obvious reasons: those human rights violations, which are taken most seriously also, involve violence.

66. See Joan Fitzpatrick, "The Use of International Human Rights Norms to Combat Violence against Women," in *Human Rights of Women*, ed. Cook, 534–40; Kenneth Roth, "Domestic Violence as an International Human Rights Issue," in *Human Rights of Women*, ed. Cook, 326–39; Dorothy Q. Thomas and Michele E. Beasly, "Domestic Violence as a Human Rights Issue," *Human Rights Quarterly* 15 (1993): 36–62.

67. CmEDAW, General Recommendation 19, A/47/38.

68. See Gayle Binion, "Human Rights: A Feminist Perspective," *Human Rights Quarterly* 17 (1995): 519.

69. In its first report on such a pilot project, *Pakistan: Violence against Women in the Name of Honour* (September 1999), however, the organization still prefers the indirect way of addressing demands to the government.

70. See Bell, "Women's Rights as Human Rights," 146; Bunch, "Transforming Human Rights from a Feminist Perspective," 14; Hilary Charlesworth, Christine Chinkin, and Shelley Wright, "Feminist Approaches to International Law," *American Journal of International Law* (1991): 635; Friedman, "Women's Human Rights," 19–20; Gallagher, "Ending the Marginalization," 290–91; Fran P. Hosken, "Toward a Definition of Women's Human Rights," *Human Rights Quarterly* 3 (1981): 2; Joanna Kerr, "The Context and the Goal," in *Ours by Right*, ed. Kerr, 4–5; Barbara Stark, "Nurturing Rights: An Essay on Women, Peace, and International Human Rights," *Michigan Journal of International Law* 13 (Fall 1991): 144–60.

71. Vienna Declaration, A/CONF.157/24, June 25, 1993, § 5.

72. UN Doc. E/1993/22, Annex III, § 5, quoted in Henry J. Steiner and Philip Alston, *International Human Rights in Context: Law, Politics, Morals* (Oxford: Clarendon, 1996), 266.

73. See Charlesworth, "Human Rights as Men's Rights," 108; Hilary Charlesworth, "What Are 'Women's International Human Rights'?" in *Human Rights of Women*, ed. Cook, 74; Mahoney, "Theoretical Perspectives," 851–52.

74. Shelley Wright, "Women and the Global Economic Order: A Feminist Perspective," *American University Journal of International Law and Policy* 10 (1995): 873–76, 885–86. This reorientation should not be limited to the work-related rights. On the need for an inclusive approach to the right to health, see Audrey R. Chapman, "Monitoring Women's Right to Health under the International Covenant on Economic, Social and Cultural Rights," *American University Law Review* 44 (1994–95): 1157–74.

75. Structural adjustment programs of the World Bank and the International Monetary Fund are frequently blamed for negatively affecting women's economic and social rights. See Rebecca J. Cook, "Women's International Human Rights Law: The Way Forward," *Human Rights Quarterly* 15 (1993) 242; Rhonda Copelon, "Bringing Beijing Home," *Brooklyn Journal of International Law* 21 (1996): 600; Adetoun O. Ilumoka, "African Women's Economic, Social and Cultural Rights—Toward a Relevant Theory and Practice," in *Human Rights of Women*, ed. Cook, 321.

76. Bunch, "Organizing for Women's Human Rights Globally," 144.

77. Coomaraswamy, *Reinventing International Law*, 20. She is referring to the frequently made subdivision of human rights in three "generations." The first generation are civil and political rights; the second are social, economic, and cultural rights; and the third are the so-called solidarity rights.

78. See Paula Abrams, "Reservations about Women: Population Policy and Reproductive Rights," *Cornell International Law Journal* 29 (1996): 1–23; Reed Boland, "Population Policies, Human Rights, and Legal Change," *American University Law Review* (1995): 1257–77; Carlota Bustelo, "Reproductive Health and CEDAW," *American University Law Review* (1995): 1145–55; Rebecca J. Cook, "International Human Rights and Women's Reproductive Health," in *Women's Rights*, ed. Peters and Wolper, 256–75; Rebecca J. Cook and Mahmoud E. Fathalla, "Advancing Reproductive Rights beyond Cairo and Beijing," *International Family Planning Perspectives* (September 1996); Sarah Y. Lai and Regan E. Ralph, "Female Sexual Autonomy and Human Rights," *Harvard Human Rights Journal* (1995): 201–27.

79. Boland, "Population Policies," 1258–61.

80. UN Doc. A/CONF.32/41, § 16.

81. UN Doc. E/CONF.60/19 (1974), 7.

82. Article 10(h) mentions the right of access to information and advice on family planning; article 11(1)(f) protects "[t]he right to protection of health and to safety in working conditions, including the safeguarding of the function of reproduction"; article 11(2) requires states to prevent discrimination based on pregnancy or maternity leave, to introduce maternity leave with pay, to encourage the provision of social services such as childcare to assist working parents, and to provide special protection to women from harmful work during pregnancy; article 12(1) deals with "access to health care services, including those related to family planning"; article 12(2) requires states to "ensure to women appropriate services in connexion with pregnancy, confinement and the post-natal period, granting free services where necessary, as well as adequate nutrition during pregnancy and lactation"; article 14(1)(b) guarantees access to family planning services for rural women.

83. Amy J. Higer, "International Women's Activism and the 1994 Cairo Population Conference," in *Gender Politics in Global Governance*, ed. Meyer and Prügl, 122–41.

84. Reproductive health is a state of complete physical, mental and social well-being and not merely the absence of disease or infirmity, in all matters relating to the reproductive system and to its functions and processes. Reproductive health therefore implies that people are able to have a satisfying and safe sex life and that they have the capability to reproduce and the freedom to decide if, when and how often to do so. Implicit in this last condition are the right of men and women to be informed and to have access to safe, effective, affordable and acceptable methods of family planning of their choice, as well as other methods of their choice for regulation of fertility which are not against the law, and the right of access to appropriate health-care services that will enable women to go safely through pregnancy and childbirth and provide couples with the best chance of having a healthy infant. In line with the above definition of reproductive health, reproductive health care is

defined as the constellation of methods, techniques and services that contribute to reproductive health and well-being by preventing and solving reproductive health problems. It also includes sexual health, the purpose of which is the enhancement of life and personal relations, and not merely counselling and care related to reproduction and sexually transmitted diseases. (UN Doc. A/CONF.171/13, § 7.2)

85. Abrams, "Reservations about Women," 32.

86. UN Doc. A/CONF.177/20, §§ 94–95.

87. Other relevant human rights include the right to life (e.g., death caused by unsafe abortion); the prohibition of sex discrimination (e.g., when women are forced to undergo abortion or family planning, or when they need the approval of a husband or a male relative to do so), the right to family life, the prohibition of torture and inhuman or degrading treatment, the right to education, and the right to enjoy the benefits of scientific progress. See Boland, "Population Policies," 1262–63; Cook, "International Human Rights and Women's Reproductive Health," 259–70; Cook and Fathalla, "Advancing Reproductive Rights beyond Cairo and Beijing."

88. Coomaraswamy, *Reinventing International Law,* 26; Lai and Ralph, "Female Sexual Autonomy and Human Rights," 201.

89. For example, Renate Klein, "The Impact of Reproductive and Genetic Engineering on Women's Bodily Integrity and Human Dignity," in *Human Rights in the Twenty-first Century,* ed. Kathleen E. Mahoney and Paul Mahoney (Dordrecht: Martinus Nijhoff, 1993), 889–904.

90. Report No 5/96, *Fernando and Raquel Mejia v. Peru,* March 1, 1996.

91. UN Doc. E/CN.4/1995/34, §§ 15–19.

92. Case of *Aydin v. Turkey,* September 25, 1997, Reports 1997-VI.

93. In full: the International Tribunal for the Prosecution of Persons Responsible for Serious Violations of International Humanitarian Law Committed in the Territory of the Former Yugoslavia since 1991, adopted May 25, 1993, amended May 13, 1998.

94. It should be noted that this is not new. Control Council Law No. 10, adopted by the Allied Powers in December 1945, already includes rape as a crime against humanity. Nicole Eva Erb, "Gender-Based Crimes under the Draft Statute for the Permanent International Criminal Court," *Columbia Human Rights Law Review* 29 (1998): 409.

95. International Criminal Tribunal for the Prosecution of Persons Responsible for Genocide and Other Serious Violations of International Humanitarian Law Committed in the Territory of Rwanda and Rwandan citizens responsible for genocide and other such violations committed in the territory of neighboring states, between January 1, 1994, and December 31, 1994.

96. See Brook Sari Moshan, "Women, War and Words: The Gender Component in the Permanent International Criminal Court's Definition of Crimes against Humanity," *Fordham International Law Journal* 22 (1998): 154–84.

97. Again, it is not new to consider rape as a war crime, as it was already treated as such by the International Military Tribunal for the Far East established in 1946 in Tokyo (Erb, "Gender-based Crimes under the Draft Statute," 410).

98. Kelly D. Askin, "Sexual Violence in Decisions and Indictments of the Yugoslav and Rwandan Tribunals: Current Status," *American Journal of International*

Law 93 (1999): 97–123. See the judgment of the Appeals Chamber of the International Tribunal for the Former Yugoslavia, in the case of *The Prosecutor v. Anto Furunzija* (July 21, 2000), the first recognition of rape as a war crime on the appeal level.

99. See Hilary Charlesworth, "Feminist Methods in International Law," *American Journal of International Law* 93 (1999): 386–94; Judith Gardam and Hilary Charlesworth, "Protection of Women in Armed Conflict," *Human Rights Quarterly* 22 (2000): 148–66. See article 27 of the Fourth Geneva Convention (1949), requiring states to protect women in international armed conflict "against any attack on their honour, in particular against rape, enforced prostitution, or any form of indecent assault."

100. See Siobhán K. Fisher, "Occupation of the Womb: Forced Impregnation as Genocide," *Duke Law Journal* 46 (1996): 91–133.

101. Rhonda Copelon, "Intimate Terror: Understanding Domestic Violence as Torture," in *Human Rights of Women*, ed. Cook, 116–52; Rhonda Copelon, "Recognizing the Egregious in the Everyday: Domestic Violence as Torture," *Columbia Human Rights Law Review* 25 (1994): 291–367; Catherine MacKinnon, "On Torture: A Feminist Perspective on Human Rights" in *Human Rights in the Twenty-first Century*, ed. Mahoney and Mahoney, 21.

102. Pamela Goldberg, "Where in the World Is There Safety for Me? Women Fleeing Gender-Based Persecution," in Peters and Wolper, 345–55; Kerr, "The Context and the Goal," 5; Erin K. Baines, "Gender Construction and the Protection Mandate of the UNHCR: Responses from Guatemalan Women," in *Gender Politics in Global Governance*, ed. Meyer and Prügl, 245–59.

103. This was recognized by a recommendation of the European Community in 1984 and a recommendation of the Executive Committee of the Office of the UNHCR in 1985, as well as the 1991 UNHCR Guidelines on the Protection of Refugee Women (Goldberg, "Where in the World Is There Safety for Me?" 348–49).

104. Goldberg, "Where in the World Is There Safety for Me?" 349–51, mentions Canada and Germany.

105. See the 1904 International Agreement for the Suppression of White Slave Traffic, the 1910 International Convention for the Suppression of White Slave Traffic, the 1921 Convention for the Suppression of the Traffic in Women and Children, and the 1933 Convention on the Suppression of the Traffic in Women of Full Age.

106. Article 1(c), quoted in A. Yasmine Rassam, "Contemporary Forms of Slavery and the Evolution of the Prohibition of Slavery and the Slave Trade under Customary International Law," *Virginia Journal of International Law* 39 (1999): 332.

107. Rassam, "Contemporary Forms of Slavery," 340–41.

108. In particular, the 1949 Convention For the Suppression of the Traffic in Persons and of the Exploitation of the Prostitution of Others.

109. Janie Chuang, "Redirecting the Debate over Trafficking in Women: Definitions, Paradigms, and Contexts," *Harvard Human Rights Journal* 11 (1998): 73.

110. Chuang, "Redirecting the Debate over Trafficking in Women," 65.

111. Chuang, "Redirecting the Debate over Trafficking in Women," 65–66.

112. Chuang, "Redirecting the Debate over Trafficking in Women," 78–79; Elizabeth F. Defeis, "Women's Human Rights: The Twenty-first Century," *Fordham International Law Journal* 18 (1995): 1753.

113. Gardam and Charlesworth, "Protection of Women in Armed Conflict," 161–62.

114. Charlesworth, "Feminist Methods," 388.

115. Bunch, "Transforming Human Rights from a Feminist Perspective," 16.

116. Kathleen E. Mahoney, "Destruction of Women's Rights through Mass Media. Proliferation of Pornography," in *Human Rights in the Twenty-first Century*, ed. Mahoney and Mahoney, 757–75.

117. Charlesworth, "What Are 'Women's International Human Rights'?" 68.

118. For example, Byrnes, "Toward More Effective Enforcement," 200; Charlesworth, "Transforming the United Men's Club"; Francine D'Amico, "Women Workers in the United Nations: From Margin to Mainstream?" in *Gender Politics in Global Governance*, ed. Meyer and Prügl, 19–40; Karen Knop, "Beyond Borders: Women's Rights and the Issue of Sovereignty," in *Ours by Right*, ed. Kerr, 75; Cecilia Medina, "Do International Human Rights Laws Protect Women?" in *Ours by Right*, ed. Kerr, 79.

119. Knop, "Beyond Borders," 76–77; Karen Knopp, "Why Rethinking the Sovereign State Is Important for Women's International Human Rights Law," in *Human Rights of Women*, ed. Cook, 159–60. In line with my concern with respect for diversity among women, and my ensuing preference for the centrality of the individual in human rights protection, I have strong doubts about the merits of this proposal.

120. Bell, "Women's Rights as Human Rights," 147.

121. Gallagher, "Ending the Marginalization," 292.

122. Binion, "Human Rights," 512. See also Byrnes, "Women, Feminism," 209–12; Charlesworth, "Feminist Methods."

123. V. Spike Peterson, "Whose Rights? A Critique of the 'Givens' in Human Rights Discourse," *Alternatives* 15 (1990): 328–32.

124. Charlesworth et al., "Feminist Approaches to International Law," 635.

125. Charlesworth et al., "Feminist Approaches to International Law," 637; Charlesworth, "Human Rights as Men's Rights," 109–10; Charlesworth, "What Are 'Women's International Human Rights'?" 75–76; Mahoney, "Theoretical Perspectives," 852–53.

126. See Rhoda E. Howard, "Women's Rights, Group Rights and the Erosion of Liberalism," in *Mistaken Identities: The Second Wave of Controversy over "Political Correctness*," ed. Cyril Levitt, Scott Davies, and Neil McLaughlin (New York: Lang, 1999), 130–45.

127. Ladan Askari, "Girls' Rights under International Law: An Argument for Establishing Gender Equality as a Jus Cogens," *Southern California Review of Law and Women's Studies* 8 (1998): 3–42; Hilary Charlesworth and Christine Chinkin, "The Gender of Jus Cogens," *Human Rights Quarterly* 15 (1993): 63–76; Christine M. Chinkin, "Remarks," *American Society of International Law Proceedings* (1991): 349–52.

128. Desai, "From Vienna to Beijing," 186; Prügl and Meyer, "Gender Politics," 6; L. Amede Obiora, "Feminism, Globalisation and Culture: After Beijing," *Indiana Journal of Global Legal Studies* 4 (1997): 359–64.

129. Chandra Talpade Mohanty, "Under Western Eyes: Feminist Scholarship and Colonial Discourses," in *Third World Women and the Politics of Feminism*, ed. Chan-

dra Talpade Mohanty, Ann Russo, and Lourdes Torres (Bloomington: Indiana University Press, 1991), 51–80.

130. Azizah al-Hibri, "Who Defines Women's Rights? A Third World Woman's Response," *The Human Rights Brief* (Washington, D.C.: Center for Human Rights and Humanitarian Law at Washington College of Law, American University, 1994).

131. Cheryl Johnson-Odim, "Common Themes, Different Contexts: Third World Women and Feminism," in *Third World Women and the Politics of Feminism*, ed. Mohanty et al., 321; see also Obiora, "Feminism, Globalisation and Culture," 372–73.

132. See Ilumoka, "African Women's Economic, Social and Cultural Rights"; Nadia H. Youssef, "Women's Access to Productive Resources: The Need for Legal Instruments to Protect Women's Development Rights," in *Women's Rights*, ed. Peters and Wolper, 279–88.

133. Charlesworth et al., "Feminist Approaches to International Law," 618–21; Julie Dimauro, "Toward a More Effective Guarantee of Women's Human Rights: A Multicultural Dialogue in International Law," *Women's Rights Law Reporter* (1996): 333–44.

134. Islamic dress is a clear example. In Western eyes, it is frequently seen as the paradigmatic expression of the cultural subordination of women. Yet both in Islamic countries and among immigrants in Europe, many women choose to wear Islamic dress and attach positive significance to it as an expression of cultural identity, nationalism, or even as an emancipatory device. With regard to the hijab (the Muslim headscarf) among immigrants in France, see Françoise Gaspard and Farhad Khosrokhavar, *Le foulard et la République* (Paris: La Découverte, 1995).

135. Coomaraswamy, *Reinventing International Law*, 24–25.

136. Halim, "Challenges to the Application of International Women's Human Rights in the Sudan," 407–10; Elene G. Mountis, "Cultural Relativity and Universalism: Re-evaluating Gender Rights in a Multicultural Context," *Dickinson Journal of International Law* 15 (1996): 113–50.

137. Rhoda E. Howard, *Human Rights in Commonwealth Africa* (Totowa, N.J.: Rowman & Littlefield, 1986), 198–200.

138. Kay Boulware-Miller, "Female Circumcision: Challenges to the Practice as a Human Rights Violation," *Harvard Women's Law Journal* 8 (1985): 171–73.

139. For example, Annie Bunting, "Theorizing Women's Cultural Diversity in Feminist International Human Rights Strategies," *Journal of Law and Society* (1993): 6–22; Nitya Duclos, "Lessons of Difference: Feminist Theory on Cultural Diversity," *Buffalo Law Review* 38 (1990): 325–81; Isabelle R. Gunning, "Arrogant Perception, World-Travelling and Multicultural Feminism: The Case of Female Genital Surgeries," *Columbia Human Rights Law Review* 23 (1991–1992): 189–248; Berta Esperanza Hernandez-Truyol, "Women's Rights as Human Rights—Rules, Realities and the Role of Culture: A Formula for Reform," *Brooklyn Journal of International Law* 21 (1996): 605–77; Tracy E. Higgins, "Anti-essentialism, Relativism, and Human Rights," *Harvard Women's Law Journal* 9 (1996): 89–126; Nancy Kim, "Toward a Feminist Theory of Human Rights: Straddling the Fence between Western Imperialism and Uncritical Absolutism," *Columbia Human Rights Law Review* 25 (1993): 49–105; Mertus and Goldberg, "A Perspective on Women and International

Human Rights"; Susan Moller Okin, "Gender Inequality and Cultural Differences," *Political Theory* (February 1994): 5–24; Joshua Cohen, Matthew Howard, and Martha C. Nussbaum, eds., *Is Multiculturalism Bad for Women? Susan Moller Okin with Respondents* (Princeton, N.J.: Princeton University Press, 1999); Elizabeth V. Spelman, *Inessential Woman: Problems of Exclusion in Feminist Thought* (Boston: Beacon, 1988). Mahoney describes this as the specialty of postmodern feminism: "Theoretical Perspectives," 826–37.

140. Radhika Coomaraswamy, "To Bellow Like a Cow: Women, Ethnicity, and the Discourse of Rights," in *Human Rights of Women*, ed. Cook, 55.

141. Rebecca J. Cook, "Effectiveness of the Beijing Conference Advancing International Law Regarding Women," *American Society of International Law Proceedings* (1997): 313; Sara Hossain, "Equality in the Home: Women's Rights and Personal Laws in South Asia," in *Human Rights of Women*, ed. Cook, 482–83.

142. Bell, "Women's Rights as Human Rights," 151; Desai, "From Vienna to Beijing," 184–85; Shefali Desai, "Hearing Afghan Women's Voices: Feminist Theory's Re-conceptualization of Women's Human Rights," *Arizona Journal of International and Comparative Law* 16 (1999): 806; J. Oloka-Onyango and Sylvia Tamale, "'The Personal Is Political,' or Why Women's Rights are Indeed Human Rights: An African Perspective on International Feminism," *Human Rights Quarterly* 17 (1995): 710.

III

THE ROLE OF
INTERNATIONAL SOCIETY

6

Human Rights in Weak, Divided, and Threatened States

Marc Weller

Human rights guarantee peace and stability within and among societies. Essential for this function are human rights connected with personal and political freedoms and the rule of law, guaranteed through a democratic system. The need for the introduction or reintroduction of a human rights culture becomes particularly pronounced where states have collapsed or are in danger of collapse. To stabilize or restore these "failed" states, liberal international theory holds that international action may be necessary to rebuild a democratic system based on the rule of law and human rights. Over the past decade, numerous and sustained attempts have been undertaken to "restore democracy" or the very integrity of a threatened state according to a set of Western-liberal values and rights. As a result, we now have a laboratory of cases to use in testing this theory against the experience of international intervention. This is the purpose of this chapter.

There have also been a number of instances of softer state transformation. These include the transitions to democracy in Central and Eastern Europe, in South America and, more hesitantly, in some parts of Africa and Asia. South Africa's campaign to overcome the apartheid legacy is also a particularly impressive example of a significant transition. Of course, the record in these instances is somewhat mixed. Some societies have not progressed as far as others. Nevertheless, these transformations are rightly seen as a vindication of the aim, and the possibility, of reconstructing societies—at times quite fundamentally—according to the democratic model of governance. The introduction of a human rights culture and the rule of law has played a crucial role in these processes. These efforts were often supported by a wide range of international agencies, from the United Nations, the Organization of American States (OAS) and the associated juridical and human rights system, the Commonwealth Secretariat, the Council of Europe and the Organization for Security and Cooperation in Europe (OSCE), to a large number of specialized nongovernmental organizations. Nonetheless, and crucially, these societies themselves had the drive and capacity to launch and sustain the process of transformation. The liberal project of reform was legitimized from the beginning by the fact that it was carried by an indigenous political movement; the element of international involvement was ancillary to, and not constitutive of, the transformation process.

State transformation is a far more controversial subject where the society in question lacks the capacity to undertake this process on its own. This is invariably the case where weak, failed, or threatened states are concerned. The situation of actual or imminent collapse is manifestly the result of the inability of the society in question to reform itself. Soft assistance of the type mentioned earlier would not be sufficient to support a transformation at that late stage. The question therefore arises whether it is possible to effect or even enforce such a transition through external intervention. Should it turn out that these attempts are forever doomed, this finding would have considerable importance for the debate about international action to transform or stabilize weak, failing, or threatened states and its legitimacy.

Before turning to a review of experience gained from recent cases of externally driven efforts at state transformation, it may be helpful to distinguish these from humanitarian interventions addressed by Nicholas Wheeler in the following chapter. Humanitarian interventions are forcible actions by foreign military forces on behalf of the population of a state without the government's consent. The operation must be aimed at averting or terminating an actual or imminent humanitarian disaster that threatens the very survival of all or a substantial portion of the population. It is axiomatic that such interventions are short-term, palliative measures. Indeed, in international legal terms, it is a requirement that the intervention is limited to action designed to avert the humanitarian emergency.

Intervention, not merely to address the immediate catastrophe but to reestablish the conditions necessary for sustaining a democratic system that guarantees human rights, is a different matter. A rushed military engagement that is strictly limited to rescuing a population from disaster is not likely to provide the conditions necessary for what has become known as state building. However, a state requiring humanitarian intervention tends to be precisely the kind of state that is in need of state building. The humanitarian emergency and the ensuing intervention will, after all, invariably have been triggered by deficiencies in the governance or in the fundamental structure of the state concerned. Unless that underlying issue is addressed, the humanitarian intervention will leave the society in question persistently vulnerable to a relapse into circumstances of humanitarian or political disaster. Humanitarian intervention and postconflict reconstruction are thus at times linked together, even though they are conceptually distinct.

Over the past decade, about twenty-five international state-building or stabilization actions have been undertaken, in contrast to just three during the Cold War period. The first of these earlier operations was the ONUC (United Nations Operation in the Congo) mission from July 1960 to June 1964. That mission was widely perceived to be a great disaster, leaving the territory in the hands of Sésé Seko Mobuto who, becoming increasingly dictatorial, ultimately led the state into disintegration and chaos some thirty years later. The second attempt—the UNSF (United Nations Security Force in Western New Guinea) operation—involved UN administration of the territory from October 1962 to April 1963. Although it helped smooth the way to integration with Indonesia, this outcome not only was an unusual method of transferring power but also remains controversial. Indeed, it has triggered a certain level of armed resistance over the past decade. Finally, there was a brief and less direct involvement of the UN in the internal conflict in the Dominican Republic in the mid-1960s. That mission, however, was overshadowed by the actions of the United States and the OAS and cannot be considered a genuine example of international state building and stabilization.

Other UN operations in the Cold War years were traditional peacekeeping missions, mainly dedicated to the separation of armed forces in state-to-state conflicts or in mixed internal/international conflicts, and therefore fall outside the scope of this chapter. Suffice it to say that these actions are generally credited with having contributed to military stabilization in their areas of deployment and in a few cases (e.g., Cyprus) also made a limited contribution to humanitarian objectives. While few of these operations led to a resolution of the underlying source of military tension, the record of traditional peacekeeping has generally been seen as positive.

Since the end of the Cold War, the United Nations has continued to manage several traditional peacekeeping missions.[1] However, these operations have been overshadowed by the acceleration of UN mandated state-building or stabilization attempts, often following on from initially more limited humanitarian intervention operations. This acceleration is all the more surprising given the apparent failure of the operations in Somalia, Angola, Rwanda, Croatia,[2] and, initially, Bosnia and Herzegovina.

These failures have exposed liberal interventionism to criticism from three directions. In the remainder of this chapter, I shall deal first with each of these criticisms—and the liberal response to them—and second with the record of international state building, its successes and failures. In both parts I shall distinguish between weak, divided, and threatened states, the three kinds of state that have been the target of international interventions. *Weak states* are those where government has effectively been destroyed by prolonged conflict; *divided states* are fractured usually along ethnic lines and characterized by the determination of the dominant group to control the state and disenfranchise its opponents; *threatened states* face the challenge of secession and/or dissolution.

CRITICISMS OF LIBERAL STATE SUPPORT OPERATIONS

The three arguments advanced against the liberal agenda of assisting in state reconstruction or stabilization are that intervention for this purpose is an illegitimate interference in the domestic affairs of a sovereign country, that it ignores the realities of power politics, and that the international community lacks the resources and capacity to achieve its objectives.

Sovereignty and Legitimacy of International Action

The liberal agenda is cosmopolitan. It assumes that all states ought to be constructed according to a basic model that must feature, at a minimum, a democratic culture, the rule of law and human rights guarantees. Democracy ensures that the authority to govern is based on the will of the governed. The rule of law ensures that public acts and intersubjective relations are conducted within the framework of the constitutional and legal environment created on the basis of the exercise of this will. Human rights ensure that individuals and groups can under all circumstances rely on basic guarantees that cannot be overturned, even through the exercise of democratic majoritarianism and the system of law that supports it. Some might also add economic considerations (i.e., the need to establish a free market economy). Any state that fails to exhibit these requirements is a failure and in need of international action.

This vision has been criticized as being culturally imperialist on philosophical/ideological and structural grounds, although both are intertwined. The philosophical/ideological objection asserts that every society must be enabled to organize itself autonomously, on the basis of the will of the governed, without reference to any imperatives that lie outside it. These external imperatives, it is argued, are invariably established by powerful states or multinational economic interests. The structural criticism refers to the international political or legal principles, which support the autonomy of societies organized as states. The self-determination of peoples, the sovereignty and equality of states, and the attendant prohibition of intervention in the internal affairs of states, all of which are laid down either in the UN Charter itself or in countless General Assembly resolutions, are invoked in support of this view.

How may such criticisms be answered? Those who object to internationalized state building overlook the fact that not every system of governance, and not every government, is necessarily an expression of the free determination of the state population. In weak, divided, or threatened states, it is, almost by definition, a construct of power that is based on anything but the will of the governed. In states weakened by prolonged internal conflict, there is no longer a system of government. Instead, there are factions exercising effective control over segments of the population. In ethnically divided states, a dominant group frequently disenfranchises other parts of the population. In other cases, the very legitimacy of the state itself is threatened by the demand for self-determination and secession of a significant proportion of its population. In all these circumstances, state building or stabilization efforts will seek to restore governmental legitimacy, often on the basis of a constitutional consensus and through democratic elections. Far from undermining international legal principle, it is the aim of these operations to restore a situation where the people can exercise their sovereign rights through a machinery of governance based on their expressed will.

It is also argued that such state-building activities violate the rights to self-determination of populations because a Western liberal state system is arbitrarily imposed. However, with the exception of Kosovo, virtually all statebuilding ventures that have ever occurred are based on an agreed settlement of the parties to the conflict. There will often be a new constitution established by the local parties, albeit with international assistance, which will be subsequently validated and filled with life through a round of elections. Essentially, therefore, this is one of the most direct methods of giving a state population the opportunity to establish the state structure it wishes for itself and to legitimize this structure through an act of will. It is possible that international attempts to support such ventures may have at times sought to encourage the parties to create a system of government unsuited to the culture and tradition of the population in question. Arguably, this was so in Somalia, but there are not many other obvious examples.

Another sovereignty-based argument is that international state building provides a means for powerful states to interfere in the affairs of the less powerful. Such a risk does exist. However, virtually all post–Cold War statebuilding attempts have been conducted under the aegis of a United Nations mandate. This has not always prevented some states from taking a lead in operations affecting states or regions of concern to them, as the United States did in Haiti; Russia, acting under the auspices of the Commonwealth of Independent States (CIS) did in Georgia; and Nigeria through its leadership of the Economic Community of West African States (ECOWAS) did in Liberia and Sierra Leone. In all three cases, however, the UN insisted on the deployment of its own missions to monitor and help shape these operations. In Haiti, the U.S.-led operation did not seek to bring to power its own candidate for government but instead sought to restore the incumbent president, who had been ousted by a military coup. A subsequent UN operation followed, to help stabilize democracy in Haiti in a more general way. In Liberia, the UN joined the initial ECOWAS operation. After some stops and starts, the end result was that Charles Taylor, the rebel leader whom Nigeria had initially sought to keep from power, was elected president. In Sierra Leone, the UN intervened in another state-building operation initially commenced by ECOWAS, perhaps with Nigerian interests at heart. Eventually, the UN was again able to ensure participation at a level that would ensure a genuine restoration of legitimate state authority. Georgia, is the one possible exception, since on this occasion, the UN was only able to dispatch a monitoring mission, and Russia, ostensibly acting on behalf of the CIS, intervened to stabilize the situation on the ground perhaps very much in accordance with its own national interests.

Overall, therefore, one may conclude that state building and stabilization are precisely aimed at revindicating the will of the governed in circumstances where governance is no longer accountable to them. This process will generally be conducted on the basis of a popular mandate. These missions will typically be conducted by the UN itself or by agencies acting within the remit of a mandate established by the UN. Hence, the risk of undue interference is reduced.

The Realist Criticism

The realist criticism appreciates the realities and also the limitations of international politics. Realists argue that certain states either are illogical constructions that cannot ever succeed or are subjected to internal conflicts so complex that they cannot ever be resolved through international action. Ultimately, it is for the society in question to reorganize itself, be it through a dissolution of state structures or through prolonged struggle for power within the state. Hence, the position of the international community can only be to isolate itself from states that are in the process of collapse and possible dissolution and perhaps to organize a minimum of palliative action.

The liberal response to this argument will differ depending on whether intervention is intended to overcome the problems of seriously weakened, divided, or threatened states. As we have seen, weak states are those where prolonged internal strife has been the result of a struggle for political power among competing armed elites. This struggle has led to a degradation of the state institutions. Authority is only based on effective control exercised by warring factions over populations and territory and especially over whatever economic resources can be rapidly converted into cash (diamonds, metals, timber, oil and gas, etc.). While these elites may, on occasion, have an ethnic basis, ethnicity is not the key issue that has led to a deterioration of state authority. Examples for these types of conflicts are the struggles for power in Liberia, Sierra Leone, the Congo, and, in its later phases, Angola.

Many realists would argue that there is no point in intervening in a conflict of this kind. A vast international intervention force would be necessary to reestablish central authority in a territory like the Congo. Such a force would find it difficult, if not impossible, to disenfranchise the opposing factions. Even if that were possible, there would be no real political alternative in place. The state would soon sink again into a factional struggle for power. More important, since no vital national interests are at stake, from the realist view, there can be no justification for launching expensive and dangerous missions of this kind.

The argument relating to feasibility is admittedly powerful, and it gains support from the list of UN failures during the 1990s. The outcome of some of the more recently launched missions also still hangs in the balance. However, as we shall see, the balance sheet is by no means as negative as is often presumed. The argument from interest is more easily countered. It is now clear that internal conflicts of this kind will often lead to a destabilization of entire regions; witness the spread of the Liberian conflict to Sierra Leone and the dangerous effect of the struggle within the Congo on its neighbors. The internal conflicts of Central America of the 1980s provided an earlier lesson of this kind. Individual states may lack an overriding national interest but can sometimes be persuaded to intervene in the interests of regional stability.

In addition to strictly national and regional interests, there exist international community interests that may need to be maintained. The prevention of massive starvation of populations suffering from civil strife, often combined with acts of violence against large numbers of civilians, is now recognized as an important aim of international policy, at least in cases so egregious that they cannot be easily ignored. This is evidenced by the fact that even after the unsatisfactory first round of complex peacekeeping operations in weak states (Somalia, Angola, Liberia, Rwanda), which significantly dampened the appetite for such missions of the United Nations Secretariat and UN force-contributing states alike, a second round was launched (Sierra Leone, Central African Republic, Congo). This development does not reflect a reborn liberal idealism but the acceptance by the major powers of the need to act in terms of realpolitik. In other words, state practice hoists realists with their own petard.

Campaigns of predominantly ethnic violence exemplify the politics of divided states. Sometimes, such campaigns amount to attempts by one group to exterminate or permanently displace another. This practice, illustrated in its most drastic form by the Rwandan genocide, is manifestly incompatible with the fundamental international interest to maintain community values, including the legal prohibition of genocide, the survival of principles of humanitarian law applicable to internal conflicts, and the prohibition of forced displacement of entire populations. Regional interests tend to be affected by the significant refugee streams that are always connected with campaigns of ethnic domination and that can lead to regional destabilization. Whether motivated by the need to maintain core international community values or by the need to prevent threats to regional stability, states have therefore found it very much in their interest to act.

Once again, the argument may be more difficult to win in terms of the feasibility of effective international intervention than in terms of its legitimacy. Ethnic conflicts are notoriously difficult to terminate, and even where this has been possible, postconflict peace building appears to be a particularly daunting task. The review of practice in the next section will address this point.

In the case of threatened states, in danger of breaking up through secession or dissolution, the international and national interest can be established most clearly. All governments share in the urgent desire to avoid any sort of precedent that might encourage secession. Their passionate attachment to the principle of territorial integrity has been repeatedly demonstrated, from Biafra to Katanga and from Chechnya to Kosovo. When it proved impossible to stabilize Yugoslavia as a whole, the international community invested massively to prevent further disintegration, underwriting the continued existence of Bosnia and Herzegovina and subjecting unruly Kosovo to international administration. Whether it can ever be feasible to address conflicts of this kind, even if national interest demands such action, will again be considered later, in the light of recent practice.

The Managerial Criticism

A final strand of criticism facing internationalized state-building or stabilization efforts concerns the ability of the organized international community to manage actions of this kind. There is doubt about the willingness to make available the resources necessary for these operations and about the long-term commitment that is required to sustain them. In addition, detailed studies of individual cases have brought out some more specific managerial lessons. Many of these were considered in a consolidated way in the United Nations Brahimi report. It may be convenient to bear in mind the following factors in this context:

- *Authority*. From the legal point of view, one may distinguish operations according to the source of authority for internationalized attempts of state construction or stabilization. In a number of cases, the origin of authority rests in a peace agreement achieved by the parties themselves who then request international support by way of a peacekeeping mandate under Chapter VI of the UN Charter, the chapter concerned with the peaceful settlement of disputes. Hence, the authority of the international element in the venture is consent based and does not exceed the consent given. This authority can nevertheless be extensive, as, for example, in the international administration of Cambodia (United Nations Transitional Authority in Cambodia [UNTAC]). A second type of mandate is partially based in Chapter VI of the Charter, but Chapter VII enforcement elements are added—for example, in relation to force protection, to sanctions enforcement or even to the protection of endangered populations. Finally, there are outright Chapter VII mandates, which involve enforcement through diplomatic, economic, or military means and locate supreme authority for the implementation of the entire mandate.

- *Actors.* There are at least four different modalities of international action covered by UN mandates. These are operations directly controlled by the UN Secretariat (e.g., United Nations Operation in Somalia II [UNOSOM II]), joint UN and regional operations (e.g., Liberia), operations managed by regional organizations or defensive alliances (e.g., Sierra Leone in the first case and Kosovo in the second), and, finally, actions undertaken by coalitions of states (e.g., Albania). These different types of actors at times perform their roles in parallel or hand on from one to the other as the mission evolves. There is a similar division of labor among UN agencies and regional agencies like the Council of Europe and the OSCE.

- *Mandates.* The attempts to stabilize existing state structures have been covered by a variety of mandates, ranging from the initially modest mandates to protect populations or create conditions for the safe delivery of humanitarian assistance, to support for individual aspects of the state structure (e.g., policing in Albania) or to very ambitious attempts to reconstruct a polity from scratch (e.g. UNISOM II). Most missions evolved, ending up with far more ambitious designs for societal reconstruction than were initially intended.

- *Tools.* The nature of the mandate determines the tools that can be brought to bear on the task at hand. The tools applied by these different types of missions include the following:

Military separation of forces, the disarming of competing armed formations and the establishment of a new military and security structure
Reconstruction of constitutional structures, the establishment of new electoral systems, and the administration or monitoring of elections
The reestablishment of administrative structures, the judiciary and other

aspects of civil and social services, and the introduction of human rights
monitoring and implementation measures

International support for economic reconstruction, including measures to
open up economic opportunities for all segments of the population and
for former combatants

Accountability mechanisms, ranging from truth commissions to the local
or even international administration of justice

There are three types of international operations. The most comprehensive
approach, at times involving all of the preceding factors, is international
interim governance. International agencies take over the functions of the
state while assisting in the process of constructing an indigenous political
system and supporting the development of a new administration. The second
and less intrusive type is a complex peacekeeping mission. The parties themselves continue to exercise governmental authority, often under an interim
power sharing agreement; the UN stabilizes the situation while assisting in
constitution building and often holds the first round of elections. Finally,
there are peacekeeping operations, where an international agency will support or take over security functions but is less involved in civil reform.

THE RECORD OF INTERNATIONAL EFFORTS

Having disposed of some of the criticisms of state-building and stabilization
efforts, it is now necessary to address the two principal objections that
remain. These are either that it is never possible to address internal conflicts
through external action or that, if this is possible in principle, the organized
international community lacks the resources and managerial skills to perform this function. These criticisms can only be assessed by reviewing the
actual cases in which the international community has been engaged, in relation to weak, divided, and threatened states. The appropriateness of the
international response in each case will be investigated in relation to the
authority under which the action is taken, the actors involved, the mandates
that specify what they are to do, and the tools they use.

It is, of course, not easy to determine whether international state building
and stabilization has succeeded or failed. Obviously, these are relative terms,
ranging from arresting further disintegration of a society to the durable reestablishment of civil society in the liberal mold, based on a democratic human
rights culture. For the purposes of this chapter, success is defined as reestablishing governance on the basis of the will of the governed. Manifestly
unrepresentative exercise of public authority is replaced by constitutional
governance that can be traced back in some form to an exercise of popular
will, even if it does not fully conform to Western liberal standards of "good

governance." In addition, a basic human rights culture is established as a result of the international operation. Success may be present when such an arrangement is stabilized over at least one electoral cycle.

Weak States

In states that have suffered from a violent and prolonged contest for central state power, international action will mostly seek to reestablish a constitutional consensus. On this basis, governmental authority is then constructed on the basis of an exercise of the will of the population through elections. There will also be a need to reestablish administrative structures and the judiciary and to introduce a human rights culture.

There are two types of weak states: those suffering from conflict driven by ideological confrontation and those where internal factions are fighting about naked power over the state structure.

Eight missions have addressed ideologically driven conflict, varying considerably in terms of authority, actors, mandate, and tools. The forms of missions varied from international interim governance to complex peacekeeping and limited peacekeeping.

Cambodia was the site of the first, and one of the most comprehensive post–Cold War state-building missions. This operation involved some twenty-two thousand military and civilian personnel, lasted from October 1991 to September 1993, and included a smaller advance stabilization operation. The authority of the operation was based on the Paris Agreements on the Comprehensive Political Settlement of the Cambodia Conflict of October 23, 1991. The Hun Sen regime, then in power over most of the territory, the former government of the Khmer Rouge that had been displaced by the Vietnamese invasion of 1978, the opposition led by Prince Sihanouk, and a further party agreed to a settlement providing for military disengagement, decommissioning of irregular units, a new constitutional structure, and internationally managed elections. The agreement established a Supreme National Council for Cambodia, "the unique legitimate body and source of authority in which, during the transitional period, the sovereignty, independence and unity of Cambodia are enshrined," composed of representatives of the principal factions. This authority was, in turn, delegated to the United Nations. Given this grant of authority, a Chapter VI mandate was sufficient.

The substance of the mandate was wide-ranging, providing for the full reestablishment of a functioning state on the basis of a new, agreed constitution. The mission conducted an election to a constitutive assembly, which drafted the constitution and then transformed itself into a parliament. In parallel, the UN mission took over supervision of public administration in most sectors, exercised administrative authority in others, and established a training program for public officials. The armed forces of the former warring factions were cantoned and integrated and policing was addressed. A human rights component was included in the mission, in the hope of improving the performance of officials. With respect to severe violations, the mission even attempted to establish a system of enforcement, including the powers of detention and trial. An economic reconstruction component was also provided. Hence, nearly the entire tool kit of state-building instruments was applied.

The mission was challenged by the refusal of the former Khmer Rouge faction to grant access to the territory under its control. Throughout the mission, patient attempts were undertaken to negotiate with this group. However, the UN never made any headway, even after sanctions were adopted to prevent the Khmer Rouge from profiting from illegal logging operations. In the end, this part of the territory, approximately 5 percent of Cambodia, did not participate in the elections. Nevertheless, a power-sharing government involving the two main parties resulted, and both the mission and the elections were judged a success. The constitutional assembly adopted a new structure of the state, providing for a constitutional monarchy. After the withdrawal of the mission, the political party headed by Hun Sen sought to oust its coalition partner from government. However, the political system by and large survived this challenge. With UN mediation, agreement was reached in April 2000 to establish an accountability mechanism relating to the Khmer Rouge period, adding the final element of possible international involvement in state building.

The UN involvement in the transfer of power in Namibia also involved substantial international governance during the transition. The territory had been under nominal UN authority, but effective South African control. The termination of the Cold War made it possible finally to implement proposals for a transition to indigenous and independent government that had been drafted towards the end of the 1970s. South Africa consented to a transitional arrangement and interim administration with a strong UN role. As in Cambodia, a Chapter VI mandate, which aimed to establish an environment for free and fair elections and the exercise of the right of self-determination, was deemed to be sufficient. A large UN mission composed of some 5,000 military, 2,000 civilian, and 1,500 police staff was dispatched. The latter element was particularly important to ensure confidence of all segments of the population in the political process and the elections. The continued use of South African administrators and of the police force established under its authority is noteworthy in this instance. An additional one thousand international monitors were drafted in to support the first round of elections.

To achieve the aims of the mission, it was first necessary to demobilize or integrate the opposition forces that had been based in neighboring territories, in parallel with the withdrawal of South African forces. This was particularly difficult, given the distrust among the parties and violations of the cease-fire arrangements. The availability of powerful and interested states, including Angola, Cuba, and South Africa, and the USSR and the United States as "observers" was important in stabilizing this process. Elections were held to a constituent assembly. In parallel, the UN mission repealed discriminatory legislation, although mainly only those elements that were relevant to the holding of elections, and engaged in the supervision of administrative activities and of policing. After this had been achieved, an indigenous government was established, under the leadership of the former national liberation movement, South West Africa People's Organization (SWAPO), which had won the majority of seats. Its authority has not been challenged.

In addition to the administration of change through international governance, a second approach that has been attempted relied on complex peacekeeping. The first series of complex peacekeeping operations were in Central America. With the withdrawal of Cold War support for the Sandinista government in Nicaragua, on the one hand, and for the right-wing governments in El Salvador and Guatemala, on the other, it became possible to negotiate peace agreement in all three states. The mandates covered a range of peace support activities, including demilitarization, the integration of formerly opposing forces, the restoration of a constitutional consensus, and the holding of a first round of elections. Significant attention was paid to institution building and the introduction of a human rights culture. In fact, the El Salvador operation was from the beginning specifically dedicated to human rights monitoring and legal reform. An important element also related to the reconstruction of the police services, which had played a particular role during the conflicts. The societies in question also sought to cover accountability, although mainly through soft mechanisms such as truth commissions with the involvement of international personalities. All operations culminated in the holding of elections that were either organized or monitored by international agents. Since the authority to act was based in peace agreements, Chapter VI mandates were sufficient. While the three missions were UN operations, they were conducted in close cooperation with the OAS.

The two post–Cold War African cases—Angola and Mozambique—proved to be even more difficult than the examples from Central America and Asia. The prospect for a settlement in Angola opened up when Cuba and South Africa agreed to withdraw their intervention forces. The initial mission, United Nations Angola Verification Mission I (UNAVEM I), was mainly dedicated to verifying this process, while a second mission, UNAVEM II, concerned itself with the agreement between the internal parties: the government of Angola and the opposition group, National Union for the Full Independence of Angola (UNITA). A third mission, UNAVEM III, followed with a similar mandate, to assist implementation of the peace accords of 1991 and later the 1994 Lusaka Protocol. The mandate of this traditional Chapter VI operation conducted by forces under UN control was mainly focused on military separation, cantonment and integration of forces. However, there was also a requirement to ensure the neutrality of the Angolan police force controlled by the government and to help establish conditions for the holding of free and fair elections. Throughout, the implementation of this mandate was threatened by deep distrust among the parties and the inability to extend UN activities fully to areas held by UNITA. Hence, the first step of implementation relating to demilitarization was never fully achieved. The withdrawal of South African and Cuban forces, on the other hand, was fully successful.

The failure of implementation led the UN Security Council to threaten the termination of the mission. However, a further effort was undertaken in 1997, with the transformation of UNAVEM III into a broader mission with a more political mandate, including the normalization of administration throughout the country and a confidence building presence to reassure all segments of the population. Even greater attention was paid to police monitoring and to attempts to integrate UNITA personnel into the police forces. A human rights component was added, dedicated to the suppression of abuses and capacity building. In the end, it was also possible to organize elections, although, when it lost, UNITA failed to recognize the result. Civil war resumed. The UN Security Council responded by imposing economic sanctions against UNITA, seeking to reduce its control over the economic resources that had enabled it to sustain itself.

A number of reasons for the failure of the mission can be advanced. First, the UN mission was from the beginning limited. The mandate only expanded as the difficulties mounted and the means placed at the disposal of the heads of the successive missions were inadequate. Nor was the mission invasive. Its mandate remained on a Chapter VI peacekeeping footing from the beginning. There was no attempt to impose compliance with the terms of the peace agreement upon the recalcitrant party, particularly important in relation to the first step of demilitarization. Instead, agreements were constantly renegotiated. Elections were finally conducted, but in an environment that was anything but politically neutral and when UNITA retained the military potential to resist implementation of the result. International efforts to cut UNITA off from its sources of funding were also inadequate and belated.

An effort was made to avoid some of these pitfalls in the United Nations Operation in Mozambique (ONUMOZ), which was based on the 1992 peace agreement concluded between the government and the Mozambiquan National Resistance (RENAMO). The operation was conducted by the UN Secretariat under a Chapter VI mandate. It encompassed demobilization, withdrawal of foreign forces, civil functions, and the monitoring of the electoral process. These functions were from the beginning seen as interrelated and deserving of equal attention. As in Angola, difficulties persisted in relation to demilitarization. However, this time, it was possible to achieve agreements on the integration of RENAMO-controlled areas and to establish an international police support mission. To ensure implementation, the UN secretary-general himself engaged in direct contact with the parties. The governments of France, Portugal, and the United Kingdom also directly supported the crucial issue of the establishment of an integrated defense force. When progress stalled, the UN Security Council sent a high-level mission, including Russia, China, and the United States, which resulted in an acceleration of implementation in advance of the elections of October 1994. The elections resulted in victory for the party of the incumbent president. A second election held in 1999 yielded a similar result.

The distinction between ideological and pure power struggles is not absolute. In Angola, what started as one degenerated into the other. There may also be an ethnic dimension to them, since more often than not the competing leaders or war lords rely on clan or tribal loyalties. Essentially, though, such civil conflicts are about the establishment of governance through force. In this respect, they represent a particularly strong challenge to liberal views about the nature of governance and the legitimacy of public authority. Operations in countries weakened by such internecine feuding have generally been conducted under Chapter VI, although in Sierra Leone, enforcement elements were added, and the Somalia operation was conducted entirely under Chapter VII.

International action to address these conflicts has at times been decisive and at times hesitant. When U.S. interests were engaged in Haiti, the threat of a military invasion resulted in a retreat of the military junta that had deposed the elected president. Those elections in turn were the result of a prolonged peace effort by the United Nations and regional organizations. Despite the apparent effectiveness of threatened force in this instance, the operation did not end with the return of President Aristide. Haiti demonstrated the need for long-term, sustained involvement. The gradual rebuilding of an administrative infrastructure and of a police and judicial system were particularly important. An initially limited U.S.-led coalition was therefore transformed into a full-fledged, complex UN peacekeeping operation. The mission not only assisted in the difficult task of maintaining law and order but also guided the state's return to constitutional rule. A priority was the formation of a new national police force and the holding of the next round of elections. When the mission terminated, a more limited support mission was established to sustain the progress that had been made. Throughout, this process was supported by a group of "friends of the UN Secretary-General for Haiti" (Argentina, Canada, Chile, France, the United States, and Venezuela), and there was full cooperation with regional agencies in seeking to introduce a human rights culture. Disappointments subsequently raised questions still difficult to answer in the case of Haiti.

The need for staying power and, when necessary, decisiveness was more effectively demonstrated in the 1997 Italian-led coalition to Albania. Initially launched with a humanitarian mandate, it was transformed into an electoral mission designed to lead Albania back to constitutional rule, following the chaotic breakdown of governmental authority. As in Haiti, the mission launched a program of police training and civil affairs management. The renewed—albeit brief—breakdown of authority a year later was addressed through international involvement. By that time, Albania had assumed a strategic significance for some Western governments, which undoubtedly made it easier to mobilize the necessary additional resources.

Attempts to reconstitute civil society after an internal conflict have proved to be much more difficult in Africa, where no such strategic interest exists. ECOWAS, led by Nigeria, has launched three operations—in Liberia, Guinea Bissau, and Sierra Leone—at times jointly or in cooperation with the United Nations. Each case called for ambitious plans for the reestablishment of a constitutional consensus, the holding of elections, integration of armed forces, and the establishment of a human rights–based civil society culture. The results were mixed.

In Liberia, a peace agreement was implemented after many false dawns, but only after elections had brought to power the brutal warlord Charles Taylor, who had launched the insurgency in the first place. In Sierra Leone, instability and civil war were initially brought about by a very small insurrection. A peace agreement followed by elections was upset by a military coup. A power-sharing arrangement, again including the leaders of the most violent opposition movement, was reached. However, when the party led by the former rebel leader, now Vice President Sankoh, resumed violence in 2000, uniquely, his treachery triggered a reasonably decisive military response by the United Nations, supported by the United Kingdom. A more aggressive Chapter VII mandate permitted action to secure freedom of movement of UN personnel and protection for civilians under threat of violence. While it is too early to tell whether the governments involved and the UN will have the determination to maintain this commitment to the peace accords, their action marks an interesting recovery from the Somali experience, which froze and doomed to failure several other peace-making operations.

Somalia itself is often quoted as the typical example of misguided Western liberal interventionism. While the initial U.S.-led humanitarian rescue mission (Unified Task Force [UNITAF]) succeeded in meeting its objective, the UN Security Council then authorized the deployment of a large UN enforcement operation charged with reestablishing civil society in Somalia, including the introduction of a human rights culture. The withdrawal of the mission in disgrace undermined the attempts that had been under way to build alternative structures of legitimacy on the basis of local tradition. It may be reasonably argued that Somali society is peculiarly unsuitable as a testing ground for international intervention aimed at the local empowerment of disenfranchised populations. But the operation was the source of several lessons concerning the management of UN operations—for example, the need for decisiveness and steadiness in response to challenges to UN mandates and for long-term staying power and commitment to operations once they have been established.

It remains to be seen whether these lessons have been learned. Since the Somali episode, there has been a second wave of African peacekeeping operations in Congo/Zaire and Central African Republic. The fact that these missions are being conducted on the basis of a very limited agreement by the parties to a civil conflict, have restricted mandates, and are severely limited in the tools and resources at their disposal must lead to some skepticism in this respect.

Divided States

In some conflicts, one ethnic group struggles against another to ensure exclusive control over the state. These conflicts are not secessionist. There is no plan for ethnic territories or groups to leave the state; instead, an ethnic group seeks to dominate the entire state under its control.

Rwanda had been under the domination of its Hutu majority when a force of the Tutsi-led Rwandese Patriotic Front (RPF) infiltrated the territory from Uganda with the aim of overthrowing the government. After Uganda gave assurances against intervention stemming from its territory, a small UN monitoring mission, United Nations Observer Mission Uganda-Rwanda (UNOMUR), was dispatched in 1993. In the meantime, the government and the RPF had managed to conclude the Arusha peace agreement, providing for a cessation of hostility, integration of armed forces, the establishment of a power-sharing interim government, followed by the holding of internationally monitored elections. There was also provision for a civil police contingent to help and to ensure a secure environment for all segments of the population. However, from the beginning, the security situation remained fraught. The interim government was also not installed, mainly due to obstruction from the incumbent Hutu head of state. His death on April 6, 1994, along with the death of the president of Burundi in an aircraft crash, was followed by an orchestrated campaign by the still Hutu-dominated government and local militias to exterminate the Tutsi population. In all, it is estimated that some eight hundred thousand Tutsi civilians were victims of this genocide. The Belgian contingent of United Nations Assistance Mission for Rwanda (UNAMIR) was withdrawn at that moment, reducing the UN presence to approximately 1,500 personnel. The UN Security Council decided to withdraw even that presence, with the exception of a small core mission of 270 to continue monitoring developments and seek to establish a cease-fire. During the ensuing chaos, no such cease-fire was possible. Efforts to intervene with an expanded UN force were frustrated in the Security Council. Only when the Hutu government appeared to fall to the advance of the RPF rebels was a French-led coalition operation launched under Chapter VII authority.

Operation Turquoise did not prevent the establishment of effective control by the RPF throughout the territory. UNAMIR was then expanded again, to assist in stabilizing the situation, support the new Tutsi-led but broad-based government in its efforts to achieve reconciliation, provide human rights support, and help establish accountability for the genocide. In the vast majority of cases, justice was pursued through local courts and in a small number of instances through an international tribunal created under Chapter VII authority. Despite the reopening of the National Assembly, the situation remained tense, mainly due to the presence of 1.5 million Hutu refugees in neighboring Zaire, purportedly under the control of members of the former Rwandan regime who were reported to be rearming. A UN Chapter VII mission to take control over these camps was long delayed. Canada agreed to lead a coalition-type operation but in the end was not deployed.

In Rwanda itself, a Human Rights Field Operation of some one hundred personnel was dispatched to assist in reconstructing the judiciary and implant a human rights culture in the new administration. The Rwandan government sought to limit progressively the role of the UN in the territory, leading to a drawing down of the military component, and later even of the civil police element, and to an emphasis on reconstruction, reconciliation, and development. Throughout, the safe return of refugees remained a priority. The mission ended in March 1996.

The initial failure of the Arusha peace process can be partially attributed to the unwillingness of the parties to settle. But the international community also failed to establish a complex peacekeeping mission that could have supported the peace process more vigorously. It was too small, its mandate too weak, and its leadership was neither willing nor able to press the parties into compliance with their own undertakings at critical junctures. There was also no significant involvement by the great powers that might have assisted in maintaining security. Instead, there was rivalry among certain states with interests in the area.

The failure of the mission to prevent the Rwandan genocide stemmed from the failure of the Security Council to change the mandate of UNAMIR from a Chapter VI to a Chapter VII operation and to boost its capacity. Senior members of the mission insist that they could have managed to prevent some of the outrages until a larger mission could have been established.

However, the reluctance of force contributing states, and even of states unwilling to contribute forces (e.g., the United States) to permit the enlargement of the UN mandate and mission in the wake of the Somalia disaster, was crucial. In any event, the international effort to reintegrate Rwandan society failed.

A more successful effort was made in eastern Slavonia, which was placed under a mixture of international administration and complex peacekeeping after Croatia obtained the means to forcibly reincorporate it. Croatia had already incorporated Krajina in 1995 by displacing the occupying Serbs. Toward the end of the year, Croatia concluded an agreement providing for the internationalized reintroduction of Croatian authority into eastern Slavonia. This was to be done in a way that would facilitate the return of ethnic Croatians without at the same time pressuring the ethnic Serb population to flee. The UN established a competent international mission, which took control over some aspects of civil administration and instituted a reform of the police system, to ensure an ethnic balance and to introduce a human rights culture. It also facilitated the gradual introduction of Croatian law in the territory and facilitated the eventual handover to full Croat administrative authority. Assurances were obtained from the Croatian government that human and minority rights would be applied to the territory, as elsewhere in Croatia, including a limited measure of cultural autonomy.

On the admittedly contestable assumption that the Dayton accords and Security Council Resolution 1244 have settled the self-determination crises of Bosnia and Herzegovina and Kosovo, respectively, at least for the time being, one might also consider them as examples of international attempts to impose human rights standards and democratic governance on divided states. In Bosnia and Herzegovina, ethnic division and politics are essentially written into the internationally drafted constitution. While a Chapter VII mandate exists, the state is not formally under international administration. A NATO-led force maintains security. Under the authority of a Peace Implementation Council of powerful and interested states, a high representative supports governance in the territory, although it was never intended that he should take over the functions of governance. A whole host of other implementation agencies, including a UN mission, are contributing to reconstruction and reintegration of society. There is an internationalized human rights monitoring system, including an international ombudsman and a Human Rights Chamber (Court).

The very wide-ranging international human rights guarantees in the Dayton accords mirror Western European standards and in some respects even exceed them. Particular attention is paid to the rights of ethnic groups and the right of return of the displaced. The mission charged with the implementation of the Dayton accords has managed to establish many of the institutions stipulated in the accords, including human rights monitoring and implementation. However, given the reality of "ethnic democracy" on the ground, the value of these provisions has been significantly undermined, and it has not always been possible to fill these provisions with life. While there is some evidence of progress in human rights–relevant areas, the structure of the Dayton accords and the approach to their implementation have contributed to a situation where ethnic division is becoming politically entrenched. The reason is that the accords only paper over the fact that the underlying tension that created the crisis and confrontation in the first place had not been addressed. This case, therefore, is one of a political solution imposed on the parties rather than supported by them. For the moment, it remains viable only for as long as it is internationally enforced.

Unhappily, the hope that the model of human rights and interethnic governance will gradually take hold and that the concerns of "real" life will generate a commitment to a multiethnic democracy appears optimistic. The efforts to make the Dayton political structure work by giving the ethnic parties incentives to cooperate in interest-led politics have thus far not fallen on fertile ground. Instead, the international high representative has been forced to exercise his supreme powers with considerable vigor, almost turning this into a case of international administration. For example, on occasions he has removed from public office anyone who engages in unhelpful ethnic politics, thus in a way disenfranchising the population the UN mission is intended to serve. The problem is, of course, that many of these politicians unfortunately enjoy a popular mandate. Nevertheless, developments in Bosnia and Herzegovina have been less discouraging than might have been expected. Military confrontation has ended, the security situation for the population has improved vastly and there is a sense of normalcy and reconciliation that is emerging in several areas.

By contrast, Kosovo was placed under direct UN administration with a Chapter VII mandate. The UN is charged with developing a system of wide-ranging self-governance. The OSCE is active in relation to democratization and the European Union (EU) exercises authority in relation to reconstruction and development. Significant efforts have been made to introduce a human rights culture into the new institutions, including the Kosovo police, the newly established judicial system that functions under international supervision, and the institutions of administration that are now being increasingly taken over by local politicians. Elections late in 2001 resulted in a power-sharing government involving all of the major ethnic Albanian parties and also those elements of the ethnic Serb community willing to cooperate. While great care was taken to ensure full and adequate representation of minority communities at all levels of governance, no firm blocking powers for ethnic communities have been introduced into the constitutional framework that was promulgated by the UN administration early in 2001.

This lesson was also applied in Macedonia by both the United States and the European Union. During the 1990s, a small UN preventative mission had been deployed to deter ethnic conflict between the majority Slav population, the sizeable community of ethnic Albanians, and several small minorities. There had always been concern that Albanians in Macedonia might attempt to secede in order to create a greater Albania. Fortunately, the local ethnic Albanian leadership had consistently limited itself to claiming full equality for its population within Macedonia. Even during the dramatic refugee crisis of the 1999 Kosovo conflict, leading to a vast and sudden influx of ethnic Albanians, the situation had maintained reasonably stable. However, at the start of 2001, an ethnic insurgency was mounted from areas close to the Kosovo border. This rapidly led to a polarization of Macedonian society.

The Macedonian government was very reluctant to admit to international intervention, even when ethnic Albanian armed formations gained ground. It argued that it was in the process of making sufficient provision for the protection of Albanian rights in its own legislation. The Albanians, on the other hand, objected to the fact that the Macedonian constitution defined the state as an ethnic state of Slavo Macedonians, that there was insufficient provision for Albanian language and education, and that there was a lack of equal economic opportunity.

On August 13, 2001 a framework agreement was concluded, addressing all of these points. It was achieved through mediation by the EU, although a breakthrough only became possible when the United States became directly engaged. The implementation of the agreement in its military provisions provided for a withdrawal of ethnic Albanian insurgents, their disarming within a short period of time, and the gradual reintroduction of Macedonian government police into areas of conflict. It was supported by a limited NATO-led force acting under a UN mandate. Provision was also made for an amnesty for Albanian fighters. Modest power sharing was introduced in the political institutions of the state, and provision made for equitable minority representation in the civil service, the judiciary, and the police. Limited powers of local self-government (territorial autonomy in disguise) were provided for. In addition, minority rights addressing language use and education are to be enshrined in legislation.

The agreement is unique, inasmuch as the ethnic Albanian community was represented in the central government throughout. It was signed by the parties in this government of national unity, created under international pressure when the conflict broke out, rather than by a government and an armed opposition. The agreement succeeded in its initial phases. The insurgency was terminated, at least for the moment. A sense of normality returned. The constitutional changes required by the framework agreement were made and other implementing legislation drafted. Because of the sensitivity of the representatives of the majority community, no significant international civil implementation was attached. Nevertheless, the EU and the OSCE have gradually and informally increased their support for reintegration in the country, although this fact may itself create problems for the future.

In Macedonia, great power intervention did succeed in arresting ethnic conflict before it took a firm grip on the country. The settlement is modest and cleverly constructed. If implemented, it may satisfy the concerns of the ethnic Albanian community, without turning Macedonia into a constitutionally divided ethnic state, along the lines of the unhappy Bosnian experiment—unhappy, that is, from a liberal point of view.

Threatened States

The international community has attempted to redress secessionist conflicts on several occasions. In the early case in the Congo, for instance, the United Nations actually militarily defeated the Katanga secession.[3] The UN peacekeeping mission then supported attempts of restoring a Congo-wide administration based on the preexisting constitutional structure. In relation to Biafra, the UN did not take action until the Nigerian armed forces had defeated the secessionist forces. A United Nations presence was introduced to provide humanitarian assistance in the wake of the reintroduction of Nigerian forces into the territory.

In the case of the former Yugoslavia—the first post–Cold War challenge of the kind—initial attempts at international crisis management also focused on the retention of the territorial integrity of the Socialist Federal Republic. When this appeared fruitless, it was hoped that the territorial integrity of the constituent republics could be maintained through international action. The intention was to achieve the orderly dissolution of the former Yugoslavia through the consent of the parties.[4] According to this strategy, ethnopolitical conflict resulting from the establishment of new boundaries and the consequent creation of new minorities was to be managed through a detailed human rights regime. This was coupled with less precise proposals for territorial autonomy, principally intended for areas mainly inhabited by Serbs that would in the future lie outside the rump Yugoslavia.

Before the strategy could take hold, Yugoslav armed forces occupied approximately a third of Croatian territory, including areas mainly but not solely inhabited by ethnic Serbs. The United Nations established a regime of so-called UN protected areas. While the UN was present under a Chapter VI peacekeeping mandate in these areas, it failed to prevent the continued ethnic cleansing committed by Yugoslav and Serb forces. Thus, an ethnically pure Serb entity was established, which claimed independence and agitated for incorporation with Serbia proper. The fact that the UN presence had left the local non-Serb population without any protection, in spite of the human rights provisions contained in the concept of operations for their deployment, considerably lessened international opposition when Croatia forcibly reincorporated these territories some three years later. The credibility of the UN as an agency, which can introduce human rights into at times violent discourse about secession, was inevitably severely dented.

After Croatia had recaptured the territory, it proved resistant to international attempts to protect the human rights of its remaining Serb population. Once again, the UN became associated with the failure to insist on the application of human rights principles, this time in relation to the exodus of most Serbs who had traditionally inhabited that area. Again, UN credibility was undermined to an extent that a far more positive example also concerning Croatia that was noted earlier (eastern Slavonia) is often overlooked.

Bosnia and Herzegovina was also the site of a sustained secessionist campaign aimed at the establishment of an ethnically pure Serb entity, which claimed independence and ultimate integration with Serbia. The Republica Srpska, was at one time established in over half of Bosnian territory through armed action by Yugoslav and local Serb military and paramilitary forces. A campaign of terror, arbitrary arrest, killing, and deportation was mounted over some three years against the mainly Muslim population. Other areas not yet captured and containing large concentrations of civilian populations, including the displaced, were subjected to humanitarian blockades and sustained military attack. In all, about two hundred thousand civilians, mainly non-Serbs, are said to have perished, and some two million were displaced.

Throughout, the United Nations maintained an international peacekeeping force with some enforcement powers in the territory. Its ineffectiveness in preventing a probable genocide while pretending to protect fundamental human values—symbolized by the fall of the so-called UN safe area of Srebrenica and the consequent slaughter—once again severely undermined the credibility of UN attempts to address ethnopolitical violence and secessionist conflicts.

Toward the end of 1995, NATO armed action and joint Bosnia government and Croat military operations brought the carnage to a provisional end, culminating in the Dayton peace agreements. A NATO-led implementation and stabilization force was established under a very wide Chapter VII UN mandate. As was noted earlier, the mission has been effective in imposing a cease-fire and the cantonment of armaments on the parties. However, the result of having created a very weak central state, which is ethnically divided, is proving very difficult to overcome. Hence, it is not entirely certain that the secessionist impetus has been curbed. In fact, in 2001, the Croat Bosnian entity within the Bosnian Federation sought to withdraw from the state.

Several attempts were made to contain the momentum toward Kosovo independence. These included the deployment of a brief OSCE long-term monitoring mission in the territory, the negotiation under the threat of force of an OSCE verification mission of several thousand unarmed observers to be deployed in the territory, and the attempt to obtain an autonomy or interim agreement between the parties through shuttle diplomacy and, finally, the proximity talks at Rambouillet in February 1999. The proposals that emerged from Rambouillet provided for a multilayered system of power sharing that would have been very difficult to implement. They also included substantive human rights guarantees, plus very wide functional autonomy for minority populations. Had the agreements been implemented, much reliance would have had to be placed on enforcement that was to be provided through a substantial UN-mandated, NATO-led force because of their complexity and the reluctance of both parties readily to embrace them. Once again, this would have been an international attempt to impose a solution, to which neither side would have been actually committed. In the end, an interim solution was imposed on the parties by force, providing for internationalized self-governance of the territory until such time as its final status can be settled. Hence, the underlying self-determination dispute has not yet been addressed.

The situation was different in relation to East Timor. Indonesia consented to the holding of a referendum on independence in that territory, being aware that the majority of the indigenous population would opt for separation. Once that outcome had been achieved in August 1999, governmental forces and affiliated militias in the territory engaged in a campaign of terrorization of the population. This triggered the establishment of a UN interim administration, charged with providing security and establishing an administration and the development of civil and social services. It was also charged with the administration of justice and with assisting in developing a sustainable capacity for self-government. This process, while fraught with difficulties and also hampered by managerial limitations on the part of the UN mission, was concluded with the holding of free and fair elections, allowing it to assume its independence after a period of interim UN administration.

An attempt was also made to address one of the few remaining cases of colonial self-determination through international action in Western Sahara. In 1988, it was finally agreed to settle the status of the territory through a referendum. A UN Chapter VI mission was established in 1991 to monitor a cease-fire, verify the reduction of Moroccan troops in the territory and the cantonment of other forces, and register voters for a referendum to be conducted by the UN. However, the work of the mission has been obstructed over the issue of registration of those entitled to participate in the referendum. Hence, it may be said that Morocco, the state exercising effective control over the territory, may have consented to a settlement assuming that it would be able to control the outcome through a manipulation of the registration process. Once that outcome was threatened, attempts have been made to inhibit the process until control over it can be removed from the UN mission. A genuine agreement on a truly international administration of the act of self-determination may therefore not have existed from the outset.

Other secessionist conflicts have been addressed with hesitant attempts to achieve stabilization through limited peacekeeping. For example, the situation in the secessionist Georgian entity of Abkhazia has been subjected to a UN monitoring mission, following agreements on a cease-fire of 1993–1994. In fact, the maintenance of the cessation of hostilities and also of the political status quo of de facto self-administration has been mainly assured by a CIS peacekeeping force with a large Russian contingent. The UN mission is principally devoted to observing the performance of that mission, given the risk of partiality in this matter on the part of the CIS forces. In addition to its military observation task, there is a UN human rights office affiliated with the mission. The 1994 agreement envisaged the negotiation of a political settlement on the basis of autonomy and power sharing for Abkhasia. However, little progress has been made in this respect, and the UN mission has therefore not been able to expand its mandate into civilian support for the reconstruction of civil authority within an agreed framework.

The international sensitivity of cases of secession is also exhibited in relation to the Somalia crisis. Although Somaliland has administered itself like an independent state over much of the past decade, the various United Nations missions have had difficulties in engaging its authorities. Care was taken to conduct such contacts through the UN structure for Somalia as a whole, and such contacts, and UN assistance, have been quite limited. Nevertheless, Somaliland has managed to provide one of the few rays of hope in Somalia, managing to provide security for its population and a modicum of economic stability.

CONCLUSION

This chapter has demonstrated that the picture regarding international attempts to reconstruct civil society in states in crisis is far less bleak than might have been expected. The large majority of missions were successful in terms of the criterion established earlier—that is, the restoration of governance on the basis of the will of the governed. It is not even possible to argue that certain types of conflicts can be addressed through internationalized state building while others cannot.

In relation to weak states, it was possible in most instances to restore a constitutional consensus. In particular, good results were obtained in cases of weak states that have emerged from a period of civil unrest and that are "ripe" for a transition. This applied especially to conflicts that had been fueled by Cold War competition. In most of these cases, the protagonists were tired of strife, their constituents were attracted by the benefits of life in an ordinary civil society, and, most important, their resource base was threatened. Under these circumstances, international actors developed a complex and sophisticated system of stabilizing the situation. It generally followed an attempt to reestablish civil society through an act of popular will, mainly in generating and approving a new constitution, accompanied by internationally managed or monitored elections. Transitional authority was exercised with international support and at times international involvement. On this basis, the evidence suggests that it is possible to evolve a new, human rights–based societal consensus. A process of national reconciliation through truth commissions or the administration of justice with international involvement can play a key role in consolidating the move from transition to stable system.

The record is marred in relation to cases in which one or more of the factions previously involved in the conflict are in danger of losing power altogether as a result of an exercise of popular will, and/or where one or more factions retain independent access to resources that permit them to sustain themselves outside the re-created state structure (Angola, Sierra Leone). Similarly, and unsurprisingly, the record of UN action is bleak where it intervenes in the absence of a consensus among the parties on the need to renew a particular society and the concrete shape of a new constitutional structure. It has rarely been possible to transform an emergency humanitarian operation into an operation that supports a long-term political transition under those circumstances.

The record in relation to divided states is also far less negative than might be expected. Where the ethnic power struggle has in some sense been decided and a dominant group has emerged (Rwanda after the victory of the RPF, Croatia after Operation Storm), international involvement can assist in protecting at least the human rights of the nondominant groups. However, from a number of other more recent instances, it appears that even ongoing ethnic conflict can be arrested. In this context, it is particularly interesting to see how lessons have been learned in the international management of ethnic division, from the initial disasters of Rwanda and Bosnia and Herzegovina to the far more advanced Macedonian settlement. The example of Macedonia also gives rise to the hope that it is possible, through international action and the encouragement of interethnic collaboration on the basis of an established human rights culture, to prevent the need to arise for a violent test of who is the dominant group in a particular state.

Threatened states also have been addressed effectively. This is, of course, most easily possible where the underlying self-determination dispute has been addressed (East Timor). On the other hand, where such an agreement may have been reached nominally but not in fact, no progress has been possible (Western Sahara). The attempts to impose a definite (Dayton) or an interim settlement (Kosovo) began amid widespread pessimism. However, some recent developments give cause to cautious optimism that the settlements can be sustained over some time. Whether they will persist when the considerable investment in international implementation wanes, or when the underlying self-determination conflict is being rekindled, is a more difficult matter.

Where difficulties have occurred, especially in relation to internal power struggles, the occasional lack of success is not due to the inability ever to address such situations. Instead, there exist managerial failings and a lack of decisiveness and investment in the necessary resources and in a lack of staying power of the international agencies involved. Given that success in these cases will tend to be obstructed by quite small elites that dominate segments of society through intimidation and violence, one might also argue that operations of this kind have not really been attempted yet. That is, if such projects are to be undertaken in the future, they will require a long-term commitment of resources and skills to the task of seeking to empower populations at present denied a participation in governance.

In terms of managerial issues, some of the apparently obvious conclusions one might reach are in fact not borne out by the analysis. A Chapter VII mandate, for instance, is not always necessary for success. In fact, it remains the rare exception, mostly associated with imposed settlements. Generally, the quality of the initial agreement of the protagonists to settle is a crucial ingredient of success. However, even defects in the commitment of the one or the other party can be overcome. To this end, it is necessary to fully engage all parties throughout the implementation process, rather than relying just on some. Steps must be taken to isolate recalcitrant groups from sources of funding and international support, and it is often very helpful to accompany UN mediation with the involvement of a contact group of states that may find it easier to bring pressure or incentives to bear on the party in question.

One of the more obvious findings of this review is that the quality of missions and outcomes depends very much on the quality of the resources and operations. Limited peacekeeping missions focusing mainly on security that have only addressed the underlying social tensions in an incidental way will also generally have only yielded limited effect. However, where the full toolbox of measures—from the restoration of a constitutional consensus, to the rebuilding of civil administrative structures, the establishment of a reliable police force, support for an independent judiciary, to the introduction of strong human rights–building element and accountability mechanisms—has been applied, results tend to be impressive. This is often done to best effect with the involvement of a significant range of specialist agencies going beyond the immediate UN family. Finally, the issue of economic reconstruction is to be considered. This element is altogether too often overlooked but crucial for the longer-term sustainability of a settlement.

Overall, therefore, we have some cause for optimism in relation to international operations aiming to stabilize weak, divided, and threatened states. However, if the record of the next fifty years of practice in this respect is to be even more positive, it will be necessary to recall that success is a matter of long-term commitment and the considerable investment of resources in stabilization measures. The question is whether the international community is willing to make such an investment.

NOTES

1. United Nations Aouzou Strip Observer Group (UNASOG) in Chad/Libya, United Nations Good Offices in Afghanistan and Pakistan (UNGOMAP) in Afghanistan, United Nations Mission of Observers in Tajikistan (UNMOT) in Tajikistan, United Nations Iran–Iraq Military Observer Group (UNIIMOG) in Iraq/Kuwait, United Nations Mission in Ethiopia/Eritrea (UNMEE) in Ethiopia/Eritrea, UNOMUR concerning Uganda and Rwanda, United Nations Mission of Observers in Prevlaka (UNMOP) in Croatia, and the United Nations Observer Mission in Georgia (UNOMIG) monitoring mission in Georgia, although, as we shall see, this operation also has a stabilization element.

2. One may perhaps also consider the UN-mandated operation in Bosnia and Herzegovina under this heading, as it is guided not by the United Nations but by a Peace Implementation Council. But the authority of this council was established through the Dayton agreements by the parties and has been confirmed by the UN Security Council.

3. This was presented as an accident at the time, due to a loss of communications between the UN forces in the field and UN headquarters.

4. This took the shape of the Carrington peace conference, which attempted to persuade the parties to agree to a treaty providing for the possibility of independence for those federal republics wishing it and regulating its modalities.

7

Enforcing Human Rights

Nicholas J. Wheeler

Securing compliance with global humanitarian norms is one of the key challenges facing the society of states in the next fifty years. The litany of atrocities perpetuated by gangster states in the 1990s and the violence inflicted on civilians as a consequence of the collapse of order in Africa's "failed states" bears powerful testimony to the continuing failure of international society to live up to its humanitarian standards. This gap between normative standards and moral practices is not new since it was a persistent feature of the international response to genocide and mass murder during the Cold War. But what makes the failure to defend human rights in the 1990s so depressing is that the end of the Cold War seemed to hold out the promise of a new era of human rights enforcement.

Consequently, the question that has to be asked is whether the story of recurrence and repetition that characterizes the international response to the "loud emergencies" of genocide, mass murder, and ethnic cleansing in the 1990s supports the claims of those who argue that the society of states is incapable of developing a collective capacity for human rights enforcement. Two voices can be heard arguing this case. First is realism, which is suspicious of governments that claim the humanitarian mantle and believes that geopolitical interests will always trump considerations of common humanity. Realism believes that state leaders have a primary ethic of responsibility to protect the national community and that while this does not rule out moral action in foreign policy, these are always subject to this overriding ethic of responsibility.

Second, pluralist international society theory (hereafter referred to as *pluralism*) believes that while states can agree on the need for order despite their onflicting conceptions of justice, any attempt to promote human rights will be subversive of that order. Although individual thinkers will straddle both categories of thought, pluralism should be differentiated from realism on the following grounds. Pluralism is committed to the idea that states recognize the existence of binding legal obligations and that these authoritative rules function to mitigate the exercise of brute power in the society of states. By contrast, realism sees rules as instrumental maxims that are only followed out of calculations of self-interest. States might adopt more enlightened conceptions of their interests as in regime theory, but their identities as rational egoists constitute the limits of interaction. Set against this, pluralism argues that state identities and interests are bound up in their membership of international society. The ethic of responsibility that guides pluralism is the construction of a set of common rules that establish a legitimate international order built on the moral principle of coexistence.

The pluralist commitment to an ethic of toleration between states reflects skepticism that states will prove capable of reaching a consensus on universal values. It follows from this that pluralism is deeply suspicious of states that set themselves up as guardians of the world common good. The worry is that Western states will employ the rhetoric of universal human rights to trespass over the principle of nonintervention in the internal affairs of states and that this will lead to a collapse of the pillars of interstate order. Such concerns would be ameliorated if there were great power consensus on humanitarian intervention, but as I show later in the chapter, contemporary pluralists oppose a doctrine of human rights intervention because this undermines order among the great powers. The moral consequences of standing aside when another government massacres its citizens has to be set against the moral consequences of unilateral action that jeopardizes great power stability and the UN Charter's fragile restraints against the use of force: the cure might be worse than the disease.

The failure of governments to act as humanitarian law enforcers is purported to demonstrate the power of realist and pluralist values in constituting the boundaries of legitimate state action. However, there is another voice in the conversation that looks to the possibilities of placing the enforcement of human rights at the center of foreign policy decision making and challenges both realism and pluralism. This is the solidarist conception of the society of states, which is predicated in Hedley Bull's words on the "solidarity, or potential solidarity of the states comprising international society with respect to the enforcement of the law."[1] Bull's traditional formulation of solidarism embraced both collective security and humanitarian intervention, but this chapter will restrict itself to the latter. It seeks to advance the solidarist project by highlighting the normative limitations of realism and pluralism and by exploring how far a foreign policy committed to the defense of human rights can reconcile the requirements of both order and justice.

It is necessary at this point to clarify how I am using the concept of enforcement. International lawyers who employ this terminology think in terms of international legal instruments that set standards and establish mechanisms for monitoring state compliance with the 1966 International Covenant on Civil and Political Rights (ICCPR) and the International Covenant on Economic, Social, and Cultural Rights (ICESCR). The key bodies here at the global level are the UN's Human Rights Committee and the UN's Commission on Human Rights. At the regional level, there are human rights instruments set up by the Organization of American States (OAS) and the Organization of African Unity (OAU, now the African Union), but the most effective and legitimate regional arrangement is the European Court of Human Rights. A crucial component in this process of holding governments accountable is the role played by the plethora of nongovernmental organizations (NGOs) like Amnesty International and Human Rights Watch. Based on their extensive networks in target states, these organizations are able to provide valuable information to the UN monitoring system about cases of human rights violations, and through persistent lobbying and the power of "naming and shaming," they are often effective in persuading governments to honor their commitments. However, when I talk about enforcement in this chapter, the reference is not to the modalities of global standard setting and compliance; rather, the focus is on the capacity of states and international organizations to employ a range of punitive sanctions against governments that grossly violate human rights.

The second qualification concerns the type of human rights abuses that are being discussed here. The failure of governments and transnational corporations to live up to the social and economic provisions of the 1966 covenants and the 1948 Universal Declaration of Human Rights poses profound challenges to the global human rights regime. But these rights cannot be defended through the use of coercive sanctions. Rather, ending these violations raises uncomfortable questions about the character of global capitalism and the growing inequalities between the global rich and poor that go beyond the scope of this chapter. The focus of this chapter is on the prospects for creating an effective capacity for human rights enforcement in cases in which governments, or other political entities, use force to repress the human rights of ethnic or political groups within the state.

The argument proceeds in four stages. First, I set up a solidarist theory of human rights enforcement that challenges realist and pluralist values. Having established the theoretical framework that will guide the subsequent investigation, the chapter explores how far solidarist values can be translated into effective foreign policy action. Here, I examine the following questions: the significance of the end of the Cold War in changing the possibilities for human rights enforcement; the problem of the selective character of humanitarian intervention; the role of economic sanctions in protecting human rights; and, finally, the question of whether force can ever be a servant of humanitarian ends. With regard to the latter, the chapter sets up some principles or guidelines for judging a legitimate humanitarian intervention, and these are then used to assess the humanitarian credentials of NATO's intervention in Kosovo.

A SOLIDARIST THEORY OF
HUMAN RIGHTS ENFORCEMENT

Realism is predicated on a particular conception of the relationship between citizens and strangers that privileges what Robert H. Jackson calls an ethic of "national responsibility."[2] States are permitted to promote moral values in foreign policy, but this permission is heavily circumscribed. Even if an action can be justified on the grounds that it saves fellow humans, it must be ruled out if it threatens vital security interests. This begs the question as to what is to count as a vital interest. Avoiding war clearly meets this category, but what about the economic costs incurred as a result of not selling arms to a government engaging in gross human rights abuses? Is a state leader failing in moral duty to protect the security of the national community if whatever actions are taken lead to some fellow nationals being made unemployed? The harder case concerns whether states should risk their soldiers' lives to save other humans in danger. Many realists would agree with Samuel P. Huntington's criticism of the U.S. intervention in Somalia when he writes, "[I]t is morally unjustifiable and politically indefensible that members of the armed forces should be killed to prevent Somalis from killing one another."[3] Pushed to its logical extreme, this position rules out risking one American life even if this could save millions of nonnationals. While few realists would endorse such a strong claim, the problem is how many of our "boys and girls" are we prepared to risk to stop cruelty and suffering?

Solidarism challenges this realist conception of ethical statecraft by arguing that humanitarian intervention is a moral duty. Solidarism agrees with realism that state leaders have a primary responsibility to protect the security and well-being of their citizens, but it parts company with it on the question of whether this obligation exhausts obligations to noncitizens. The debate within solidarism is over the nature and character of these obligations. States committed to human rights principles—"good international citizens"[4]—are not required to sacrifice vital interests in defense of human rights, but they are required to forsake narrow commercial and political advantage when these conflict with the protection of human rights. A solidarist ethic requires governments to refrain from selling arms to repressive regimes, even if this creates unemployment at home, and to rigorously enforce sanctions against gross violators, even if this leads to the loss of lucrative contracts. Given these criteria, the Blair government clearly failed this test in selling Hawk aircraft to the Indonesian regime in 1997–1999 while it was brutally repressing the human rights of the East Timorese resistance movement.[5]

The hard question is whether solidarism permits state leaders to risk and lose soldiers' lives. The solidarist battle cry that state leaders "are burdened with the guardianship of human rights everywhere"[6] begs the question as to how this duty should be balanced against their responsibility to protect the lives of citizens, including those who serve in the armed force. The argument defended here is that soldiers' lives should be risked in cases of what I call "supreme humanitarian emergency." This argument borrows from Michael Walzer's notion of "supreme emergency" in *Just and Unjust Wars* and applies it to the moral choices facing state leaders in decisions on humanitarian intervention. Walzer's book is a powerful defense of the principle of noncombatant immunity in the just war tradition. But having built up the argument as to why war cannot escape moral discourse, he argues in chapter 16 that situations arise where the survival of the state requires leaders to violate the prohibition against the deliberate killing of civilians. A supreme emergency exists when the danger is so imminent, the character of the threat so horrifying, and when there is no other option available to assure the survival of a particular moral community than violating the rule against targeting civilians. He gives the example of British political and military leaders employing strategic bombing against German cities in 1940–1941 as the only defense against the evil of Nazism.[7]

Applying this framework to a solidarist theory of humanitarian intervention, the survival of our state is not on the line (and in that sense it is not a supreme emergency in the way it was for Britain in 1940), but it is a supreme emergency for those human beings facing genocide, mass murder, and ethnic cleansing. A supreme humanitarian emergency exists when civilians in another state are in imminent danger of losing their life or facing appalling hardship, and where the only hope of rescue is outside military intervention. It is important to distinguish between cases like Sierra Leone where substate actors perpetrate abuses and the government would like to act but is unable to do so, and cases like Kosovo where the source of the violations is the government itself.[8] What counts as a supreme emergency is open to interpretation, and naming a situation as an emergency will always be open to political manipulation, but it is also evident that some interpretations will be more persuasive than others. Justifying the use of force on humanitarian grounds requires persuading other governments, domestic publics, and the wider transnational citizenry committed to human rights that the scale of the human rights violations warrants military intervention.[9]

Western state leaders increasingly found themselves confronted with supreme emergencies in the 1990s, and when they did, they faced the ultimate choice between realist and solidarist conceptions of moral responsibility in statecraft. The latter demands that state leaders override their primary responsibility not to place citizens in danger and make the agonizing decision that saving the lives of civilians beyond their borders requires risking the lives of those who serve in the armed forces. This still leaves unanswered the appalling moral dilemma of what counts as unacceptable losses. As Hugh Beach puts it, "How many Dutch lives was it worth to protect Srebrinica?"[10] The bar is considerably higher for solidarism than realism, but how much higher? How many casualties are we prepared to accept to save *x* number of civilians being slaughtered by either their government or other armed groups within the state?

Even if it is agreed that there is a moral duty of humanitarian intervention in conditions of supreme humanitarian emergency, there is the pluralist objection that this will issue a license for unilateral intervention that will place in jeopardy the foundations of international order. The pluralist argument is predicated on the assumption that the society of states lacks a substantive value consensus on what level or type of human rights violations should trigger intervention and that in the absence of this, it is the powerful who will decide whether intervention is justified. Reflecting on the lack of support in state practice for a doctrine of humanitarian intervention during the Cold War, Bull encapsulates this pluralist argument:

> The reluctance evident in the international community even to experiment with the conception of a right of humanitarian intervention reflects not only an unwillingness to jeopardize the rules of sovereignty and non-intervention by conceding such a right to individual states, but also the lack of any agreed doctrine as to what human rights are.[11]

One standard objection to creating a legal right of humanitarian intervention is that states will abuse such a right by cloaking state interests in the garb of humanitarian rhetoric. However, Bull's pluralist objection is a different one: the argument is that since there is no consensus on the substantive values that would govern the exercise of such a right, this practice should remain outlawed by the society of states. Moreover, it is not the case that pluralism thinks that such a consensus should be sought since it is claimed that any attempt to create one will run into the fundamental difficulty that states hold very different understandings of the meaning and content of human rights.

It can be agreed with pluralism that enforcement action on humanitarian grounds will remain in the hands of the powerful without succumbing to the view that such actions must lead to an erosion of order. Enforcement action by individual states is unlikely to be disruptive of order if it has the authority of the UN Security Council behind it. A threat to order only arises when intervention is undertaken where the permanent members disagree on the merits of the action and where it threatens the vital security interests of one or more of these states.

Article 2(7) of the Charter bans the UN Security Council from intervening in matters that are "essentially within the domestic jurisdiction of any state," but this prohibition does not apply to matters that the Security Council determines under Article 39 of Chapter VII as posing a threat to "international peace and security." During the Cold War, the Council had refused to define human rights emergencies inside state borders as constituting a threat to international security, restricting this to cases of interstate aggression. This conception of the Council's policing role belongs to a pluralist ethic of coexistence. A solidarist ethic of humanitarian responsibility would interpret article 39 as permitting UN-authorized humanitarian intervention. As I show later, this solidarist ethic did not shape Security Council practice in the Cold War, but it has been increasingly evident since the end of the Cold War. Growing international pressure for effective UN action to stop gross and systematic human rights abuses led the Security Council to stretch the traditional meaning of a threat to "international peace and security" to legitimate international intervention in the internal conflicts in northern Iraq, Somalia, Bosnia, and Haiti. In the cases of Somalia, Bosnia, and Haiti, the Council delegated to UN member states its Chapter VII authority to use force to protect human rights.

Bull has defined solidarism in terms of the enforcement of the law, but this is too narrow a definition since the prior discussion illustrates that pluralism is compatible with Security Council enforcement action. What distinguishes pluralism from solidarism is not the capacity for enforcement action per se but the ethical position underpinning intervention. In the case of pluralism, enforcement action is only justified if it upholds international order and is sanctioned by the Security Council. By contrast, solidarism maintains that humanitarian intervention is valued as an *end* in itself, and there may be cases in which intervention is permissible even in the absence of UN authorization.

The problem with the UN Charter's ban on the use of force (except for purposes of self-defense and collective enforcement action under Chapter VII) is that it makes an intervention to end genocide dependent on prior Security Council approval. This issue was posed starkly over Kosovo because Russia and China made it clear that they would veto any draft resolution that sought authority for NATO to use force against the Federal Republic of Yugoslavia (hereafter Yugoslavia). NATO's decision to bypass the Council and justify its use of force on human rights grounds challenged the authority of core Charter principles. This prompted UN secretary-general Kofi Annan to invite the General Assembly to debate the legitimacy of humanitarian intervention in cases in which the Security Council was unwilling or unable to act (hereafter also referred to as unilateral humanitarian intervention).[12] In opening the debate, Kofi Annan posed the following hypothetical question to the General Assembly:

> If, in those dark days and hours leading up to the genocide [in Rwanda], a coalition of States had been prepared to act in defence of the Tutsi population, but did not receive prompt Council authorisation, should such a coalition have stood aside and allowed the horror to unfold?[13]

Annan did not answer this question, but a solidarist reply would be that a decision whether to intervene in cases of supreme humanitarian emergency cannot be hostage to the exercise of veto power in the Security Council. Consequently, the challenge is to devise rules or guidelines to cope with those exceptional cases in which the conscience of humanity cries out for intervention but the Council is blocked by the veto from acting. I will return to this question of how to legitimate unilateral humanitarian intervention when I discuss the case of Kosovo later in the chapter.

THE SIGNIFICANCE OF THE END OF THE COLD WAR FOR THE ENFORCEMENT OF HUMAN RIGHTS

Has the end of the Cold War transformed the possibilities for enforcing human rights in international society? To explore this question, I consider how far the international response to genocide and state sponsored slaughter changed in the 1990s, focusing on the cases of the "killing fields" in Cambodia in the 1970s and the Rwandan genocide in the 1990s.

The adversarial relationship between the United States and the Soviet Union ensured that when the stakes were high enough, local conflicts were always interpreted and played out in terms of their impact on the superpower competition. The people of Cambodia were one of the many peoples to suffer as a consequence of this geopolitical dynamic. Their fate demonstrates how the Cold War dynamic constrained humanitarian intervention. The story of the terrible brutalities inflicted on the Cambodian people by the Khmer Rouge, with up to two to three million people perishing between 1975 and 1979, has been told many times, and our interest lies in why it was that humanity abandoned the Cambodians to their fate. Realism tells us that Cambodia's misfortune was to find itself a pawn in the game of superpower politics. The Carter administration wanted to balance Soviet power in the region, fearful that Vietnam was acting as a Soviet proxy. This led the United States to align with China, which in turn was allied with the Pol Pot regime in Cambodia. The Carter administration was very uncomfortable with the gross human rights violations taking place inside Cambodia as news of these began to leak out of Cambodia in late 1977 and early 1978, but there was no question of the United States taking military or any other kind of action against Pol Pot.

Moreover, when the Vietnamese decided for their own security reasons to end the Pol Pot regime—saving the Cambodian people from the appalling excesses of the Khmer Rouge—the U.S. response was to condemn Vietnam's action. The fact that Cambodians had welcomed the intervention as a liberation was ignored by American policymakers who focused solely on what they perceived as growing Vietnamese and Soviet expansionism in the region. The U.S. position was supported by its European allies, China, and the regional states of the Association of Southeast Asian Nations (ASEAN), who were especially fearful of Vietnam's expansionist ambitions. Vietnam should not have been praised for its intervention since the humanitarian benefits were an inadvertent outcome of actions taken for nonhumanitarian reasons. But because its motives and the means employed were not incompatible with a positive humanitarian outcome, it should not have been condemned by wider international society.[14]

Realism will reply that the United States and China had no choice but to emphasize geopolitical imperatives because their security depended on containing Soviet power in Southeast Asia. Similarly, for states like Malaysia, Singapore, and especially Thailand, it was the fear of Vietnamese expansionism that dictated the response to the overthrow of the Pol Pot regime. The problem with this argument is that by treating Vietnam as a pariah, the Western bloc, China, and ASEAN only succeeded in pushing Hanoi even more into the arms of the Soviet Union. What is more, by continuing to economically and militarily support the Khmer Rouge's ongoing war against the new government in Phnom Penh, a chance was lost to pursue the alternative path of trying to persuade Vietnam that its long-term security would be enhanced if it accepted a neutralization of Cambodia. In short, the geopolitical justifications for opposing Vietnam are open to the charge that these were not only morally bankrupt but also myopic and self-defeating in terms of promoting regional security.

In arguing that Vietnam's action should have been excused because it ended the killing fields, there is the pluralist objection of order to consider. Had Vietnam's action been approved on the grounds that it rescued the Khmer people from the murderous clutches of Pol Pot, would this have set a precedent that could be used by the powerful to enforce their cultural and ideological values on weaker states? This brings us back to the question of whether humanitarian intervention can be legitimate if it lacks Security Council authorization. In the case of Vietnam's intervention in Cambodia, it is clear that had the government in Hanoi tried to secure a mandate from the Council, either this move would have failed to secure the necessary votes, or it would have been vetoed by the West and China.

If governments can plead that they were constrained by Cold War imperatives from intervening in Cambodia, then they have no such justification to explain their nonintervention in the Rwandan genocide. The end of the Cold War changed the context for humanitarian intervention in three key ways: first, the newfound cooperation between East and West transformed the possibilities for the Security Council to live up to its Charter responsibility of maintaining "international peace and security"; second, it appeared to eliminate the worry that intervention might lead to a superpower crisis risking nuclear war; and, finally, it left the United States as the global hegemonic power that, under the Clinton administration, professed a commitment to defend human rights around the world. Yet the notion that humanitarian values became elevated in the hierarchy of U.S. foreign policy principles in the 1990s runs immediately into the grim reality that it was the Clinton administration that decided to do nothing while over a million Rwandans were killed in the genocide that began in April 1994.

It can only be speculated how the Clinton administration would have reacted to events in Rwanda had this been the president's first African humanitarian crisis. As it was, the ghost of the eighteen Rangers lost in a Somali firefight in October 1993 haunted the U.S. government, with the president ruling out any options that placed American personnel in harm's way. In response to the Somali debacle and congressional concerns that the United States was acting as the world's police officer, the president signed Presidential Decision Directive (PDD) 25 that was made public at the beginning of May. This attempted to establish strict limits to American participation in future UN peacekeeping operations by stating that the United States would only contribute to operations where its national interests were engaged and that its soldiers would always remain under national command and control. Although several commentators have suggested that the Tutsis were the first to suffer the consequences of Clinton's PDD 25,[15] the document is sufficiently indeterminate to have been invoked by the administration to justify sending U.S. soldiers to Rwanda. As Oliver Ramsbotham and Tom Woodhouse point out, the directive states that it is in the U.S. national interest to support peace enforcement operations where "there is a threat to or breach of international peace and security . . . defined as one or a combination of the following: international aggression; or urgent humanitarian disaster coupled with violence . . . or gross violation of human rights coupled with violence; or threat of violence."[16]

Consequently, the Clinton administration could have defended military intervention in Rwanda in the first two weeks of April on the grounds that halting genocide was a moral duty and in the national interest. Unfortunately, the president—who on his trip to Rwanda four years later apologized for the international community's failure to save Rwanda—lacked the moral courage to take the lead in arguing the case at home that U.S. soldiers should be put at risk in defense of common humanity.

Despite the changed geopolitical context, realism has no difficulty in explaining why Rwanda was abandoned. The plain truth is that no Western state that had the military capability to make a difference cared enough about the fate of Africans in a faraway continent to risk their soldiers' lives to end the genocide. What is apparent is that the deployment in the early weeks of April 1994 of a multinational force of five to ten thousand well-armed soldiers could have significantly halted the killings. However, no Western state came forward with the offer of troops, and when African states volunteered to send forces to Rwanda in the period May to June, the United States failed to provide the necessary logistics to fly these forces into Kigali. The Clinton administration would not land heavy transports into Kigali without a prior cease-fire because it feared for the safety of U.S. air crew and ground controllers.

The barrier to intervention in Rwanda was not any doctrinal disagreement among members of the Security Council as to the priority to be accorded human rights over sovereign rights in the post–Cold War order. Instead, as UN secretary-general Kofi Annan acknowledged in his 1999 annual report, "[T]he failure to intervene was driven more by the reluctance of Member States to pay the human and other costs of intervention, and by doubts that the use of force would be successful, than by concerns about sovereignty."[17] The appalling failure of Western governments to end the killings in Rwanda demonstrates that even in a case in which there is good reason to think that the use of force would have been successful, with only limited casualties, Western leaders decided to privilege their responsibilities to protect citizens over the moral claims of other humans in danger.[18]

Had any state sought a Security Council mandate in April 1994 to end the genocide in Rwanda, there is little question that this mandate would have been forthcoming. The end of the Cold War created a context in which there is a "developing international norm" in support of UN authorized forcible humanitarian intervention. However, this emergent norm does not make humanitarian intervention a duty of individual states or the society of states. The development of a new norm enables new practices of intervention that were previously unthinkable, but this does not determine that intervention will take place when it is desperately needed as in Rwanda.

How to persuade state leaders that they have a moral responsibility to "pay the human" costs of intervention is the challenge for a solidarist theory of international society. The fact is that no Western government has intervened to defend human rights in the 1990s unless it has been confident that there was little risk of casualties. The implication of this is that state leaders will accept anything other than minimal casualties only if they believe vital national interests are at stake, and this means that practices of humanitarian intervention will always be subject to the vagaries of geopolitics.

THE POLITICS OF SELECTIVITY

The selectivity argument is the most popular reason advanced against humanitarian intervention. But while it unites realist and radical critics, these groups have very different perspectives on this question. For sophisticated realists like David Hendrickson, a selective approach to the application of human rights reflects the voice of prudence in foreign policy decision making. Reflecting on why more was not done to end the Turkish genocide against the Armenians in 1914, he considers that in the circumstances of World War I, "it is difficult to see what outside powers might have done." William Rubenstein echoes this conclusion in his persuasive study of how the Allied powers could not have done more to save Jews during World War II.[19] Realism reminds state leaders that acting as a force for good in the world must always be balanced by a recognition of the moral consequences of such actions.

At the other end of the spectrum is the claim of public intellectuals like Noam Chomsky that Western states are guilty of moral hypocrisy in their protestations of what he calls the "new military humanism."[20] The charge of double standards is a powerful one: Chomsky points to the blatant selectivity of U.S. military action to defend the human rights of the Kosovars with its deafening silence over Colombia and Turkey's gross violations of human rights. The explanation for these radically diverging responses to human rights abuses is that U.S. security and commercial interests dictate action in one case and inaction in the others. The belief that humanitarian claims on the part of the West are always a cover for the pursuit of selfish interests is one of the principal arguments advanced by Russia, China, and India against Western attempts to legitimate a doctrine of humanitarian intervention in international society. Therefore, any progress in reaching a consensus on the enforcement of human rights principles depends on addressing the problem of selectivity.

In thinking about the problem of selectivity, solidarism argues that a distinction should be made between actions that are selective because states privilege selfish interests and those that are selective because of prudential concerns. This does not resolve the problem because there will always be scope for debate over whether governments are acting prudently or selfishly in particular cases, but what matters is that this debate is a public one in which citizens can articulate their views and hold governments accountable for the decisions taken in their name. I argued earlier that the West should not have put Cold War imperatives prior to the human rights of the Cambodian people, but others would argue that prudence required U.S. decision makers to act in this way given the threat posed by the Soviet Union to U.S. security interests at the end of the 1970s.

A harder case than the Cambodian one is the question of how to deal with Turkey's use of force against Kurdish civilians living within its eastern borders and inside northern Iraq. Going well beyond Milošević's ethnic cleansing of the Kosovars in 1998–1999, it is reported by human rights groups inside and outside the country that the Turkish government has killed several thousand Kurdish civilians in its quest to wipe out the PKK, the guerrilla movement committed to Kurdish independence. Turkey denies deliberately killing civilians and invokes the justification of maintaining the territorial integrity of the state to legitimate its use of force against rebel forces. This is the same rationale as that employed by the Milošević regime and the Russian government to justify their respective attacks against the Kosovo Liberation Army (KLA) and separatist forces in Chechnya.

If solidarism requires that governments always pay a heavy price in diplomatic, political, and especially economic terms for gross violations of human rights, then Turkey's allies in NATO have failed this test by turning a blind eye to its human rights violations. Turkey continues to buy arms from its NATO partners, including the U.K. government, which conveniently overlooks the fact that Turkey breaches the guidelines for arms sales laid down by Foreign Secretary Robin Cook in July 1997. The case of Turkey illustrates the complex trade-off involved in trying to promote human rights in foreign policy. The paradox is that while Turkey is guilty of indiscriminately using force against Kurdish civilians, it is from Turkish bases that U.S. and British jets police the "no-fly" zone imposed by the latter over northern Iraq in the immediate aftermath of the 1991 Gulf War. This provides an important measure of protection for the Kurds against any attempt by Saddam Hussein to remove the limited de facto autonomy they gained as a consequence of the creation of the "safe havens" in April 1991. Putting pressure on Turkey to stop its campaign of violence might jeopardize these "basing" rights, and NATO strategists are well aware that Turkey would be vital as a logistic staging base in any future conflict with Iraq.

Turkey's pivotal geopolitical position in the Middle East and the lucrative market it offers for Western arms sales protect the Turkish government from serious international pressure. Trying to persuade the Turkish government to adopt a more restrained policy has clearly failed and it is arguably time for tougher measures. One step that should be taken is that NATO members should cease supplying the Turks with any military equipment that is tailored specifically for internal repression. This would be little more than a symbolic step since it would not stop Kurdish civilians being killed by indiscriminate Turkish air attacks against rebel bases. Turkey justifies its acquisition of strike aircraft on the grounds that this is a legitimate requirement of self-defense, but states committed to the principles of good international citizenship should not sell weapons to any government, which is committing gross human rights violations. Threatening to apply this principle to Turkey—or even applying it—would clearly create a major crisis in the alliance. Without the pressure of this sanction, it is hard to see what incentive Turkey has to moderate its use of force against the Kurdish guerillas. Employing the sanction of restricting arms sales to Turkey would not guarantee an improvement in the human rights situation, but it would address the charge of selectivity.

What is required is that like cases be treated alike. This does not mean taking the same action in every like case because prudence demands different responses in different situations. Western military intervention to end gross abuses of human rights is unthinkable in places like Chechnya and Tibet because it would risk war—including nuclear war—with Russia and China. The problem is that if these states are seen to be able to abuse human rights with impunity, then the dangerous signal is sent that the way to avoid becoming a target for humanitarian intervention is to develop weapons of mass destruction that will make the costs of military intervention prohibitive.

Solidarism requires that Russia's indiscriminate killing of civilians in Chechnya be treated as a violation of global humanitarian norms. However, what was striking about the Western response to Russia's action in 2000 was how muted it was compared to the position taken a year earlier over human rights abuses in Kosovo. With military intervention clearly ruled out, the world was left with only two sticks by which to alter the Russian government's behavior: diplomatic censure and economic sanctions. The decision by the Parliamentary Assembly of the Council of Europe in April 2000 to suspend Russia's membership was an attempt to signal to the Russian leadership that its use of force against civilians placed it outside the standards of European civility. This limited sanction failed to persuade the Russian political and military leadership to stop bombing the capital of Grozny, which was causing the exodus of hundreds of thousands of civilians. The fact that the Russian leadership was not inhibited by concerns about Russia's moral standing is further grist to the realist mill that states only respect international legal standards when it is convenient to do so.

Should Western governments have done more to enforce global humanitarian norms against Russia for its actions in Chechnya? The United States, and especially the U.K. government, decided that the best hope of protecting the Chechens lay in initiating a dialogue with the new Russian president Vladimir Putin. The latter visited the United Kingdom in April 2000 and after the sharp downturn in relations over Kosovo, the prime minister and foreign secretary were keen to improve relations. Tony Blair raised the subject of Chechnya with Putin at their meeting on April 17, and he defended the decision to invite the Russian leader to London in the following terms: "Some say that because of our concerns about Chechnya we should keep some distance from Moscow. I have to tell you that while I share those concerns I believe that the best way to register those concerns and get results is by engaging with Russia and not isolating Russia."[21] Set against this, there is no evidence that this attempt at dialogue had any significant impact on the ground in Chechnya. The Russian president rightly calculated that the United Kingdom and United States placed a good relationship with Russia ahead of concerns for the plight of the Chechens. Although Western states had little room for maneuver over Chechnya, did Blair's decision to invite Putin to London send the wrong signal to the Russian leadership? The decision certainly left the U.K. government open to the accusation that it was applying double standards in its treatment of governments that violate human rights. Peter Bouckaert of Human Rights Watch leveled this charge. He stated, "During Kosovo, Mr Cook said Europe could not stand by and watch atrocities being committed or it would be complicit. But that is exactly what he is doing with Chechnya."[22] Western governments never tried to make the case for imposing a tough sanction against the Putin government, and this perhaps reflected the fact that the only stick available was economic sanctions. As I discuss later, these achieved little in the 1990s in protecting human rights, and it is not surprising that the United States and United Kingdom were reluctant to select this instrument of coercion when it came to Chechnya.

ENFORCING HUMAN RIGHTS
THROUGH SANCTIONS

Utilizing economic sanctions as a means of defending international human rights standards poses two key problems. First, there is the question of whether it can ever be effective in changing the cost–gain calculations of the target government. Second, there are the ethical consequences of a strategy that is justified on humanitarian grounds but which might be likened to the contemporary equivalent of siege warfare.[23]

For sanctions to work the following conditions must be satisfied. First, a government must be heavily dependent on one or a number of commodities that can be cut off without alternative sources being found by the regime. Second, the sanctions must undermine the domestic legitimacy of the regime. Third, the costs imposed by sanctions must be sufficiently high that they outweigh the benefits that the regime gains from its repressive policy. Satisfying these conditions in practice has proved very difficult as the case of sanctions against the Milošević regime shows.

The UN Security Council imposed mandatory economic sanctions against Yugoslavia in the early 1990s. However, there is no evidence that this moderated Milošević's policy of ethnic cleansing in the Balkans. The coercive pressure represented by sanctions was insufficient to compel the Milošević regime to change policy in Bosnia or Kosovo. The regime's political survival was too bound up with its policy of ethnic cleansing to be influenced by the use of this weapon. The same problem existed in the case of Chechnya. Russia would have been affected by Western governments cutting off financial aid in response to its conduct in Chechnya. But the Russian government's overriding security interest in preventing Chechnya seceding from the union far outweighed any costs that the West could inflict through a policy of economic coercion. Many Russians are resentful at the West for not doing more to help Russia economically through the 1990s, and the fact that Western economic support has been so limited undermines the leverage that can be extracted from this kind of action.

The one case in which it is argued sanctions worked to bring about a fundamental change of domestic policy is South Africa. Sanctions were an important factor here because there was a strong body of opinion in the business community and among voters who were hurt by the sanctions and who sought radical political change.[24] Growing public opposition to apartheid by whites within South Africa coupled with sustained pressure from outside created the context that made possible the transition to black majority rule. This process did not happen in the case of sanctions against Yugoslavia in the 1990s, nor is there any evidence of it in relation to the sanctions imposed against Iraq. Rather, in both these examples, sanctions created an impoverished people who lined up behind regimes that were very effective in representing the adverse humanitarian consequences of the sanctions as the fault of the West.

The fact that economic sanctions proved ineffective in the 1990s as an instrument for enforcing human rights is even more worrying given that sanctions raise profound ethical dilemmas. It is the case of sanctions against Iraq that illustrates this most graphically. The strongest supporters of sanctions, Britain and the United States, justify the sanctions, imposed against the Iraqi government after its invasion of Kuwait in August 1990, on the grounds that Iraq has not complied with UN Security Council resolutions that require Iraq to disarm its chemical, biological, and nuclear capabilities. Critics of the sanctions point to the UN estimate that since they were imposed there have been 720,000 deaths in Iraq beyond the normal rate. The worst hit are children, who are less able to cope with malnutrition and the lack of medicines.[25] Although the UN established an "oil for food" program that allows the Iraqi government to sell oil and spend some of the money on food and vital medicines, diphtheria vaccines and chemotherapy medication remain on the banned list. They are prohibited because the United Kingdom and the United States argue that they could be used in Iraq's chemical weapons program.[26]

The U.K. position is that Saddam Hussein is deliberately allowing the Iraqi people to suffer in order to get the sanctions lifted without having to accept any weapons inspections regime, a claim that is not without some foundation.[27] But whatever the Iraqi government's complicity in aggravating the impact of the sanctions on Iraqi civilians, the United Kingdom and the United States have supported a policy that has had the effect of killing hundreds of thousands of Iraqi civilians over the last ten years. It is little wonder that this policy has lost all legitimacy in the eyes of the wider society of states and world public opinion. The alternative strategy would be to lift sanctions and allow the return of foreign investment to Iraq in return for a limited degree of UN monitoring of Iraqi disarmament.

There is also plenty of evidence that neighboring governments are breaching the sanctions. This confirms for realism how sanctions will never work because some governments are always tempted to place selfish advantage prior to the effective implementation of sanctions. There is some validity to this claim, but what is overlooked is how breaches of the sanctions regime against Iraq have increased as the policy has lost what little international legitimacy it possessed. The worrying conclusion to be drawn from this view is that Iraq might well be able to obtain over the longer term the materials it needs to further its ambitions of acquiring chemical, biological, and even nuclear weapons. Ewen MacAskill, citing Western sources in Baghdad, considers that "at the Jordanian border only one in 20 trucks is being checked by UN inspectors: on the Turkish border, about one in 200; and the Iranian border is the most porous of all."[28] Lifting the sanctions would increase the opportunities for Iraq to acquire weapons of mass destruction, but one possibility suggested by MacAskill is to restrict the embargo to arms.[29] However, this recommendation overlooks the problem that much of the controversy about what to allow into Iraq revolves around the question of whether such materials could be used for military applications. It will be many more years before Iraq is in a position to challenge its neighbors, and while a nuclear-armed Iraq would change the risks for Western policymakers in any renewed conflict with Iraq, it is not morally acceptable for governments committed to human rights to use Iraqi civilians as a means to the end of containing Iraq.

The key conclusion that emerges from this discussion of sanctions is that in the cases of Iraq and Yugoslavia, sanctions failed to hurt those whom they were targeted at. Saddam Hussein has been able to continue to live a life of luxury, diverting money into palace building programs and protecting those in the army on whose loyalty he relies to stay in power. Sanctions also had little or no impact on Milošević and his supporters because they did not damage the financial and business interests of the regime. As a result of the ethical and practical failure of comprehensive sanctions in both these cases, the Clinton administration moved toward the idea of "smart sanctions" that are designed to hurt those individuals who are directly responsible for gross human rights abuses.

Three possible strategies suggest themselves here. First, travel restrictions could be imposed on named members of the regime. This would turn individuals into international pariahs. Second, strenuous efforts could be made to freeze the assets held outside the country by members of the leadership. These are important measures, but once a regime is committed to a policy that involves gross and systematic human rights abuses, they are unlikely to be sufficient to compel it to change course. The third and most promising sanction is the creation of a regime of universal jurisdiction for crimes against humanity. The knowledge that individuals cannot leave their countries because of fear of prosecution, or the worry that a change of power at home could lead to them being tried for crimes against humanity, might deter future leaders from committing such criminal acts.

In May 2000, the International Criminal Tribunal for the Former Yugoslavia (ICTY) issued a war crimes indictment against Milošević for his command responsibility for Operation Horseshoe (the alleged plan prepared by Serb generals for ethnically cleansing Kosovo of its Albanian population). After being swept from power by Vojislav Kostunica in the elections in September 2000, Milošević was subsequently handed over to the ICTY. The victory of Kostunica might be cited as evidence of the long-term effect of economic sanctions and international isolation in eroding the domestic legitimacy of authoritarian leaders. The destruction inflicted by NATO planes against the civilian infrastructure of the Yugoslav state probably also played a significant role in leading the Serb people to reject Milošević as their leader. His trial began on February 12, 2002, in The Hague, the first prosecution for war crimes of an ex-head of state. There can be no guarantee that the criminal case will succeed against Milošević. At the time of writing, he has refused any formal legal defense, relying on the claim that the court is illegal and has no authority to try him.[30] If he does subsequently provide a detailed legal defense, it is likely to rest on the claim that NATO and not the Serbian army and security forces are responsible for the mass expulsion of Kosovars during Operation Allied Force. In his opening statements to the court, he alleged that NATO political and military leaders are guilty of war crimes for launching a bombing campaign against Yugoslavia that killed hundreds of Serb civilians.[31]

It is highly unlikely that such a plea by Milošević will be accepted by the ICTY. Nevertheless, the uncertainties of relying on legal processes in determining violations of human rights and international humanitarian law led seven governments (including the United States) to oppose the signing in July 1998 of the Rome statute that founded the International Criminal Court

(ICC). Another 21 states abstained, but 122 states supported the principle of universal jurisdiction for war crimes. However, the limits of the advance that human rights have made over state sovereignty since the Nuremberg and Tokyo tribunals is illustrated by the limitations imposed on the ICC. First, cases can only be referred to the prosecutor if there is consent by the state where the crime is committed or the accused is handed over by its own government to the court. The Security Council can also refer cases, but this opens the door to the possibility of permanent members vetoing resolutions.[32]

The Clinton administration initially refused to sign the Rome statute because powerful critics in the U.S. Congress like Jesse Helms, then chair of the Senate Foreign Relations Committee, indicated that it would be dead on arrival if placed before the Senate for ratification. For Republicans like Helms, it is unacceptable that an international court should have jurisdiction over U.S. soldiers serving with the UN. In the last weeks of his presidency, Clinton signed the treaty, perhaps in the hope of locking in president-elect George W. Bush, who is strongly opposed to the ICC.[33] The treaty is unlikely to be placed before the Senate for ratification on Bush's watch, and this does not augur well for the long-term viability of the ICC. The ICC does take us further along the road to universal jurisdiction begun in 1946 and carried forward with the creation of the tribunals for the former Yugoslavia and Rwanda. But it does so against a backdrop of power considerations that continue to set limits to the solidarist vision of a universal system of criminal law enforcement.[34]

For all their problems and limitations, sanctions are generally viewed as a more acceptable alternative to the use of force. As Larry Minear points out, it might be erroneous to think that "military action is necessarily less civilian-friendly or morally justifiable than economic coercion."[35] The civilian suffering inflicted by economic sanctions should always be proportionate to the humanitarian ends of the policy, a test that was clearly failed in Iraq. A decade of sanctions has further destroyed the infrastructure that was already badly damaged after the air strikes against Iraq in the 1991 Gulf War. In cases in which it is believed that sanctions will, or are, contradicting humanitarian ends, it is necessary for policymakers to consider whether force might be a more ethical instrument in defending human rights values.

ENFORCING HUMAN RIGHTS BY FORCE[36]

Can it ever be ethical to kill in the name of defending the human rights of civilians in another state? For pacifists committed to a deontological ethic of nonviolence, there are no circumstances in which it is justified to kill to stop crimes against humanity. This absolute prohibition on killing is a morally respectable position, but it deprives governments of the threat or use of force to end gross violations. If the principle is recognized that it is ethical to kill to save other humans in danger, then the logical corollary of this is that the intervening state must be prepared to place at risk its service personnel. Since policymakers can never know in advance whether force will produce a surplus of good over harm, and there is always the risk that intervention will lead to an escalation of the killing, it is vital that criteria be arrived at for judging a legitimate humanitarian intervention. A solidarist theory of humanitarian intervention establishes four key criteria, derived in part from the just war tradition that should govern a duty of humanitarian intervention. Later I explore how far NATO's intervention in Kosovo met these requirements.

First, there must be a just cause, or what I called earlier a "supreme humanitarian emergency." Genocide and state-sponsored mass murder are the most obvious cases, but I also want to include ethnic cleansing. The latter can be defined as the mass expulsion of individuals belonging to a particular racial or ethnic group, where men of fighting age are either imprisoned or killed. Humanitarian intervention is justified in these cases, but if we wait until thousands have been killed or hundreds of thousands expelled, rescue will come too late for those whom we want to save. This raises the problem of how early intervention should be. Even though it is easier to justify a military intervention after blood has been spilt on a significant scale, governments should not wait for thousands to die before they act. Here, I agree with Michael Bazyler that the "intervening nation or nations need not wait for the killings to start if there is clear evidence of an impending massacre."[37] This does not resolve the problem of deciding in particular cases what counts as "clear evidence," and these assessments will always be open to dispute.

Critics of NATO's intervention in Kosovo charge that the situation had not reached the point where the use of force was justified. They argue that Serbian security forces were not the only party to the conflict and that the Kosovar Liberation Army (KLA) was also guilty of committing atrocities. They buttress their argument with the proposition that NATO failed to exhaust all peaceful means. Indeed, it is argued by some that the United States and United Kingdom deliberately set terms at the talks in Rambouillet that they knew Milošević would not accept, thereby legitimating the decision to go to war.[38] The problem with this criticism is twofold. First, it rests on the proposition that no sovereign state would have consented to the type of restrictions that the "Interim Agreement" imposed on Yugoslavia's control over Kosovo. But this overlooks the crucial point that the only way to safeguard the human rights of the Kosovars was to limit the sovereignty of the Yugoslav state in this way. Second, it ignores the evidence that Serb ethnic cleansing was taking place under the cover of the negotiations. NATO's justification for intervention was to prevent an impending humanitarian catastrophe, and it was argued by the leading alliance governments prosecuting the war that intelligence intercepts indicated that the Milošević regime was preparing to embark on an operation to expel Albanians from Kosovo. In the absence of the intelligence intercepts that NATO was working with (some of which were handed over to the Hague Tribunal's chief prosecutor prior to her decision to indict Milošević as a war criminal), it is hard to reach a definitive judgment as to whether the use of force was the only means of preventing a humanitarian catastrophe.

It is too demanding to require state leaders to exhaust all peaceful remedies since every day's delay risks an ever-increasing death toll. However, what is required to meet the second criterion of last resort is that policymakers are confident that they have considered all avenues that are likely to prove successful in stopping the cruelty. If there is doubt on this score, then state leaders are morally required to continue to pursue their humanitarian ends through nonviolent means. The use of force can promote good consequences, but it should never be forgotten that it always produces harmful ones as well.

If the fateful decision is taken to use force, then state leaders must adhere to the absolutist principle in the just war tradition that civilians cannot be deliberately targeted no matter what the proclaimed beneficial consequences of such attacks. Nevertheless, it is accepted within the tradition and enshrined in the 1977 Additional Protocol 1 to the 1949 Geneva Conventions that civilians can be harmed if this is an inadvertent consequence of attacks against legitimate military objects and where the civilian deaths are not excessive in relation to the anticipated military advantage. In the case of NATO's bombing of Yugoslavia, were NATO's attacks against bridges, the TV station, and the electricity grid in conformity with the laws of war? The alliance had a team of lawyers scrutinizing each target and defended its targeting policy on the grounds that its targets all had military related applications. However, the charge raised during the war by critics, including Mary Robinson, the UN's human rights commissioner, and afterward by Human Rights Watch and Amnesty International is that the civilian deaths were out of all proportion to the military advantage gained. No one is claiming that NATO deliberately targeted civilians. But the legal stipulation that they be protected as far as possible from the exigencies of war begs the question as to whether NATO's determination to win the conflict led the alliance to attack targets that stretched the rule of noncombatant immunity to a breaking point.

The controversial decision to attack the headquarters of the radio and television station on April 23, which killed sixteen technicians, was justified by NATO on the grounds that it was supporting the Serbian war effort, and hence a legitimate military target. Equally controversial was the strike that took out the power grid on May 24, putting the lights out all over Belgrade and demonstrating that NATO could hit at the heart of the regime. As Michael Ignatieff points out, it was the power grid that also supplied the hospitals, and he cites one NATO lawyer as saying, "We'd have preferred not to have to take on these targets. But this was the Commander's call."[39] There can be no final objective judgment as to whether NATO breached the laws of war over Kosovo; international humanitarian law establishes the legal norms for deciding this issue, but it does not resolve the issue in specific cases.

What is apparent after Kosovo is that governments, which seek to justify their use of force as humanitarian, must make every effort to uphold the laws of war. And where their targeting decisions are strongly contested, they should be prepared to publicly defend these choices, perhaps even submitting them to a process of judicial review by the International Court of Justice (ICJ) or the International Criminal Court (ICC). It is only through this process that a body of case law will be built up establishing the legal norms that should govern the conduct of humanitarian wars.

The fourth criterion in deciding whether to intervene is whether there is a reasonable prospect of a successful outcome. This is the proportionality requirement and it is satisfied only if the destruction produced by the use of force is outweighed by the good that is achieved. Intervention must save more lives than would have been lost by a policy of nonintervention, and politicians and military leaders confront agonizing moral dilemmas in formulating these ethical judgments without the benefit of hindsight. In judging the success of a humanitarian intervention, the Argentinean international lawyer Fernando Teson defines a successful humanitarian intervention as one that rescues "the victims of oppression, and [where] human rights have subsequently been restored."[40]

How far, then, does NATO's intervention in Kosovo meet Teson's criterion? Within weeks of the start of the bombing, it is estimated that approximately three thousand Kosovar Albanians were killed by Serb forces (this is based on the discovery of bodies after the conflict, but there could be many more who will never be found); half a million were driven from their homes to become refugees in neighboring countries, and hundreds of thousands found themselves internally displaced within Kosovo itself. U.S. Deputy Secretary of State Strobe Talbott conceded in October 1999 that the bombing campaign "accelerated" the ethnic cleansing.[41] NATO leaders stand accused, then, of exacerbating the humanitarian disaster that their intervention was justified as averting.

Having failed to prevent a humanitarian catastrophe, bombing did play a significant, though not decisive, role in producing a political settlement. Russia's refusal to come to the aid of Milošević and NATO's developing plans for a land invasion of Kosovo were equally significant factors in compelling Milošević to agree to the NATO-led international force for Kosovo entering the province. This enabled the refugees to return home and provided them with a substantial measure of political autonomy that they would have been denied in the absence of NATO intervention. Jonathan Steele, writing from Pristina in July 1999, declared, "Those Western critics who condemn the bombing for turning a humanitarian crisis into a catastrophe get short shrift in Kosovo. Albanians were the primary victims and there is an almost universal feeling that although the price was far bloodier than expected, it was worth paying for the sake of liberation from Serb rule."[42]

On the other hand, NATO's intervention is problematic as a model for future humanitarian interventions because it has not succeeded in restoring human rights to the people of Kosovo. It might be argued that this is too demanding a test of humanitarian intervention and that what matters is to end the atrocities. Intervention that prevents or ends supreme humanitarian emergencies is clearly preferable to inaction, but if the withdrawal of the intervening forces leads to a resumption of the violence within a short space of time, this diminishes the humanitarian credentials of an intervention. The international community has taken on, through its peacekeeping force and the UN's transitional civil administration, the challenge of addressing the political causes that produced violence between the Serb and Albanian communities. Unfortunately, the results have not been encouraging: The international force failed to stop a new round of ethnic cleansing as thousands of Serbs fled in fear of Albanians seeking revenge. Those who remain live in ghettos, fearful of traveling to work or school without protection. This ragged end to Operation Allied Force is reflected in the limited moral commitment to postwar reconstruction. Western governments, which spent millions prosecuting the war, have failed to provide the necessary resources for the rebuilding of Kosovo. This demonstrates the gap between the rhetorical commitment of NATO governments to human rights and their willingness to accept the costs of protecting these rights in the postconflict environment.

Even if potential intervenors are satisfied that their proposed action meets the requirements of just cause, last resort, noncombatant immunity and has reasonable prospect of success, there is the question as to whether such action should take place in the absence of a supporting Security Council resolution. This question was crucially raised over NATO's bombing of Yugoslavia. One interpretation of NATO's use of force is that it violated international law because only the Security Council can authorize the use of force for purposes of collective enforcement action. This was the view taken by Russia, China, and India in the Security Council debates on March 24 and 26, 1999. They argued that the action represented a direct assault on the principles of international order.[43] NATO governments replied that it is legitimate for states to use force in those exceptional cases of extreme humanitarian necessity without explicit Security Council authorization.[44] This argument challenges the power of the veto in the Security Council. The pluralist justification for the insertion of the veto into the Charter was to prevent the UN from taking action in situations where the great powers were divided. As Robert Jackson writes, "The veto is a legal recognition that armed intervention by international society must rest on a great power consensus."[45] On this view, NATO was behaving recklessly in splitting the five permanent members of the Council into opposing camps in order to save the Kosovar Albanians.

It is obviously desirable to have the authority of the Security Council behind humanitarian intervention, and the challenge is to make the Council work more effectively to defend human rights in the future. However, solidarism cannot accept that a strict legalism should trump the defense of human rights in cases of human rights emergency. Instead, it wants to distinguish between responsible and irresponsible uses of the veto. The solidarist claim that the right to the veto carries with it concomitant responsibilities was raised by the Slovenian permanent representative during the Security Council debate over NATO's action on March 24, 1999. He implied that Russia and China were abusing their power of veto by refusing to support military action to protect the Kosovar Albanians and prevent the conflict in Kosovo from escalating. He contended that NATO's action was justified because "not all permanent members were willing to act in accordance with their special responsibility for the maintenance of international peace and security."[46] The task for the future is to persuade the permanent members of the Council, and the wider UN membership, that it is illegitimate to exercise the power of the veto in cases of supreme humanitarian emergency.

CONCLUSION: A NEW AGE OF HUMAN RIGHTS ENFORCEMENT?

This chapter has mapped the challenges facing the global human rights community when it comes to enforcing minimum standards of common humanity. Crucially, it has asked whether governments are capable of acting as humanitarian law enforcers or whether the constraints set out by realism and pluralism continue to limit the possibilities for the solidarist project of enforcing human rights. On the one hand, the end of the Cold War opened up new possibilities for giving human rights law the enforcement arm it has lacked: the Security Council was freed from its Cold War paralysis, and the creation of the tribunals for the former Yugoslavia and Rwanda brought nearer the day when there will be a regime of universal jurisdiction for all war crimes. On the other hand, progress is blocked by a realist and pluralist mind-set that leads powerful governments to refuse to accept the principle of universal jurisdiction for war criminals, remains stubbornly defensive of the prerogatives of state sovereignty, and is selective in its protection of human rights. Some liberal-democratic governments such as Canada and the United Kingdom have been prominent in trying to give their foreign policies an ethical dimension. But while the Blair government can take credit for joining the majority of states in supporting the ICC against the opposition of the United States, its other forays into this territory have been less successful. It has found itself increasingly isolated over its strong support for the sanctions policy against Iraq, and its decision to sell the Hawks to Indonesia contradicted its position that it would not sell arms to repressive governments. The United Kingdom failed the test of good international citizenship because it privileged contracts in the aerospace industry over human rights. In making this decision, there is every reason to think that the Blair government believed that it would not face a public outcry. Consequently, if governments are to be persuaded and cajoled into placing a greater priority on human rights, it will be necessary for domestic and international public opinion to make itself heard on this issue. The progress made in banning land mines and in creating the ICC owed much to the activism of human rights groups in mobilizing public pressure. Yet it is also clear that this pressure is most effective in changing global norms when governments committed to the principles of good international citizenship support it. For example, the ex-Canadian foreign minister Lloyd Axeworthy played an important catalyzing role in translating the pressure from transnational civil society into an international agreement to ban land mines.

Realism argues that state leaders only espouse a commitment to defend human rights when this does not conflict with important political, economic, or security interests. Thus, it is easy for Canada to take a leading role in banning land mines because this approach does not affect its interests. However, this underestimates how far states committed to internationalist values can raise humanitarian claims that lead to normative change in the society of states. The ICC is a very good example. After weeks of negotiating, the draft treaty advanced by human rights groups and a broad coalition of western and southern states was eventually put to the vote and, against the wishes of the United States, a majority of states voted their approval.

The realist argument that states are only interested in pursuing their security interests overlooks the solidarist claim that human rights and security need not be opposed values. The thesis of good international citizenship is predicated on the proposition that states have a long-term national security interest in protecting human rights everywhere. The reason that NATO found itself using force in Kosovo was because international society failed to act to end the human rights violations against the Kosovars in the late 1980s. As Marc Weller shows in his chapter in this volume, preventive military deployment on the part of the UN can be effective, as it was in Macedonia, in defusing ethnic conflict that threatens to explode into violent conflict. However, it is hard to generalize from this case since the deployment of UN peacekeepers to Macedonia has to be located in the context of worries about the war in Bosnia spreading to engulf Macedonia. Moreover, the Macedonian government consented to the operation. However, preventive action is frequently required in cases in which a state refuses to accept intervention or the state has collapsed, as in Somalia and Liberia. The problem is that justifying preventive military action to domestic and international publics is very difficult in a context in which there is no compelling evidence that the situation constitutes a supreme humanitarian emergency. But if intervening states wait for such evidence before they act, many lives will already have been lost, and the risks and costs of ending the emergency are likely to be greater than if action had been taken earlier.

In arguing that the concerns of national security, international order, and human rights can often be reconciled, it is necessary to acknowledge that there will be situations in which order has to be privileged over justice. But even in cases such as Chechnya where military intervention was rightly ruled out as unthinkable, responsible statecraft requires governments to express their strongest regret at human rights violations. And if state leaders believe there are good reasons for not publicly censuring and/or sanctioning governments that violate human rights, they should be prepared to explain and justify these choices in the wider public sphere.

The problem with pluralism is that it all too often exaggerates the dangers to international order posed by the practice of unilateral humanitarian intervention. This is reflected in Robert Jackson's contention that "the stability of international society, especially the unity of the great powers, is more important, indeed far more important, than minority rights and humanitarian protections in Yugoslavia or another country."[47] This pluralist argument is open to two rejoinders. First, NATO's action was recognized by many states as an exceptional one that could only be invoked as a precedent where it could be plausibly argued that a similar set of circumstances pertained. A key aspect of NATO's justification was the prior existence of three Security Council resolutions adopted under Chapter VII that defined the Milošević regime's violation of international humanitarian standards as a threat to the peace. In the absence of similar Council determinations in future cases, states would not be able to claim, as NATO did, that enforcement action to protect human rights was taken on behalf of the purposes set out in successive Council resolutions.

The second reply to Jackson is that NATO's action did not threaten great power stability in the way he suggests. The alliance was able to trample over Russian and Chinese sensitivities for two reasons: first, Western power is dominant in the global arena; second, neither Russia nor China would have risked war with NATO over Kosovo since this area was not a core security interest for either of them. The more pertinent question to ask over the rupture of relations among the permanent members of the Security Council at the end of the last decade is whether this action could have been avoided. The deterioration in relations with Russia can be traced to the failure of the West to draw Russia into a genuine security partnership. The decision of the alliance to admit Poland, Hungary, and the Czech Republic as full members was a key turning point in this process. It has to be asked whether a different approach to Russia in the years before Kosovo might have led Russia to bring more concerted pressure to bear on the Milošević regime in the run-up to hostilities. Indeed, it is not entirely far-fetched to think that NATO and Russia could have imposed a joint military protectorate over Kosovo in late 1998 as an alternative to war.

The argument that NATO was able to act in the case of Kosovo because of its preponderant power raises a troubling issue for solidarism. The worry is that Operation Allied Force might have sent the dangerous signal that states wishing to resist Western power should develop weapons of mass destruction. To prevent NATO's first humanitarian war being interpreted as a new form of Western imperialism, it is important that the society of states forge a new consensus at the UN on the substantive and procedural criteria that should govern Security Council authorized humanitarian intervention. This will not resolve the problem of deciding in specific cases whether these principles have been met, but it will establish a common language within which the argument can take place. This debate will have to address what should happen if the Security Council cannot act because of the exercise of the veto by one or more of the permanent members. This is a very sensitive issue at the UN, but it is hard to see how this question can be avoided in any future dialogue on this issue.[48]

The UN Charter commits states to solving their conflicts by peaceful means. But, as I have argued, once a government begins massively violating the human rights of its citizens, little leverage is provided by nonviolent actions, including economic sanctions. Even on the most optimistic assumptions, by the time sanctions work, those whom we are trying to save will be dead. The best recent example of the limits of nonviolent humanitarian intervention is the Rwandan genocide: the only realistic means of halting the frenzied killing after April 6 was armed intervention. The reason that Western governments failed to act was because they did not believe that there were any interests at stake that justified risking western soldiers to save Rwandan strangers.

The Kosovo intervention does not alter this conclusion. NATO believed that it could compel the Milošević regime to accept its terms through the use of air power and that this strategy risked few alliance casualties. Critics argue that NATO could have saved the lives of more Kosovar Albanians and avoided killing so many Serb civilians had it relied on a land invasion. However, this position is rejected by many military strategists who argue not only that a land invasion would have produced much greater military losses on both sides but also that many more Kosovar Albanians would have been killed. This is a counterfactual question that is open to debate, and other military experts have advanced different views. What can be said with greater certainty is that there was no support among NATO political leaders for a ground operation that risked significant casualties. Had the only military option been a land invasion, it seems that NATO would not have acted over human rights abuses in Kosovo. Michael Walzer fundamentally challenges this conception of risk in Western military operations:

> *You cannot kill unless you are prepared to die.* . . . . Political leaders cannot launch a campaign to kill Serbian soldiers, and sure to kill others too, unless they are prepared to risk the lives of their own soldiers. They can try; they ought to try to reduce those risks as much as they can. But they cannot claim, and we cannot accept, that those lives are expendable, and these are not.[49]

Robert Jackson argues that the promotion of human rights in international society is limited by pluralist ethics.[50] However, it was not pluralist ethics that led Rwanda to be abandoned or NATO to employ bombing with all its attendant moral ambiguities in Kosovo. These choices owe nothing to pluralist concerns about the dangers of privileging human rights over considerations of international order. Instead, it represents the triumph of realist ethics over solidarist ones. The future of human rights depends on persuading state leaders to change this mind-set and embrace a solidarist ethic of humanitarian responsibility.

NOTES

I am grateful to Tim Dunne for his comments on an earlier draft of this chapter.

1. Hedley Bull, "The Grotian Conception of International Society" in *Diplomatic Investigations: Essays in the Theory and Practice of International Politics*, ed. Herbert Butterfield and Martin Wight (London: Allen & Unwin, 1966), 52.

2. Robert H. Jackson, "Political Theory of International Society," in *International Relations Theory Today*, ed. Steve Smith and Ken Booth (Cambridge: Polity, 1995), 123.

3. Quoted in Michael J. Smith, "Humanitarian Intervention: An Overview of the Ethical Issues," *Ethics and International Affairs* 2 (1989): 74.

4. The idea of states as "good international citizens" was first employed by the former Australian minister for foreign affairs and trade, Gareth Evans, to describe his pursuit of a foreign policy that reconciled "enlightened self-interest" and "idealistic pragmatism." The concept was first developed by Andrew Linklater in "What Is a Good International Citizen?" in *Ethics and Foreign Policy*, ed. Paul Keal (Canberra: Allen & Unwin, 1992). Tim Dunne and I argue that the test of "good international

citizenship" is how well states live up to the solidarist ethic of acting as guardians of human rights everywhere. See Nicholas J. Wheeler and Tim Dunne, "Good International Citizenship: A Third Way for British Foreign Policy," *International Affairs* 74, no. 4 (October 1988): 853–56.

5. Wheeler and Dunne, "Good International Citizenship," 862–65.

6. Bull, "The Grotian Conception," 63.

7. Michael Walzer, *Just and Unjust Wars* (London: Allen Lane, 1977), 251–68.

8. British foreign secretary Robin Cook made this distinction on July 19, 2000, in his speech to the American Bar Association, London. See www.fco.gov.uk/news/speechtext.asp?3989.

9. For a fuller discussion, see Nicholas J. Wheeler, *Saving Strangers: Humanitarian Intervention in International Society* (Oxford: Oxford University Press, 2000).

10. Hugh Beach, "Secessions, Intervention and Just War Theory: The Case of Kosovo," *Pugwash Occasional Papers* 1, no. 1 (February 2000): 29.

11. Hedley Bull, "Conclusion," in *Intervention in World Politics,* ed. Hedley Bull (Oxford: Oxford University Press, 1984), 193.

12. I follow W. Michael Reisman in defining "A 'unilateral action' is an act by a formally unauthorized participant, which effectively preempts the official, decision a legally designated official or agency was supposed to take. Yet the unilateral action is accompanied by a claim that it is, nonetheless, lawful." The defining characteristic of a unilateral act is that the legal procedure by which it should have been taken has been disregarded, but the actor claims that the act is a lawful one on substantive grounds. See W. Michael Reisman, "Unilateral Action and the Transformations of the World Constitutive Process: The Special Problem of Humanitarian Intervention," *European Journal of International Law* 11, no. 1 (March 2000): 7. Consequently, it is clear that when we are talking about unilateral acts in international law, we are not referring to a singular state or entity. Multilateral groupings of states can act unilaterally on this understanding of the term.

13. Secretary's General Annual Report to the General Assembly, Press Release SG/SM7136 GA/9596, srch 1.un.org:80/plweb-cgi/fastweb, September 20, 1999.

14. This argument and the background to the Vietnamese action are developed more fully in Wheeler, *Saving Strangers.*

15. For example, Alain Destexhe, "The 'New' Humanitarianism," in *Between Sovereignty and Global Governance: The United Nations, the State and Civil Society,* ed. Albert J. Paolini, Anthony P. Jarvis, and Christian Reus-Smit (London: Macmillan, 1998), 97.

16. PDD 25 Executive Summary, 4. Quoted in Oliver Ramsbotham and Tom Woodhouse, *Humanitarian Intervention in Contemporary Conflict* (Cambridge: Polity, 1996), 141.

17. Kofi A. Annan, *Preventing War and Disaster: A Growing Global Challenge* (1999 annual report on the work of the organization) (New York: United Nations, 1999), 21.

18. For a powerful and compelling account of the West's failure over Rwanda, see Linda Melvern, *A People Betrayed: The Role of the West in Rwanda's Genocide* (London: Zed, 2000).

19. David C. Hendrickson, "In Defense of Realism: A Commentary on Just and

Unjust Wars," *Ethics and International Affairs* 11 (1997): 43, and William Rubenstein, *The Myth of Rescue: Why the Democracies Could Not Have Saved More Jews from the Nazis* (London: Routledge, 1997).

20. Noam Chomsky, *The New Military Humanism: Lessons from Kosovo* (Monroe, Me.: Common Courage, 1999).

21. Quoted in Ewen MacAskill and Graham Diggines, "Russia Evades Human Rights Issues," *The Guardian*, April 18, 2000.

22. Julian Borger, "Generals Accused of War Crimes," *The Guardian*, February 26, 2000.

23. I owe this point to James Mayall.

24. This argument is advanced by Jonathan Freedland, "Compromised," *The Guardian*, March 8, 2000.

25. For an authoritative examination of this issue, see Eric Herring, "Between Iraq and a Hard Place: A Critique of the British Government's Case for UN Economic Sanctions," *Review of International Studies* 28, no.1 (January 2002): 39–57.

26. Freedland, "Compromised."

27. Peter Hain, "I Fought Apartheid. I'll Fight Saddam," *The Guardian*, January 6, 2001.

28. Ewen MacAskill, "So Drop Your Vendetta and Give Iraqi Kids a Break, Peter," *The Guardian*, April 3, 2000.

29. MacAskill, "So Drop Your Vendetta."

30. Ian Black, "Milošević: A Lust for Power Driven by Medieval Savagery," *The Guardian*, February 13, 2002.

31. Ian Black, "I'm Being Crucified, Says Milošević in Four-Hour Diatribe to Court," *The Guardian*, February 15, 2002. Human Rights Watch's detailed investigation on the ground puts the figure of Serb civilians killed at between 489 and 528. See Civilian Deaths in the NATO Air Campaign, hrw.org/reports/2000/nato/Natbm200-01.htm.

32. For an excellent discussion of the ICC, see David Wippman, "Can an International Criminal Court Prevent and Punish Genocide" in *Protection against Genocide: Mission Impossible?* ed. Neal Rimer (London: Praeger, 2000), 85–105.

33. Julian Borger, "US Will Join World Court," *The Guardian*, January 1, 2001.

34. Geoffrey Robertson, *Crimes against Humanity: The Struggle for Global Justice* (London: Penguin, 1999), 324–67.

35. Larry Minear, "The Morality of Sanctions," in *Hard Choices: Moral Dilemmas in Humanitarian Intervention,* ed. Jonathan Moore (Oxford: Rowman & Littlefield, 1998), 238.

36. The arguments in this section draw heavily on my other published works in this area. See Wheeler, *Saving Strangers*, 275–81, and Nicholas J. Wheeler, "Humanitarian Intervention after Kosovo: Emergent Norm, Moral Duty or the Coming Anarchy," *International Affairs* 77, no. 1 (January 2001): 113–29.

37. M. Bazyler, "Reexamining the Doctrine of Humanitarian Intervention in the Light of the Atrocities in Kampuchea and Ethiopia," *Stanford Journal of International Law* 23 (1987): 600.

38. See Chomsky, *The New Military Humanism.*

39. Quoted in Michael Ignatieff, *Virtual War: Kosovo and Beyond* (London: Chatto & Windus, 2000), 108.

40. Fernando Teson, *Humanitarian Intervention: An Inquiry into Law and Morality* (Dobbs Ferry, N.Y.: Transnational, 1988), 106.

41. Strobe Talbott was speaking at a conference organized by the Royal Institute of International Affairs and the Institute of World Economy and International Relations Russian Federation on "NATO Development in Partnership: Engagement and Advancement after 2000" held at Chatham House, London, October 7–8, 1999.

42. Jonathan Steele, "Confused and Still in Denial, Serbs Have a Long Way to Go," *The Guardian*, July 9, 1999.

43. S/PV.3989, March 26, 1999, 6.

44. S/PV.3989, March 26, 1999, 5; S/PV.3989, March 26, 1999, 3. For a fuller discussion of these arguments, see Nicholas J. Wheeler, "Reflections on the Legality and Legitimacy of NATO's Intervention in Kosovo," in *The Kosovo Tragedy: The Human Rights Dimensions*, special issue of *International Journal of Human Rights* 4, nos. 3/4 (Autumn/Winter 2000): 145–64.

45. Robert H. Jackson, *The Global Covenant* (Oxford: Oxford University Press, 2000), 284.

46. See S/PV.3988, March 24, 1999, 6–7.

47. Jackson, *The Global Covenant*, 291.

48. For a discussion of these issues, see Nicholas J. Wheeler, "Legitimating Humanitarian Intervention: Principles and Procedures," *Melbourne Journal of International Law* 2, no. 2 (2001): 550–67.

49. Quoted in Mikulas Fabry, "The Defeated Feat: The Legality, Justice and Ethics of the NATO Intervention over Kosovo," paper presented at the British International Studies Association annual conference held at the University of Bradford, December 16–18, 2000, 18–19.

50. Jackson, *The Global Covenant*, 289.

8

Human Rights and International Politics

James Mayall and Gene M. Lyons

In our introductory chapter, we discussed the central problem that we confront in this book: The international human rights regime that has emerged since approval of the Universal Declaration on Human Rights has generally focused on individual rights and yet recent violations of rights have, in large measure, resulted from the individual's identity with a group, be it ethnic or religious, an indigenous people or as women. This leads to two questions that we address in this concluding chapter: first, whether we need to extend the human rights regime to include specific protections for group rights; second, how the international community can effectively respond to violations of group rights, especially in cases of divided societies where governments have failed and political leaders have actually authorized violations as a matter of official policy.

In his chapter, Jack Donnelly agrees that the regime is centered on individual rights, but he goes on to argue that no further elaboration of group rights is necessary so long as the collective nature of rights is recognized—that is, that freedom of association or of religion, for example, cannot be exercised unless the rights of groups with which one associates, are also protected. Other contributors—Jennifer Jackson-Preece on minorities, Hurst Hannum on indigenous people, and Eva Brems on the human rights of women— nonetheless advocate the promulgation of group rights that obligate governments to comply with specific obligations. Wherever they stand on this issue, all of our contributors agree that a major issue for the future is the enforcement of human rights: to develop strong incentives for governments to comply with treaty obligations and to bring pressure, including where necessary, military pressure, to bear when there is evidence of gross violations of human rights, especially violations that constitute crimes against humanity or genocide. In this regard, the years since the end of the Cold War have provided what Marc Weller calls a "laboratory" of experience in which the international community, usually (but not always) working through the UN Security Council, intervened in the affairs of states in which governments were failing and in deeply divided societies often mired in cruel ethnic conflict.

In their chapters, both Weller and Nicholas Wheeler point to the uneven results of international intervention, either in terms of bringing stability to troubled states or creating the infrastructure for the protection of human rights. There has been, as Weller testifies, limited success but also abysmal failure, principally because of the reluctance of major states in the international system to accept the long-term commitments that such enterprises require and the equally long time that it takes for internal groups that have been at war with each other to reconcile their differences and develop a democratic consensus that a working government requires. It is this realistic assessment that leads Wheeler to ask whether the international community, as presently constituted and motivated, is capable of enforcing the international human rights regime, or whether it has to move closer to a more "solidarist" consensus on common principles.

In this conclusion, we want to elaborate further on the positions taken by our colleagues on the questions of group rights and international intervention. We believe that these issues cannot be treated as purely technical, legal, or even discrete issues. In both cases, the answers that are likely to emerge in practice will be deeply influenced by the more general climate of ideas. We start, therefore, with the evolution of ideas about international society. Our purpose is to identify the ideas connecting international society, democratic government, and human rights. These links, we believe, must be understood before we can effectively confront violations of the rights of groups.

THE EVOLUTION OF
INTERNATIONAL SOCIETY

The idea that all human beings are endowed with rights essentially by virtue of their humanity is deeply attractive, but it is not self-evident. It rests on philosophical foundations that are contested. Nor is the philosophical argument—in particular between those who rest their case on *a priori* assumptions and those who locate human rights within a historicist understanding of human development—susceptible to final resolution. It is for this reason that protection of human rights depends so crucially on the law. Once a set of principles has been legally codified, it is placed, for all practical purposes, beyond the reach of normative and philosophical dispute. The law is not, of course, static, inscribed for all time, like the commandments, in stone. Nor can it be expected to command respect if it attempts to ride roughshod over custom and social consensus. Ultimately, it can be challenged, ignored, overthrown, or rewritten. Nonetheless, in the meantime, it provides society with a framework of stability, predictability, and order and at least a partial guarantee that power will not be exercised arbitrarily over those who have no redress.

Just as law in general is indispensable to any society but is not synonymous with it, so international law is a central institution of international society from which it draws its authority but should not be confused with it. With respect to human rights, this is an important distinction, because it shows that it will not be possible to establish an international order on the basis of human rights by legal means alone. Respect for the law, which is deeply engrained in most societies, may well act as a powerful incentive to harmonize international standards and practices, but if it gets too far ahead of the political consensus on which it rests, it will fail. If this holds for domestic legislation, where governments can use the law to buttress their authority, it is even more important at the international level where the law depends on interstate agreement and self-policing. The evolutionary potential of international society—and its direction—are, therefore, crucial preconditions for the development of a global human rights culture.

Traditional international society from the seventeenth century on was a minimalist association. It was concerned with the mutual recognition of European sovereigns, but with little else. Before the nineteenth century, there was no conception of international progress or of sovereigns engaging in cooperative projects to advance the welfare of their subjects. Hedley Bull has described changes that then occurred:

> The century following the Congress of Vienna witnessed the experiment in management of the international system by a concert of great powers, the regulation of diplomatic precedent and protocol, the steady professionalization of international law, dramatic successes in communications and transport, the deeper involvement of many societies in an expanding international economy, the rise of technical organizations, the first stirrings of internationally organized action about human rights in relation to the slave trade, and new ideas about disarmament and the peaceful settlement of international disputes.[1]

In the twentieth century, international society further expanded in two major ways: first, by the impact of advances in science and technology that dramatically increased the interactions of states and societies; second, by the participation of an increasing number of states from Asia, Africa, and the

Americas that began to influence the international society that Europeans had initiated. As Bull and Adam Watson have indicated, these new participants "accelerated the pace of decolonization or national liberation, and brought about a new legal and moral climate in world affairs in which colonial rule and by extension rule by settler minorities, came to be regarded as illegitimate."[2] These developments expanded international society but not necessarily a new spirit of international cooperation. The enthusiasm with which non-European governments embraced international society and sought entry to it as a mark of their freedom from colonial rule largely stemmed from its grounding in the legal principle of sovereignty rather than common interests with the major powers in the north.

Sovereignty has always been more highly regarded by the weak and vulnerable than by the strong. It is not surprising, therefore, that in the contemporary world those who believe most strongly in the minimalist, static conception of international society are to be found in Africa and Asia. Like new entrants before them, they fear that they may lose their independence as the result of intervention, allegedly sanctioned on grounds of international solidarity but in fact masking the economic and political interests of stronger states. This retreat to a strict reading of sovereignty may also have been hastened by the failure of newly independent developing countries in the 1970s to influence changes in international society to emphasize the redistribution of resources and redress what they saw as the inequalities of the world economy. Their efforts to translate United Nations resolutions calling for "a new international economic order" into political reality failed and the gap in living standards and life chances enjoyed by the population of rich and poor countries has continued to widen. It is not surprising, therefore, that arguments about the need to make international society more responsive to the people and their rights continue to be regarded at best with ironic skepticism, and often with deep suspicion in the non-Western world.

Nevertheless, the evidence that international society has evolved is compelling. Modifications in the original conception followed the economic and strategic integration of the world as the result of the industrial revolution and Western imperialism. In reaction to the relentless globalization of the world economy, there has been a tendency, throughout the twentieth century, to transform the quasi-constitutional order of international society into an enterprise association—that is, one that exists to pursue substantive goals of its own such as economic development or the protection of human rights. The commitment of states to a pluralist framework—and the continuing importance of sovereignty as the foundation of international law— continues to block the way to a fully fledged transnational society of this kind. As we argued in the introduction, however, the fact that most governments accept that people have positive as well as negative rights—and have been prepared to sign and ratify treaties binding themselves to uphold them—illustrates the extent to which international political thought and practice have been penetrated by solidarist assumptions.

The case for a compromise between the principles of pluralism and solidarism emerges as soon as we consider the origins of solidarist claims and the problems of implementation. The idea of international solidarity, like the political doctrine of nationalism that gave rise to it, took shape in the wake of the American and French Revolutions. The nationalization of the state was accompanied, almost everywhere, by the socialization of the nation. The partial and awkward exception is the United States. It is partial because for reasons that relate to the period when the American nation took shape and to the fact that atypically it was a nation of immigrants, it largely avoided the collectivism that was a feature of the assertion of popular sovereignty elsewhere. It is awkward in that American exceptionalism, combined with American power, has, in recent years, given U.S. governments a virtual veto over forms of international cooperation (and/or standard setting) of which it disapproves.

In the majority of other states, the claim that sovereignty was being exercised by the nation and on its own behalf led ineluctably to the view that the national economy had to be brought under national control and freed from foreign interference and exploitation. The underlying idea—and on this issue the United States concurs—was the right of *all* people to manage their own affairs. But if this was a right, it necessarily implied the existence of an exclusive domain from which outsiders could be legitimately excluded.

The impact of nationalism on the evolution of international society was thus paradoxical. On the one hand, it introduced the progressive idea of popular representation—if the state existed to serve the interests of the people, international society had to be a society in which the rights of all peoples to self-determination were recognized. On the other hand, popular sovereignty reinforced the traditional concept of exclusive jurisdiction. It is true that the exclusive domain has shrunk under pressures from many directions, including demands for the international protection of human rights. But as long as the state remains the dominant political form—and there is no serious evidence that it is withering away—it cannot be ignored altogether. Indeed, international progress, if possible at all, depends on its recognition.

The implications of this observation for the future of the human rights regime can best be illustrated by analogy. Experience of the Great Depression and world war led the major powers to conclude at the Bretton Woods conference in 1944 that economic welfare required the creation of institutions to lubricate the world economy with capital and credit, and police the liberalization of world trade. The aim of the Bretton Woods institutions (and the General Agreement on Tariffs and Trade [GATT]) was to develop a rule-based diplomacy—and hence in a sense to depoliticize economic affairs—but not at the expense of national well-being. It was conceded, for example, that in a crisis the government's duty to maintain full employment would take priority over international obligations.

A concern for popular rights and welfare, in other words, sets practical limits to the evolution of international society in the direction of cosmopolitan solidarity. In 1944, not only was there no alternative source of authority to the state, but there was no interest in seeking one. If economic order was to be maintained by a reciprocal exchange of most favored nation rights, there had to be national governments to make the exchange. The difficulties faced by the World Trade Organization (WTO) today arise not from a rejection of this principle but from doubts about whether it can provide sufficient protection to those vulnerable states and communities—or indeed to the environment—that are on the losing end of global economic integration. In parentheses, one might note that if it cannot, the problem of expanding respect for human rights beyond the minority of affluent states will be greatly complicated if not rendered insoluble.

The same logic covers other aspects of contemporary world politics. For example, under the UN Charter, it covers the establishment of regional and standing alliances in the absence of a credible system of collective security. On grounds of human solidarity, all governments have to refrain from aggressive war, but there have to be governments not only to do the refraining but to maintain a deterrent against potential aggressors. It applies also to human rights. It did not need the chapters in this book to establish that many governments regularly abuse the human rights of their citizens, but it is also governments that uphold them. Indeed, notwithstanding the importance of public opinion and the NGOs that seek to mobilize it as an instrument of pressure on government, it is ultimately only through governments that the international human rights regime can be deepened and extended.

DEMOCRACY, HUMAN RIGHTS, AND INTERNATIONAL SOCIETY

The proposition that international society would be more "solidarist" if made up of democratic states is not new. It has been around at least since the establishment of the League of Nations. What is new is the defeat, with the end of the Cold War and the collapse of communism, of the only large-scale ideological rival to liberal democracy. This has led some to argue that the major remaining obstacle to global democracy has been removed and others to see the absence of democracy as the principal source of violent conflict in the contemporary system. Since these conflicts are generally associated with massive human rights violations, it follows, in this frame of thought, that the protection of human rights will be made easier within a democratic environment.

Whatever the evidence in support of the claim that international society is evolving in this direction, many international lawyers and human rights advocates—including some of the authors of this volume—are reluctant to concede that there is a necessary relationship between human rights and democracy. One can see why. If human rights exist, they belong to all human beings, regardless of the nature of the regime under which they live. To tie them too closely to democracy, it may be argued, is to let tyrants off the hook; they will be able to argue that rights are ideological, conditional on a particular political philosophy and culture, rather than being truly universal, and thus in a sense above and beyond politics.

There is a further problem that comes with treating human rights as an instrument of foreign policy in a democracy. The attempt to pursue an ethical foreign policy with human rights objectives almost inevitably leads to accusations of double standards, as President Jimmy Carter discovered in the United States in the 1970s and the Blair government discovered in Britain in the 1990s. A higher standard of public behavior will be demanded of the weak and vulnerable than of the strong and economically powerful. The standard riposte to this criticism is that the best should not be made the enemy of the good, that just because human rights cannot be protected everywhere should not stop action against their abuse where it is possible. Perhaps, but somehow this sounds a more convincing defense with respect to, say, famine relief, than with human rights. In the former case, the famine may or may not be accompanied by human rights violations, and the decision to send or withhold assistance may quite reasonably be conditioned by practical considerations, such as access, distance, intelligence, and capacity. In the latter case, some of the greatest offenders have been able to claim immunity merely by reference to their power.

Moreover, the very powerful—China, for example (potentially if not actually)—are often protected by an ancient civilization that is grounded on different standards of public and private behavior than those that underpin the Universal Declaration of Human Rights. Of course, this proposition will be contested, not least by many brave people in the countries whose leaders claim the protection of alternative value systems. But there is little doubt that Western governments feel more constrained in dealing with representatives of so-called world civilizations than with smaller states, many of which were shaped by Western imperialism and only recently released from its clutches.

It is for reasons of this kind that scholars such as Donnelly see that it is states that must, finally, implement human rights and that the essential role of the international community involves standard setting, the promotion of debate, and patient advocacy. On this view, the protection of human rights—and where appropriate, their extension—requires vigilance in stable liberal democracies and not merely in collapsed states and those ruled by tyrannical autocrats. It is possible, he believes, to accommodate most claims for group rights that have been pressed since the end of the Cold War by ensuring that existing individual rights are properly interpreted and, if necessary, by extending their range.

However, other authors in this volume have variously challenged his position; they are at one with Donnelly in believing that the ultimate aim is the creation of a human rights culture that, whatever its basis, will remove the protection of people's fundamental freedoms from the arena of political contestation. We share this hope. Nonetheless, in the meantime there is a more immediate political reason for taking seriously the pressures for group rights. It is intimately linked to the preconditions for democratization in deeply divided societies. Whether or not a right of free association necessarily implies democratic government, it clearly creates the possibility, particularly when combined with the one collective right recognized within the current regime—namely, the right of all peoples to self-determination. The problem arises especially in deeply divided societies, where, however regrettably, people refuse to subordinate their ethnic, national, or religious identity to their identity as citizens.

Two nineteenth-century authors—Lord Acton and John Stuart Mill—considered the social preconditions that had to be met if a democracy was to function properly but drew radically opposite conclusions. For Acton, the ideal was a society consisting of as many separate social groups as possible. If the social mix was sufficiently heterodox, he believed, people would see no advantage in mobilizing along ethnic or communal lines. On the contrary, they would have every advantage to identify themselves as citizens. The Actonian model projected onto the contemporary political landscape bears a striking family resemblance to the United States.[3]

Mill's commitment to democratic freedoms was no less than Acton's, but he drew an opposite conclusion, or, more accurately, he based his analysis on a different but arguably more widespread social configuration. He believed that if a divided society—presumably he was thinking of the United Kingdom—had developed a political culture over a long period of time during which no one enjoyed civil and political rights, then when eventually the demand for democratic representation prevailed, the issue of social, religious, or ethnic origins, in a word of blood line and ancestry, would be irrelevant.[4]

It was not that people would necessarily forget whether they were English, Scots, or Welsh or consider this aspect of their identity unimportant but rather that it would not define their political loyalties. On the other hand, if the demand for national and democratic freedoms arose simultaneously in a society that was divided between two ethnonational communities of approximately equal size, then, he believed, a democratic constitution would inevitably result in both communities mobilizing to capture the state through the ballot box. In a winner-take-all situation, the winner would use all available means to eliminate the loser. Projected onto the contemporary political landscape, Mill's vision bears an uncomfortably close resemblance to the former Yugoslavia and to many other troubled societies around the world. The implications of the Mill/Acton contrast for a would-be democratic world order are clear. If democracy is not only to be regarded as a good in itself, but as an instrument of conflict resolution and an enabling mechanism for a human rights culture, there are two plausible lines of development. The first is to accept—as Mill did, although only up to a point—that the promotion of democracy may require partition. The second is to accept the position (largely prevalent in today's world) that there is no right of secessionist self-determination and that unless partition is agreed between the parties, it is illegal. If this path is followed, the only way to reconcile territorial integrity with democratic freedoms is to accept the right of communities to democratic representation on their own behalf and to engineer the democratic constitution accordingly.

There are admittedly formidable problems that need to be addressed if democratization is to be pursued by way of this second alternative. Mill was not prepared to accept the right of secessionist self-determination for any but the largest and therefore most indigestible of stateless national communities. Yet if minority rights really are human rights, how logically can this be denied? It is presumably because this is indeed recognized to be the case that, even in Europe, governments still refuse to translate their political commitment to minority protection into a legal right that could in theory be used to challenge their authority. If, as Hurst Hannum suggests, indigenous peoples have made more substantial progress in putting their rights on a legal basis than minorities, this is partly because they have dealt with practical problems of discrimination and eschewed the problem of definition, but it is mainly because they mostly cannot entertain serious ambitions of separate statehood.

Extending the human rights regime to meet the special needs of women can similarly be best approached by addressing problems of discrimination as they arise within the state, along the lines outlined by Brems, rather than by engaging in philosophical confrontation. The political problem that underlies Jackson-Preece's chapter on minorities, on the other hand, is that it is much more difficult to avoid such confrontation; in other words, it is difficult to avoid the problem of definition and, in the present state of international society, difficult to address minority fears in a way that will not be perceived by state authorities as a threat to their sovereignty. If a way could be found to head communal conflict off at the pass, prior to democratization, then we could justly claim that international society had evolved a workable compromise between the principles of solidarity that underpin the human rights regime and of pluralism that is implied by the concept of a society of sovereign states. If prevention of this kind is not available, then it is unclear that securing minority rights will be sufficient to resolve the issue.

HUMAN RIGHTS AND
INTERNATIONAL CRISIS

Against this background, let us turn to the two problems that we suggested in the introduction had posed the most serious challenge to the human rights regime in the years following the Cold War: the increasing evidence of group identity as a principal source of civil conflict and hence of human rights violations, and the role of the international community in confronting gross violations of rights in situations of extreme emergency. We already argued that the problem of group rights could not be avoided if international efforts at democratization were to have any realistic chance of bearing fruit. Here, by contrast, our concern is with the record since the end of the Cold War and thus not with the theoretical problem but with what has actually happened.

Both of these problems are in many ways related to the results of the Minorities at Risk Project, which Ted Robert Gurr has now reported in his book, *Peoples versus States*. His analysis is based on tracking a worldwide series of ethnic conflicts from the mid-1980s to 1999. He concludes that by the end of the 1990s, "armed conflict within states had abated," and "there was a pronounced decline in the onset of new ethnic wars and a shift in many ongoing wars from fighting to negotiation."[5] Leaving aside the hostages to fortune that he takes, these conclusions are more optimistic than one might deduce from the number and intensity of civil conflicts that have continued into the twenty-first century.

To be fair, Gurr himself does not deny that internal conflicts continue to be a major threat to international peace and security. Nonetheless what is of special interest in relation to the problems discussed in this book are the reasons that Gurr offers for concluding that there has been a "general decline in ethnic wars." First, he argues, we have now passed through the initial "shocks" caused by the fall of the Soviet Union and the disintegration of the Soviet sphere of influence. The breakdown of Soviet control, together with the fragmenting of communist authority in the former Yugoslavia, opened up new—and revived old—ethnic rivalries in Eastern and Central Europe.

If we compare the transition in Eastern Europe and the former Soviet Union with the previous major international upheaval—the transfer of power from the European imperial powers to successor states in Asia and Africa—his analysis seems convincing, at least up to a point. Then, too, there were a series of postcolonial crises and conflicts after which the situation stabilized, although very often as the result of the consolidation of authoritarian governments. In the present case, however, it is claimed that democracy has itself helped to stabilize the emerging order. Even if we conclude that, in some cases, ethnic rivalries have been restrained by the emergence of embryonic democratic regimes, it is difficult to ignore the continued tensions in Bosnia and Kosovo (where such stability as has been achieved is the result of *de facto* international trusteeships rather than local democracy), let alone in Chechnya, Georgia, and a number of other former Soviet Republics.

Gurr also provides two more general reasons for the decrease of ethnic conflicts that extend the analysis to the rest of the world: one is the spread of democratic societies that "are less likely to rely on strategies of assimilation and repression" and "more likely to follow policies of recognition, pluralism and group autonomy"; the second is that "states and international organisations, prompted by intense media attention and the activism of nongovernmental organisations, have been more willing to initiate preventive and remedial action."[6] These are large claims. A more skeptical set of assumptions about the capacity of political and social structures to transform themselves overnight, in the first case, and attention to how post–Cold War enthusiasm for humanitarian intervention has become more ambiguous might have led to rather different conclusions.

Gurr himself seems fully aware of the thinness of the ice on which he skates. He sensibly warns us that ethnic tensions will certainly continue to erupt into violent conflict, that democratic regimes are often weak and vulnerable, and that international organizations (and the states that support them) often "walk away" after preliminary intervention and leave unattended the long-term objectives of political and economic stability. His conclusions at best are only conditionally positive. We are still confronted with the formidable obstacles facing "pluralist" societies (in the democratic rather than international sense of that term) that both Jackson-Preece and Hannum discuss, as well as the obstacles that arise in connection with a more active and persistent international role that Weller and Wheeler analyze.

The fact is that the two problems at the center of our study strongly reflect the interaction between domestic and international politics. The search for "pluralist" society in which diverse collective rights are, at a minimum, protected and, beyond that, promoted is essentially a matter for domestic society. The protection of the language and culture of minorities and indigenous peoples and the exercise of affirmative action to grant them a leg up in the ranks of society (the American and in the end still assimilationist option) or a separate space in which they are politically autonomous yet remain within the state (the European and/or multicultural option), all depend on government policies and public programs. At this level, as we noted earlier, the role of international society (in which governments and NGOs both participate) ranges from standard setting to general exhortation and "shaming." Insofar as informed debate may influence domestic human rights policies, the effect of "international public opinion" cannot be discounted, but it remains impossible to measure. At the same time, international enforcement is only accepted under extreme conditions and, even then, difficult to carry out.

Nevertheless, it is when governments fail to promote pluralism and leave minorities and indigenous peoples in deprivation without hope or expectations, that the seeds of conflict are nourished. The failure to meet pluralist aspirations not only threatens the stability of domestic society but calls into question the solidarity of international society, first through its impact on the immediate region and then more broadly through the processes of contemporary globalization.

The "internationalization" of domestic conflicts has been widened and intensified by the growth of the global economy beyond the universality of the international human rights regime. What does this statement mean? First, the global economy, characterized by the interpenetration of national economies, has, in several ways, a direct impact on human rights. The great disparity between rich and poor across the world encourages the migration of tens of thousands from the less developed to the more industrialized countries. There they often constitute substantial minorities, their numbers swollen by the demand—in defiance of national immigration laws—for low-paid workers.

The problem is that more often than not the rational need of the labor market is at odds with the interests of the general population, many of whom are likely to perceive the newcomers as a threat to their own jobs and way of life and to resent them for all their "differences." Such has certainly been the case with the influx of workers from Central and South America into the United States; from Turkey, Eastern Europe, and the former Soviet Union into Germany; from north Africa into France; and from the Indian subcontinent and the Caribbean into Great Britain.

Globalization has also encouraged the flow of investment into less-developed countries as multinational corporations seek cheap labor and production facilities. They are also attracted to countries where workers rights are less rigorously enforced than in the industrialized world and where the standards of environmental protection are lower. This process has had both positive and negative results for the host countries. On the one hand, foreign private investment has fueled development and locked developing countries into the international division of labor on which the global economy depends. On the other, it has increased corruption among local entrepreneurs and political leaders and abused workers' rights through lower standards of compensation and, in some cases, the exploitation of child labor. The most flagrant cases have become the focus of the world media and voluntary human rights advocates. Their pressure has in turn led major corporations to adopt "good conduct" agreements to protect workers rights and secure equivalent standards and benefits in developing countries as in their "home" plants and factories.

There is an inevitable tension between the development needs of poor countries and the attempt to establish a universal standard of positive as well as negative rights. It is precisely because countries are poor that labor is cheap and therefore attractive to foreign investors. Consequently, workers in industrialized countries are likely to claim that they are being subjected to unfair competition and to join forces with human rights advocates in claiming that differential labor standards amount to a nontariff barrier—in other words, a hidden form of protection. Even the attempt to ban child labor may seem discriminatory in cultures where the family has always been regarded as an economic as well as a social unit and where training for craft manufacture—for example, in the hand-woven carpet trade—was tradition-ally done "on the job" and began at a very early age.

This is not to condone exploitative practices, let alone to suggest that children in developing countries do not have a right to education, but rather to point out the practical difficulties that may arise and the scope for cross cultural misunderstanding in the attempt to harmonize standards worldwide. Despite such difficulties, such companies as Walt Disney, Gap, Levi, Reebok, Nike, as well as Shell, British Petroleum, Texaco, and Wal-Mart have signed "good conduct" agreements. In the end, however, the enforcement of standards—and the working out of sensible compromises between different national practices—depends on the construction of stable, responsible governments.

BY WAY OF CONCLUDING

The world, in effect, has become increasingly interconnected. The recent intensification in the process of globalization has reinforced the tendency, to which we referred earlier, to regard international society as an enterprise association. In other words, it has increased the incentive of states to find common interests and to cooperate to meet shared objectives. Common interests have two major sources: the one pragmatic, emerging from common concerns about material resources and relations of military power, the second more doctrinal in the sense of creating standards of conduct, which are recognized by most states as the test of a government's legitimacy.

There is, as we also suggested, a deep structural problem in moving in any final way from a pluralist society of states to a solidarist community of peoples. The real question, at least for the foreseeable future, will be what kind of compromise between the two principles will be struck. For the time being, Donnelly was surely right to argue that "political legitimacy in the post–Cold War world is increasingly judged by and expressed in terms of internationally recognised human rights." It may not be an exaggeration to add "democratic processes" to this formulation. Certainly this view is supported by the tests that have been established for entry into the European Union, the Commonwealth, and even, in theory, the (newly constituted) African Union, as well as the new version of political conditionality increasingly exercised by the World Bank and the International Monetary Fund (IMF). It is also supported by the stated objective of fair and equitable elections repeatedly stipulated by the UN Security Council in establishing peacekeeping forces to intervene in civil conflicts.

Since the end of the Cold War, the protection of group rights, which had been virtually ignored after 1945, reemerged as a central issue in the debate about the future of the human rights regime. Arguably, it has already become part of the growing doctrine against which the activities of governments are evaluated. Donnelly maintains that the existing international human rights regime can be easily extended to encompass the legitimate interests of groups within an expanded version of liberalism. This will maintain the existing priority given to individuals but *inter alia* integrate political and civil rights, on the one hand, with economic, social, and cultural rights, on the other. We have already argued that there may be instrumental reasons why it may be necessary to recognize groups as a distinct category of rights holders—for example, by expanding the scope of democratic government in deeply divided societies where, in the absence of such recognition, democracy may contribute to social conflict rather than resolve it.

In her chapter, Jackson-Preece goes even further, advocating the promotion of group rights as desirable ends in themselves, as much as their protection. Moreover, despite the qualifications that she prudently enters, she sees considerable progress in the 1992 passage of the UN Declaration of the Rights of Persons Belonging to National or Ethnic, Religious and Linguistic Minorities, the action in Europe on a Charter for Regional or Minority Languages, and the policies of the Organization for Security and Cooperation in Europe (OSCE) in focusing on the collective rights of minorities. Hannum demonstrates, equally effectively, how indigenous peoples have been successful in promulgating international agreements to put pressure on national governments to adopt policies that will sustain their autonomy. Their arguments lend weight to the view that the international human rights regime, like international society itself, is not static. On the contrary, it is continually evolving, a process that is further driven by the kinds of transformation that Brems indicates are being pressed on behalf of women, especially the extension of rights into private relations.

These are the positive signs of progress. They are worthy of attention but should not tempt us into unreal euphoria. The protection, let alone the promotion, of group rights is also meeting resistance at various levels of domestic as well as international society. Despite the advances that Jackson-Preece reports in Europe, for example, there is strong opposition to immigration in the industrially advanced countries with outbreaks of xenophobia that frequently lead to violent attacks against new immigrants. In the United States, a country built up through periodic waves of immigration, the myth of the "melting pot" has been replaced by the more inclusive if vaguer image of multiculturalism. Yet, simultaneously, there is continuing resistance to bilingual education, proposals to establish English as the official national language, and opposition to affirmative action.

The problem is complicated by the fact that, while conservative and even reactionary forces may drive such campaigns, it is not self-evident that the ends that they seek are necessarily reactionary. If the result of multicultural education is to make it easier for the majority to marginalize minority communities in linguistically sealed ghettos, the cause of human rights will not have been well served. The problem is even more acute in many parts of the developing world. In much of Africa, for example, assimilationist policies, adopted in the name of nation building, have led to the rights of minorities being systematically abused, a situation that has not been noticeably improved by the reintroduction of democratic elections.

Throughout Central and South America, the condition of indigenous peoples remains dismal and unresolved, while policies to redress the miseries of the indigenous people of Australia and the Maori in New Zealand have polarized the European populations in both countries. The history of national policies with regard to American Indians in the United States is no less discouraging, and only marginally better in Canada. It is difficult to be overly optimistic, therefore, about the future of group rights, particularly against the background of continuing ethnic rivalries in the Balkans and the states of the former Soviet Union; the revival of intolerant fundamentalism in Christianity, Judaism, and Islam; and the frightening poverty in large parts of Asia and Africa that pits group against group in the struggle for scarce resources.

The protection of group rights, in this regard, is far from being fully accepted as part of the normative framework of international society. We can only reiterate that unless progress can be made in building minority protection into effective preventive diplomacy, prior to the outbreak of violent conflict, it might prove to be too late afterward. Nonetheless, the violation of the rights of minorities—and in some cases of majorities that have been excluded from power by the minority—remains a trigger for international action by organized human rights movements, by the mass media, and, it must be admitted often reluctantly, by governments. Nevertheless, all of the above not withstanding, the fact is that the permanent members of the UN Security Council have been in retreat from the readiness with which they accepted the idea of humanitarian intervention in the immediate aftermath of the Cold War.

There is, nevertheless, a question whether a change in direction might be marked by NATO's intervention in Kosovo; by the establishment of, first, a peacekeeping operation and then a *de facto* trusteeship in East Timor, both in 1999; and, more recently, by the commitment of the international community to the long-term rebuilding of Afghanistan once the ruling Taliban were overturned and the al Qaeda camps for training terrorists destroyed. With regard to the willingness of the international community to address mass violations of human rights, these cases have admittedly ambiguous implications. It is true that, in Kosovo, NATO—whose bombing campaign dramatically increased the flow of refugees—insisted that it was motivated by humanitarian considerations. No doubt it was, but it was also concerned to carve out a role for itself after the Cold War that would justify its recent enlargement and to prevent any further encroachment by the UN—a body that many, in the United States in particular, regarded as unreliable—into the security field.

The East Timor operation was not initially triggered by violent human rights abuse but by a decision of the UN Security Council to allow the territory, a former Portuguese colony, the right of self-determination that other colonies had enjoyed but that in this case had been prevented by the Indonesian annexation of 1974. Self-determination as decolonization was the conventional interpretation of the concept that emerged after 1945. However, in the context of the American withdrawal from Vietnam in the 1970s, the Western powers had turned a blind eye on Indonesia's aggression, although only Australia—ironically the country that led the 1999 peacekeeping operation—had ever recognized Indonesia's incorporation of the territory.

There had undoubtedly been serious violations of human rights in East Timor during the occupation, as indeed there had been in other parts of the Indonesian archipelago wherever ethnic minorities opposed the domination of the Javanese. But only in East Timor, where it was possible to claim that a rightful transfer of power had been denied, was the UN prepared to act. Arguably, moreover, the UN's action initially made the human rights situation worse. By organizing a referendum on independence in circumstances that left the Indonesian military, the one organization in the country that remained implacably opposed to independence, in charge of security, it effectively guaranteed that there would be attempts to terrorize the population into opposing secession.

The major powers were also drawn into Afghanistan, which they had abandoned after the retreat of Soviet forces more than a decade earlier, in response to the terrorist attacks against the United States in September 2001. The problems that they faced were formidable, not least the difficulties in creating and supporting a unified government in a country that is severely divided into a number of historically antagonistic groups, separated by forbidding geographic formations and the absence of any kind of connecting transportation system. Developing a democratic regime will require strong protection for the interests of the several groups that make up the population of the country and will not otherwise give up their autonomy.

The evidence since the end of the Cold War thus strongly suggests that while violation of group rights may trigger international action, it is not sufficient to ensure timely and effective enforcement. The real lesson of recent cases may be different. Kosovo, East Timor, and Afghanistan all indicate how, despite their reluctance, the major powers, acting either through the UN or outside it, are still likely to find themselves drawn into international crises that involve humanitarian catastrophe, *whether they want to intervene or not.*

The question posed by this possibility is this: If humanitarian intervention is unavoidable, does this mean, as Wheeler urges, that international society should develop along solidarist lines? Indeed, does it imply that it will necessarily have to do so? It is impossible to give an unambiguously positive answer to these questions. Wheeler argues, persuasively, in our view, that the reason NATO felt compelled to act in Kosovo outside the UN Security Council, was that, in seeking the enlargement of the alliance, the United States and its allies had failed "to draw Russia into a genuine security partnership." The implication is that had this been done, possibly by admitting Russia or by eschewing the idea of enlargement altogether, it might have been possible "to forge a new consensus at the UN on the substantive criteria that should govern Security Council authorized humanitarian intervention." But, even if we concede the counterfactual hypothesis—namely, that had there been a different decision on enlargement, "a solidarist ethic of responsibility" might have taken hold—it would still have been taken on a view of state interests. Such a decision would have reflected a more enlightened pluralist conception of international relations than the one that was in fact adopted, but it would still not have been based on solidarist principles: whatever else it is, NATO remains a nonuniversal defensive alliance.

There is nothing reprehensible in suggesting that the moral improvement of international society should be pursued crabwise rather than via a direct confrontation between principle and interest. The most celebrated advance in applied international ethics—the abolition of the slave trade—was brought about in precisely this manner. Unfortunately, in the present case, the analogy is imperfect. The comparison with humanitarian intervention works better if one considers international action against slavery itself. This was a much harder nut to crack. In the end, given power and the will to use it, the slave trade could be stopped on the high seas. Slavery, which was deeply embedded in the political culture of slave-owning societies, was much less susceptible to external pressure. By analogy, the reason why Western governments failed to act in Rwanda was not merely, as Wheeler argues, "that they did not believe that it was worth sacrificing Western soldiers to save Rwandan strangers," although that was no doubt part of the story; it was also because *they did not know what to do*. What is there to suggest that they would be better placed to act if a similar emergency were to arise in the future?

Western leaders do not know what to do because, for understandable reasons, they are unwilling to accept that the logic of humanitarian intervention is imperial: it involves the setting up of a government and administration to replace discredited institutions associated with the catastrophe, and a willingness to stay as long as it takes to build local support for institutions that are both more stable and more representative than those they replace. As Weller demonstrates, in many humanitarian crises, it is not true that nothing can be done, although, as he also concludes, "the record of UN action is bleak where it intervenes in the absence of a consensus on the need to refound a particular society and on the concrete shape of a new constitutional structure."

The logic of humanitarian intervention is not one that the governments of the major powers find attractive because it is expensive, open-ended, and likely to prove unpopular. If governments, nevertheless, continue to be drawn into such crises—and we believe they will—it behooves them to think long and hard about what they are getting into. Collateral damage is an inevitable consequence of any military action, which makes it all the more important that enforcement action be sanctioned only when there is a reasonable prospect of relieving human suffering, even if it is not always possible to achieve a resolution of the underlying conflict. Defying the dangers of predictions, our own conclusion is that, into the twenty-first century, international society will move painfully in the direction of solidarist principle. Nevertheless, any advance will proceed without relinquishing the essence of pluralism: the continued existence of separately organized sovereign states that pursue their interests in a world divided by the struggle for material resources and ideas about what the good life is all about.

NOTES

1. Hedley Bull, "The Emergence of a Universal International Society," in *The Expansion of International Society*, ed. Hedley Bull and Adam Watson (Oxford: Clarendon, 1984), 125.

2. Hedley Bull and Adam Watson, "Conclusion," in *The Expansion of International Society*, ed. Bull and Watson, 428.

3. Lord Acton, "Nationality," in *Essays on Freedom and Power* (Gloucester, Mass.: Smith, 1972), 141–70.

4. J. S. Mill, "Of Nationality as Connected with Representative Government," in *Utilitarianism, Liberty and Consideration on Representative Government* (New York: Everyman's Library, 1972), 359–68.

5. Ted Robert Gurr, *People versus States: Minorities at Risk in the New Century* (Washington, D.C.: United States Institute of Peace Press, 2000), viii.

6. Gurr, *People versus States*, xiv.

Index

About the Contributors

Eva Brems is a professor of human rights law at the University of Ghent in Belgium. Her research interests include most areas of human rights law, in European and international law, as well as in Belgian and comparative law. Most recently, she is the author of *Human Rights: Universality and Diversity* (Martinus Nijhoff, 2001).

Jack Donnelly is the Mellon professor in the Graduate School of International Studies at the University of Denver. He has published widely in the field of human rights. His works include *The Concept of Human Rights* (St. Martin's, 1985); *Universal Human Rights in Theory and Practice* (Cornell, 1989); *International Human Rights* (Westview, 1998, 2d ed.); *Realism and International Relations* (Cambridge, 2000).

Hurst Hannum is a professor of international law and codirector of the Center for Human Rights and Conflict Resolution at the Fletcher School of Law and Diplomacy at Tufts University. He has served as counsel in cases before the European and Inter-American Commissions on Human Rights and is the author of *Autonomy, Sovereignty and Self-Determination* (University of Pennsylvania Press, rev. ed., 1996) and editor of *Guide to International Human Rights Practice* (Transnational, 3d ed., 1999).

Jennifer Jackson-Preece is currently a lecturer on nationalism in Europe at the London School of Economics and Political Science. Recent publications include *National Minorities and the European Nation-States System* (Oxford University Press, 1998) and "Ethnic Cleansing as an Instrument of Nation-State Creation" (*Human Rights Quarterly*, 1997).

Gene M. Lyons is a senior fellow of the John Sloan Dickey Center for International Understanding at Dartmouth College. He has served with the National Research Council and UNESCO and been a visiting professor at the University of Paris (Sorbonne). He has recently been coeditor and contributor to *Beyond Westphalia: State Sovereignty and International Intervention* (Johns Hopkins University Press, 1995) and to *The United Nations System: the Policies of Member States* (United Nations University Press, 1995).

James Mayall is a professor of international relations and director of the Center of International Studies at the University of Cambridge. He was for many years a member of the faculty of the international relations department at the London School of Economics and Political Science. His publications include *Nationalism and International Society* (Cambridge University Press, 1990), *The New Interventionism 1991–1994* (Cambridge University Press, 1996), and *World Politics* (Polity, 2000).

Marc Weller is an assistant director of studies in the Centre of International Studies of the University of Cambridge, a fellow of the Lauterpacht Research Centre of International Law and of Hughes Hall, and a director of the European Centre for Minority Issues. His research interests lie in the areas of international law and the management of conflict and of the developing international constitutional order.

Nicholas J. Wheeler is a senior lecturer in the Department of International Politics at the University of Wales in Aberystwyth. He has served as a research associate at the International Institute for Strategic Studies and is coeditor of *Human Rights in Global Politics* (Cambridge University Press, 1999). He has recently published *Saving Strangers: Humanitarian Intervention in International Society* (Oxford University Press, 2000).